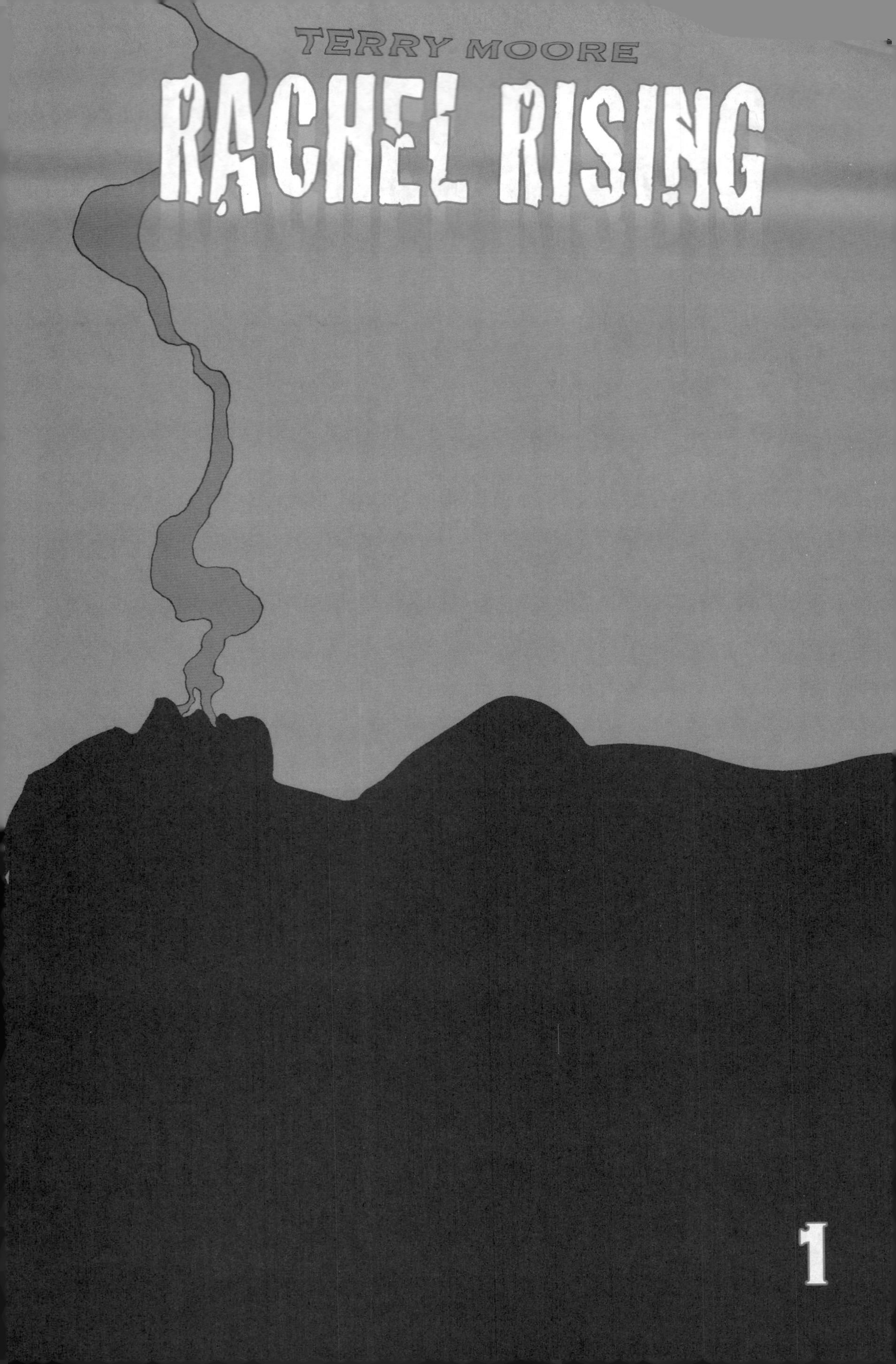
TERRY MOORE
RACHEL RISING
1

DEATH IS NOT THE WORST THING
THAT CAN HAPPEN TO YOU.
—PLATO

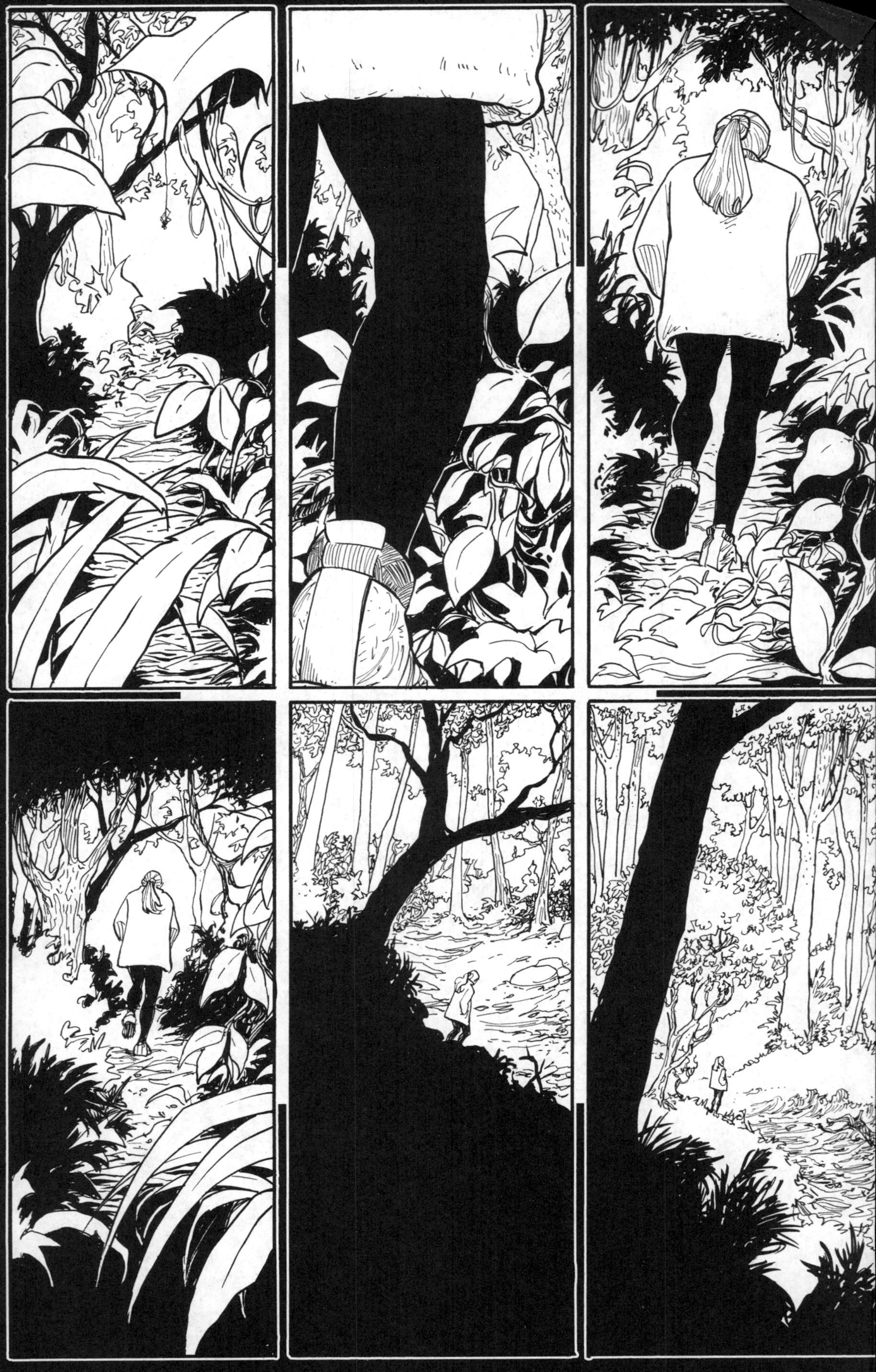

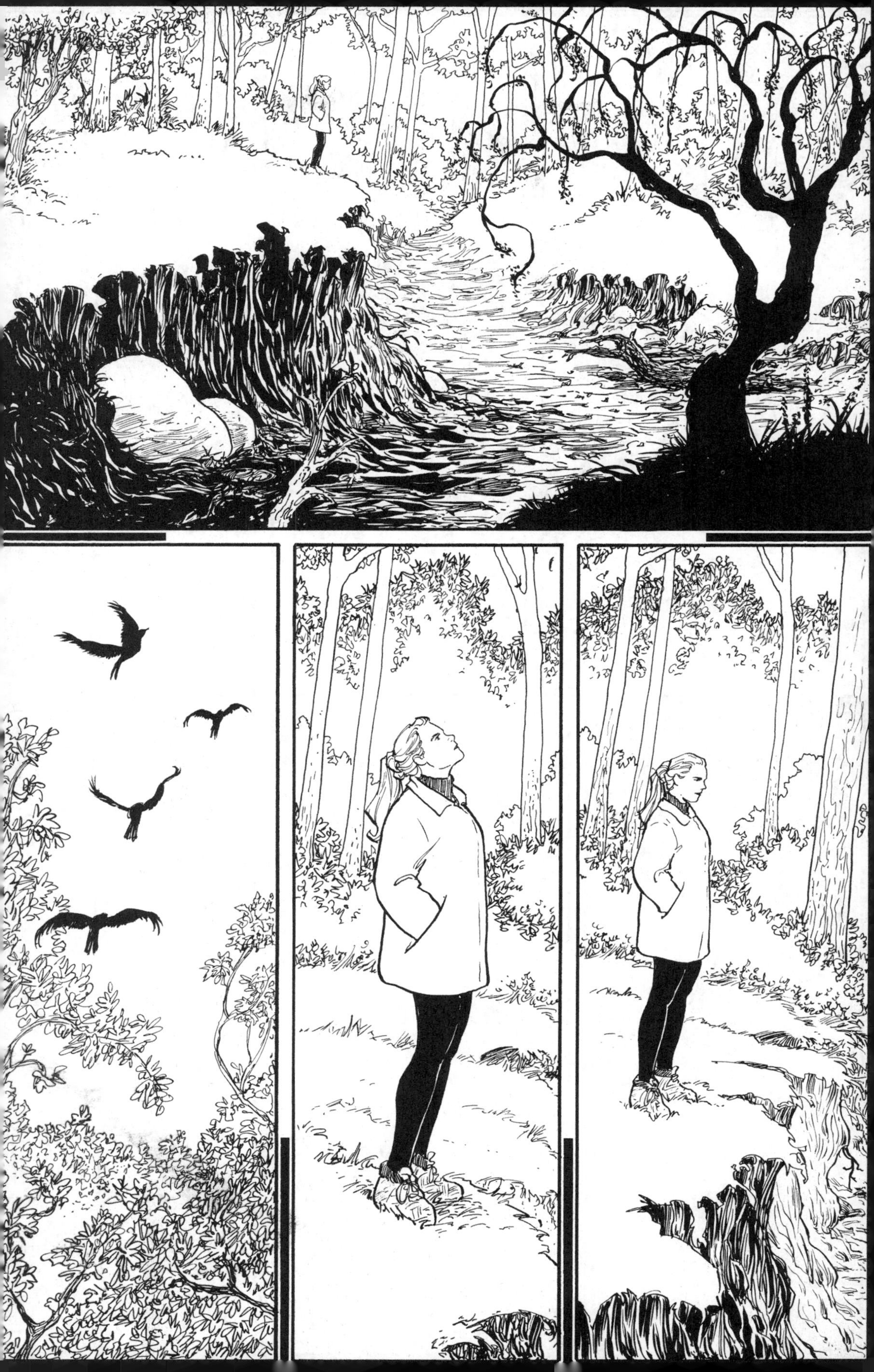

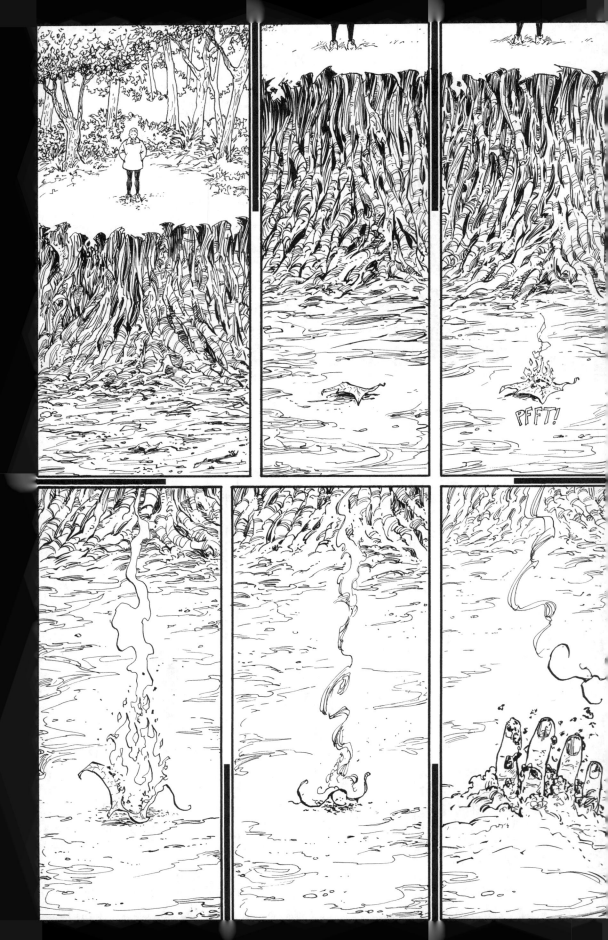

PFFT!

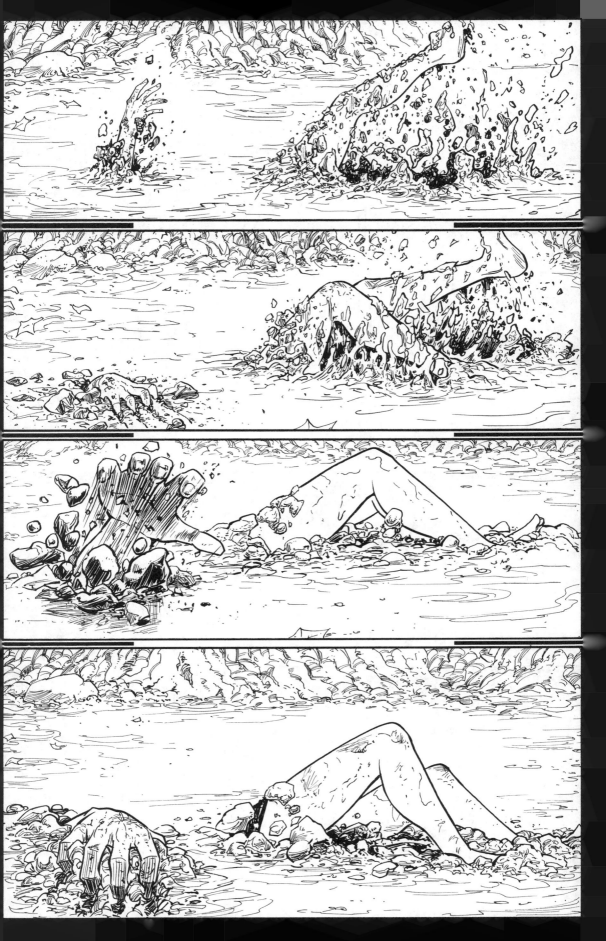

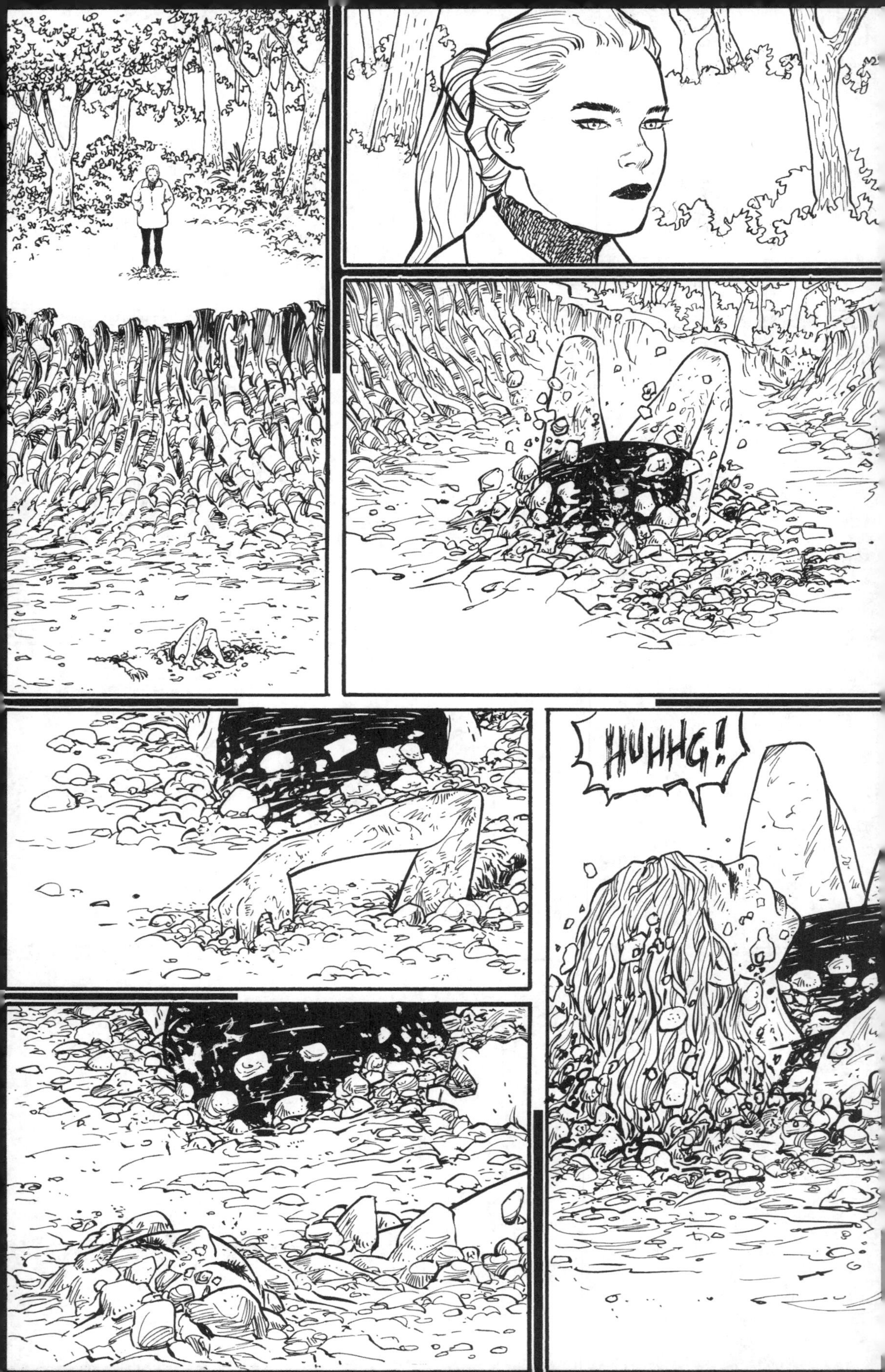
HUHHG!

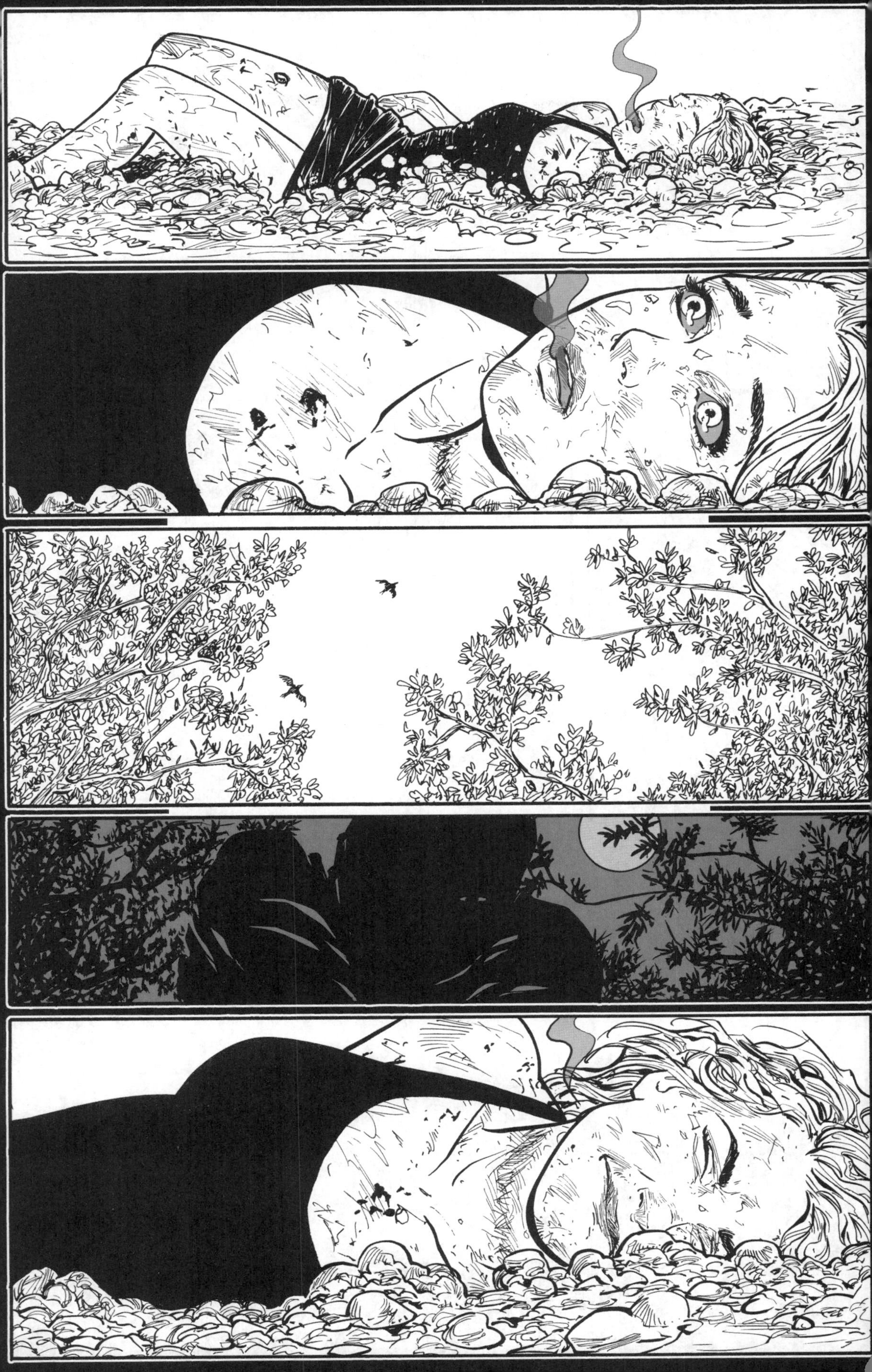

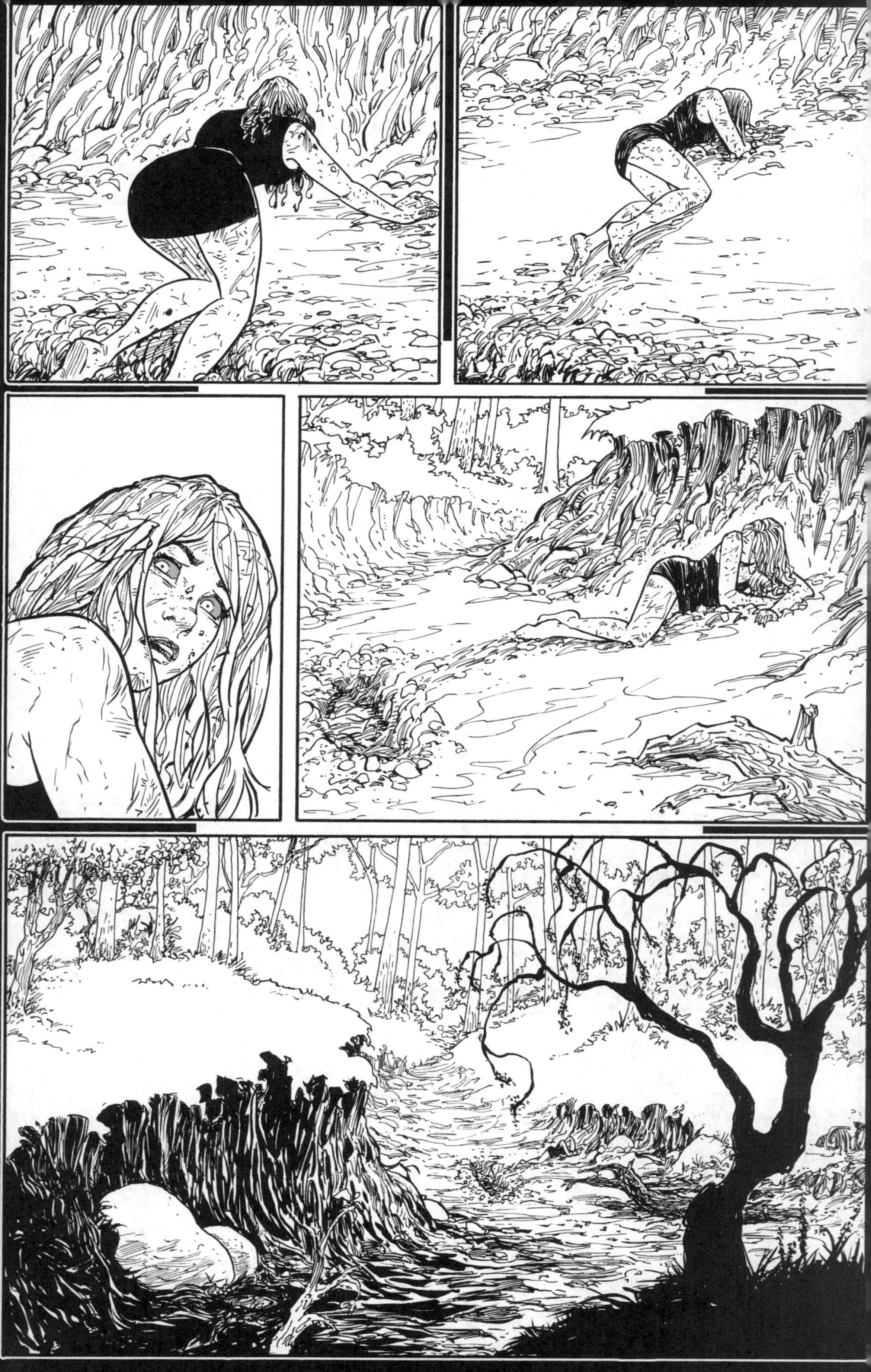

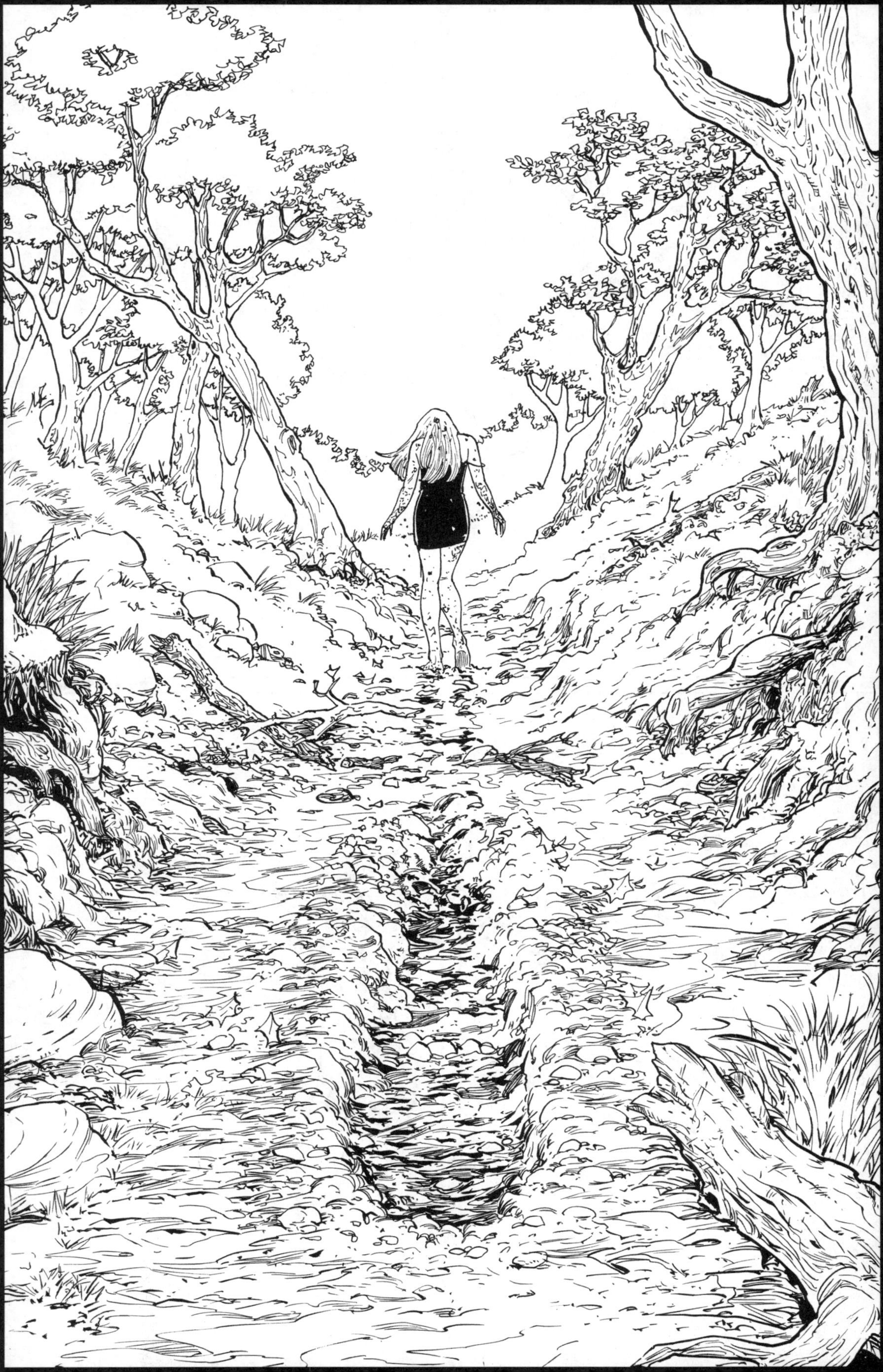

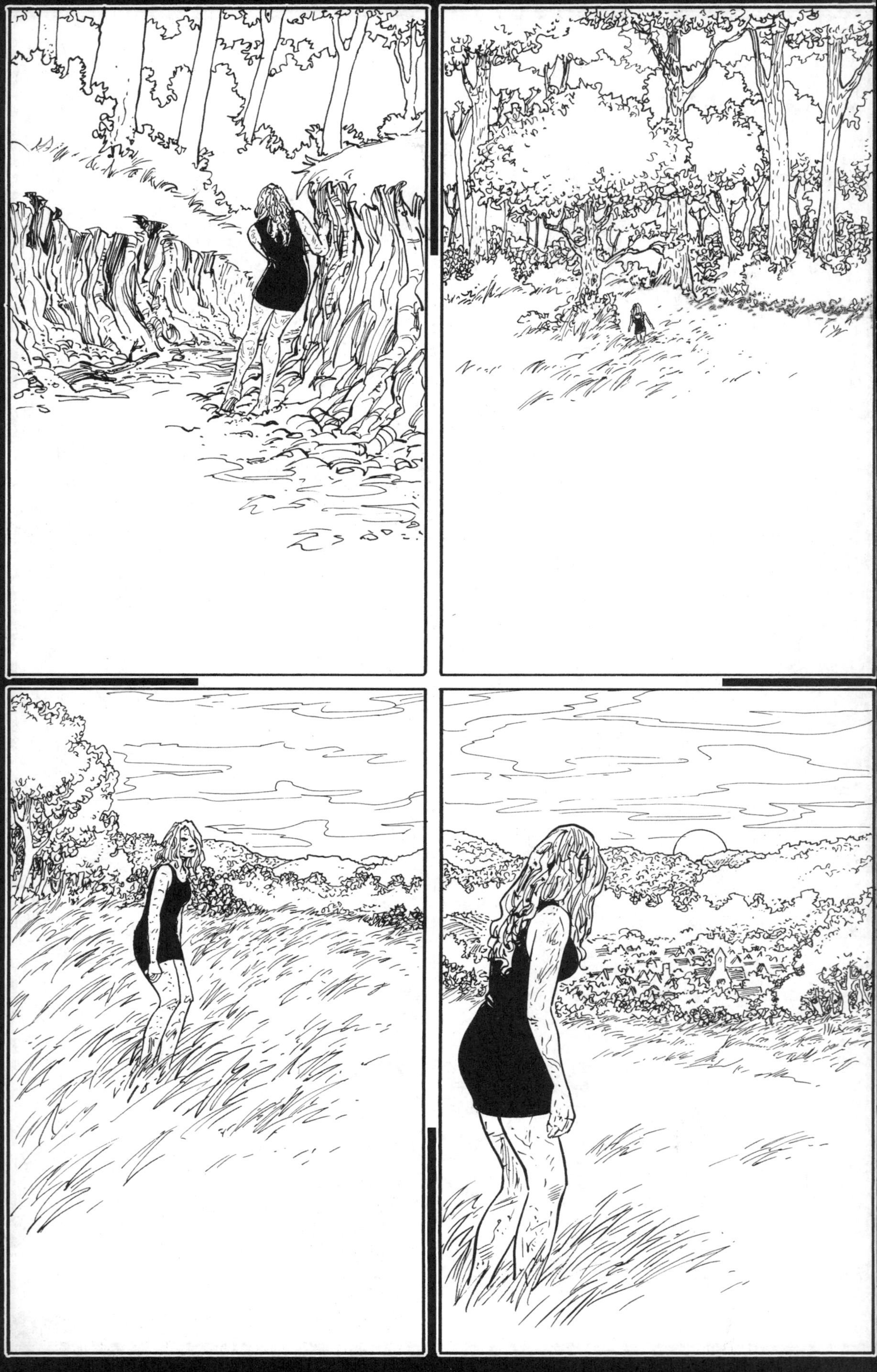

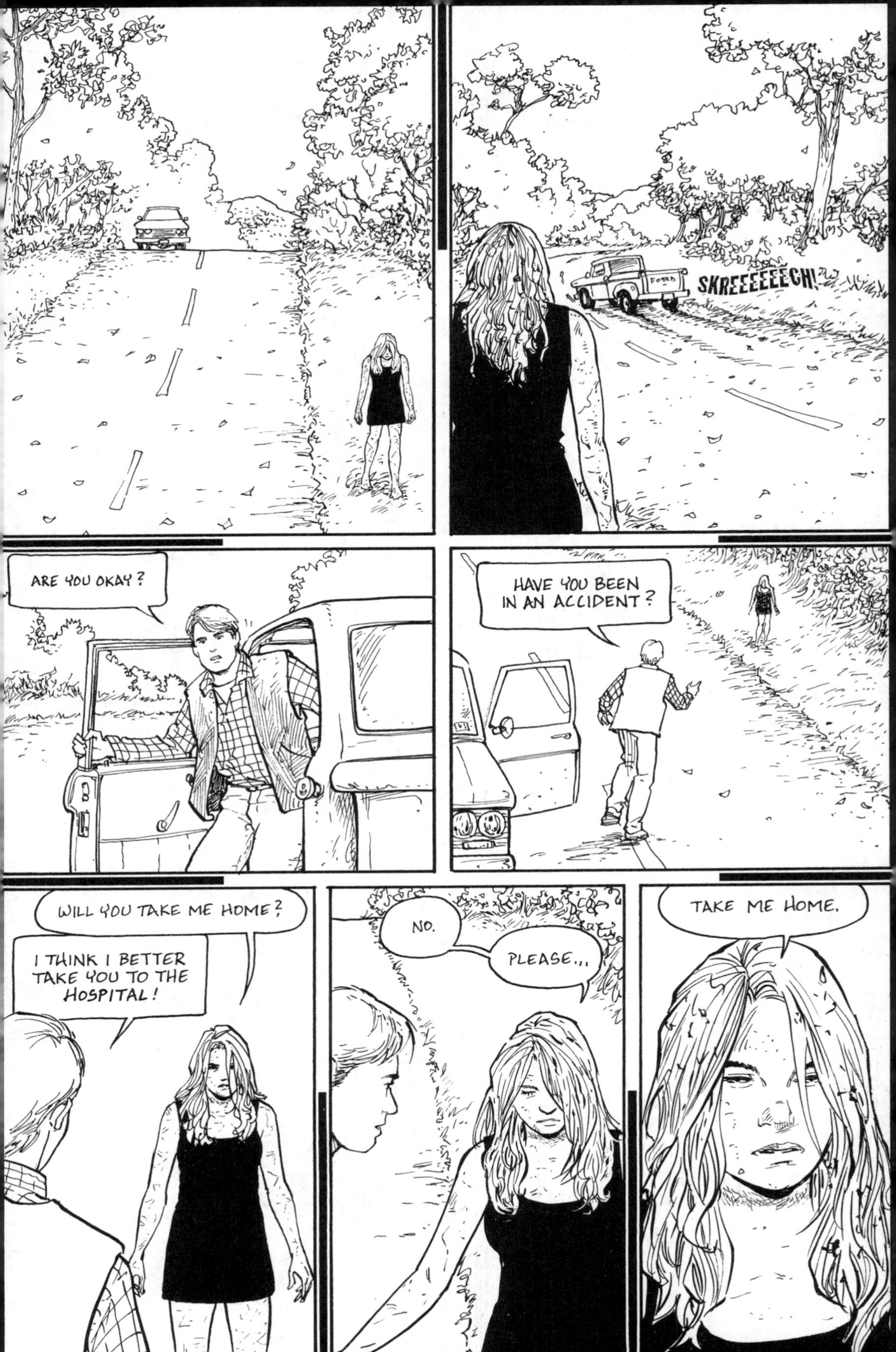
SKREEEEEEECH!
FORD
ARE YOU OKAY?
HAVE YOU BEEN IN AN ACCIDENT?
WILL YOU TAKE ME HOME?
I THINK I BETTER TAKE YOU TO THE HOSPITAL!
NO.
PLEASE...
TAKE ME HOME.

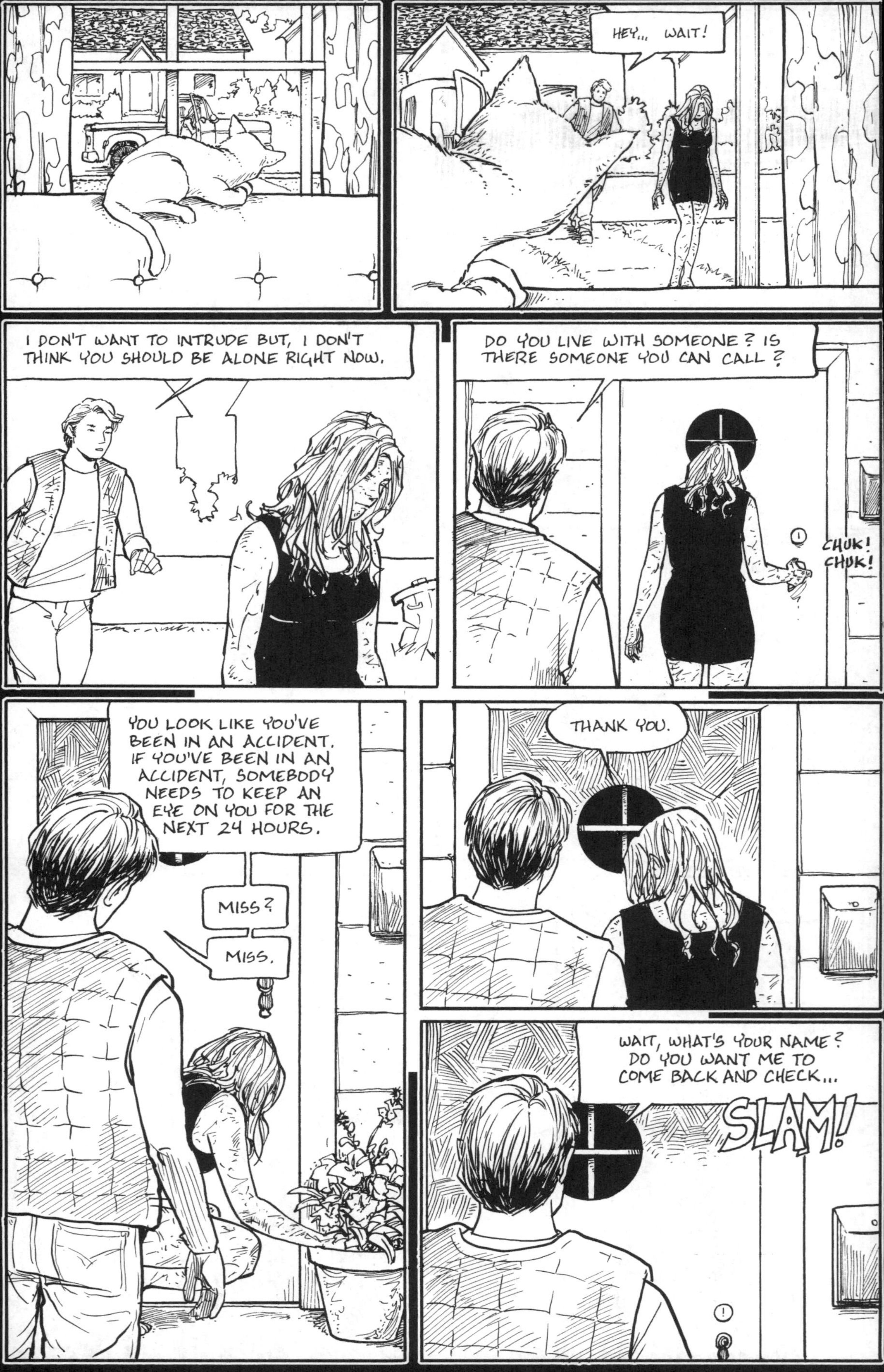

HEY... WAIT!
I DON'T WANT TO INTRUDE BUT, I DON'T THINK YOU SHOULD BE ALONE RIGHT NOW.
DO YOU LIVE WITH SOMEONE? IS THERE SOMEONE YOU CAN CALL?
CHUK! CHUK!
YOU LOOK LIKE YOU'VE BEEN IN AN ACCIDENT. IF YOU'VE BEEN IN AN ACCIDENT, SOMEBODY NEEDS TO KEEP AN EYE ON YOU FOR THE NEXT 24 HOURS.
MISS?
MISS.
THANK YOU.
WAIT, WHAT'S YOUR NAME? DO YOU WANT ME TO COME BACK AND CHECK...
SLAM!

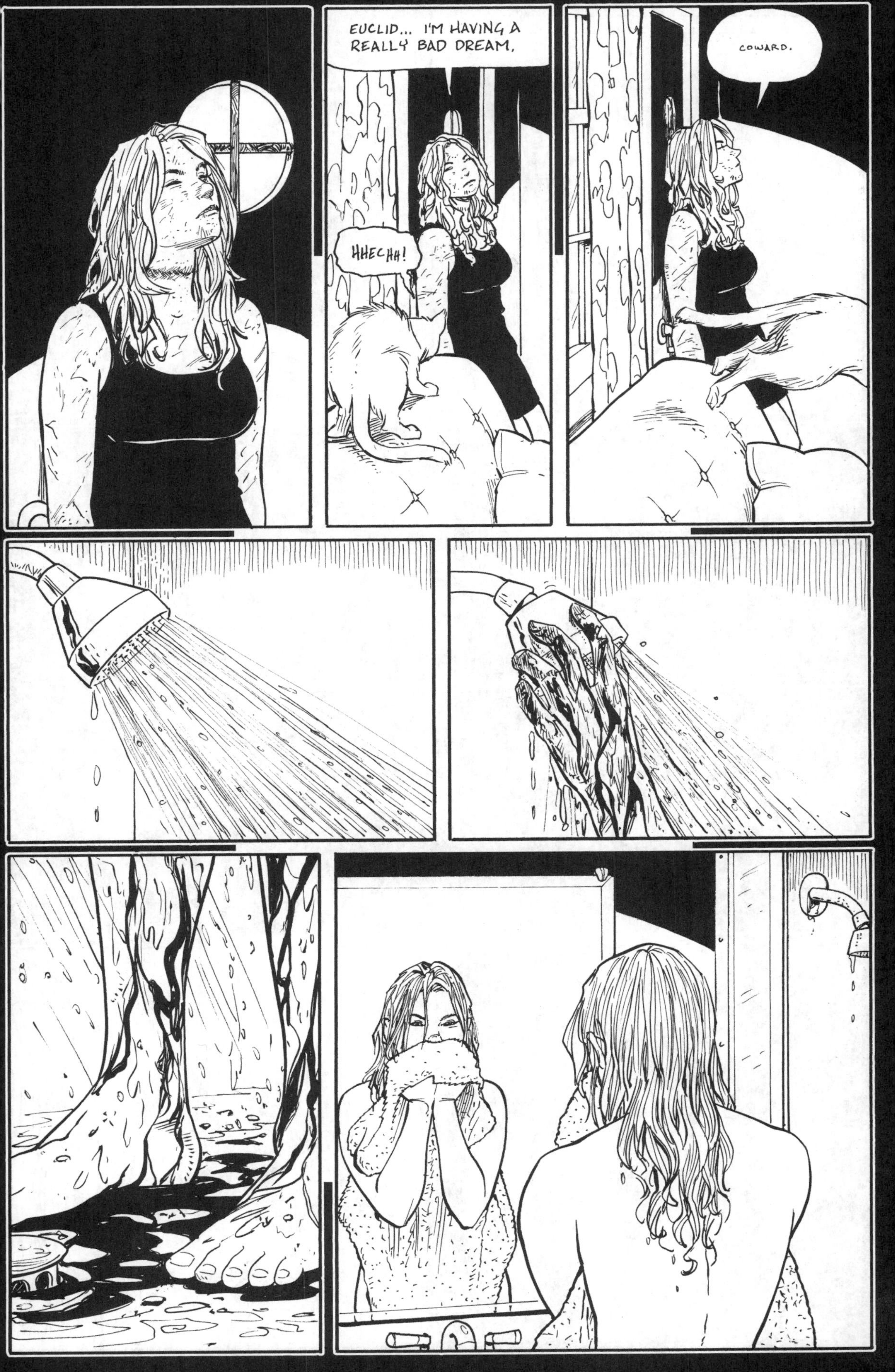
EUCLID... I'M HAVING A REALLY BAD DREAM.
HHECHH!
COWARD.

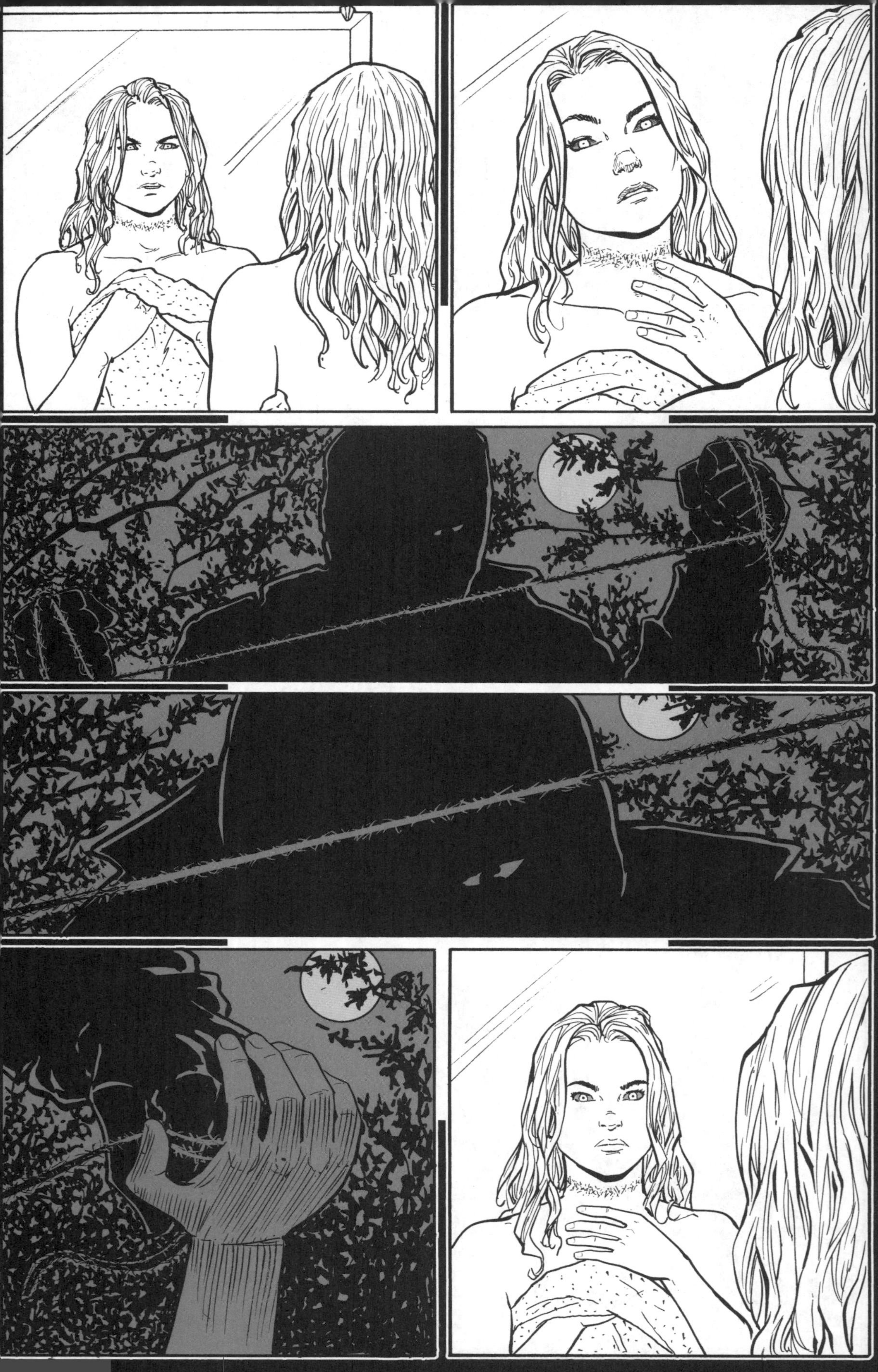

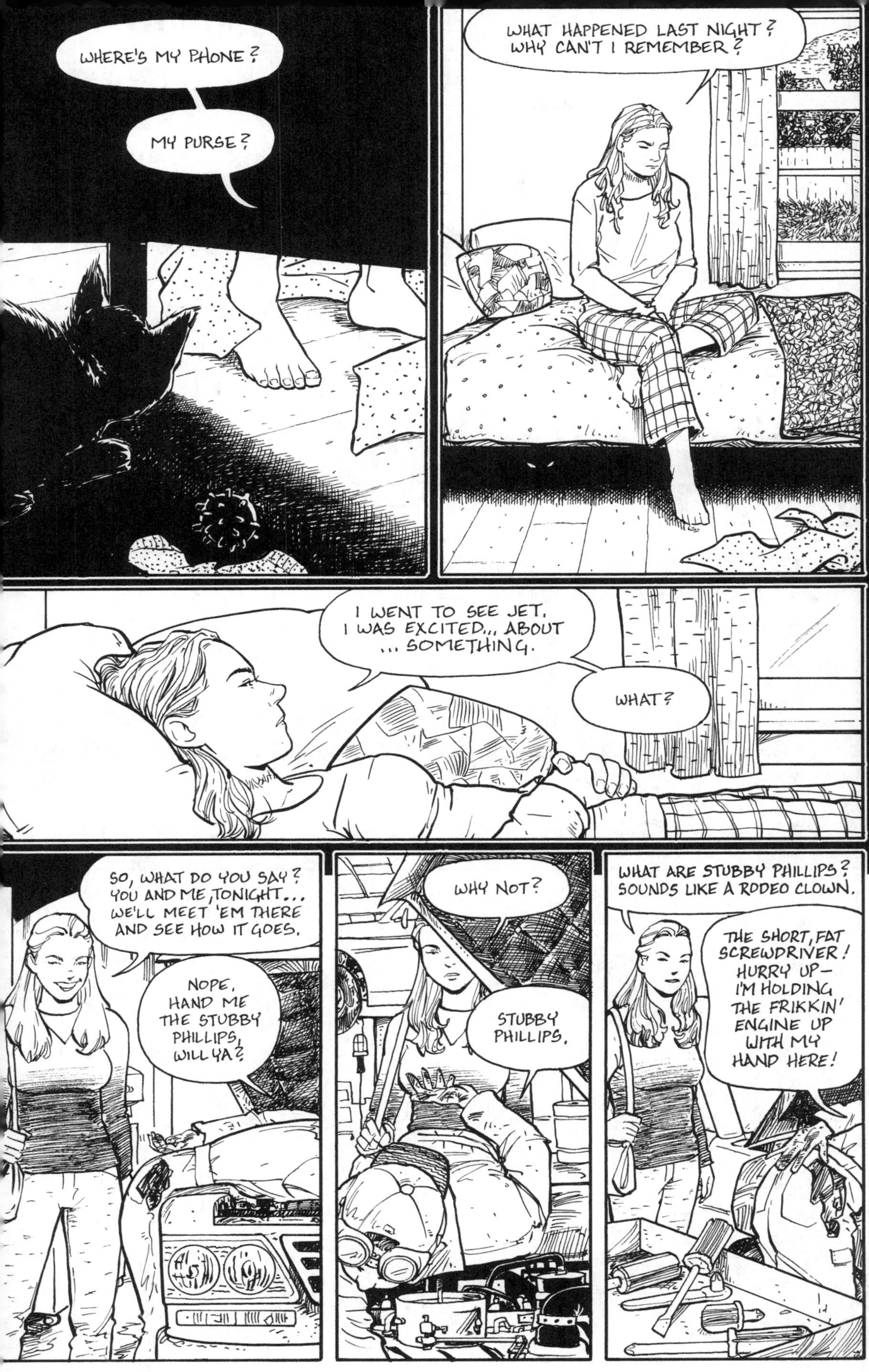
WHERE'S MY PHONE?
MY PURSE?
WHAT HAPPENED LAST NIGHT? WHY CAN'T I REMEMBER?
I WENT TO SEE JET. I WAS EXCITED... ABOUT ... SOMETHING.
WHAT?
SO, WHAT DO YOU SAY? YOU AND ME, TONIGHT... WE'LL MEET 'EM THERE AND SEE HOW IT GOES.
NOPE, HAND ME THE STUBBY PHILLIPS, WILL YA?
WHY NOT?
STUBBY PHILLIPS.
WHAT ARE STUBBY PHILLIPS? SOUNDS LIKE A RODEO CLOWN.
THE SHORT, FAT SCREWDRIVER! HURRY UP— I'M HOLDING THE FRIKKIN' ENGINE UP WITH MY HAND HERE!

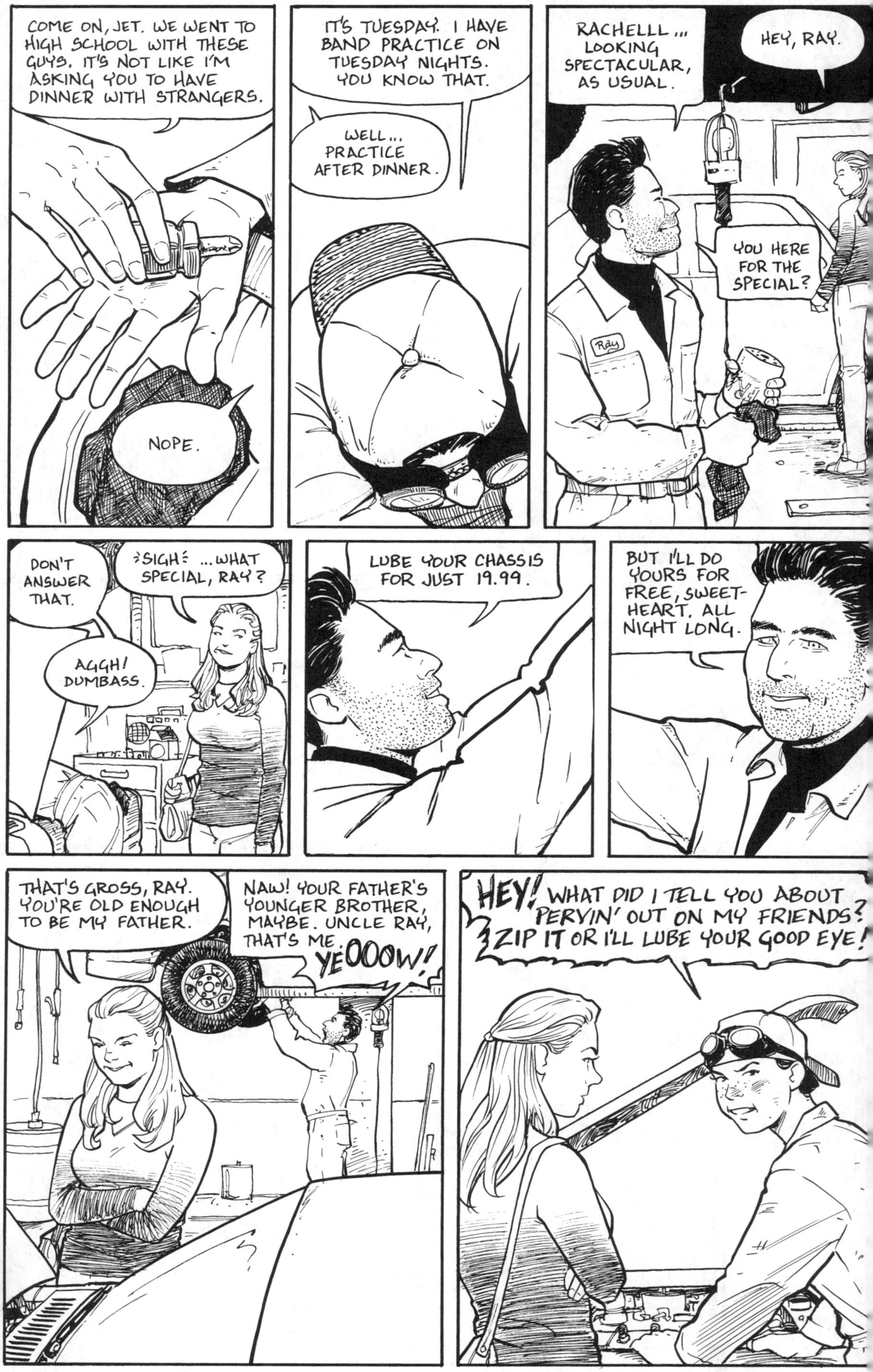
COME ON, JET. WE WENT TO HIGH SCHOOL WITH THESE GUYS. IT'S NOT LIKE I'M ASKING YOU TO HAVE DINNER WITH STRANGERS.
NOPE.
IT'S TUESDAY. I HAVE BAND PRACTICE ON TUESDAY NIGHTS. YOU KNOW THAT.
WELL... PRACTICE AFTER DINNER.
RACHELLL... LOOKING SPECTACULAR, AS USUAL.
HEY, RAY.
YOU HERE FOR THE SPECIAL?
RAY
DON'T ANSWER THAT.
:SIGH: ...WHAT SPECIAL, RAY?
AGGH! DUMBASS.
LUBE YOUR CHASSIS FOR JUST 19.99.
BUT I'LL DO YOURS FOR FREE, SWEET-HEART. ALL NIGHT LONG.
THAT'S GROSS, RAY. YOU'RE OLD ENOUGH TO BE MY FATHER.
NAW! YOUR FATHER'S YOUNGER BROTHER, MAYBE. UNCLE RAY, THAT'S ME.
YEOOOW!
HEY! WHAT DID I TELL YOU ABOUT PERVIN' OUT ON MY FRIENDS? ZIP IT OR I'LL LUBE YOUR GOOD EYE!

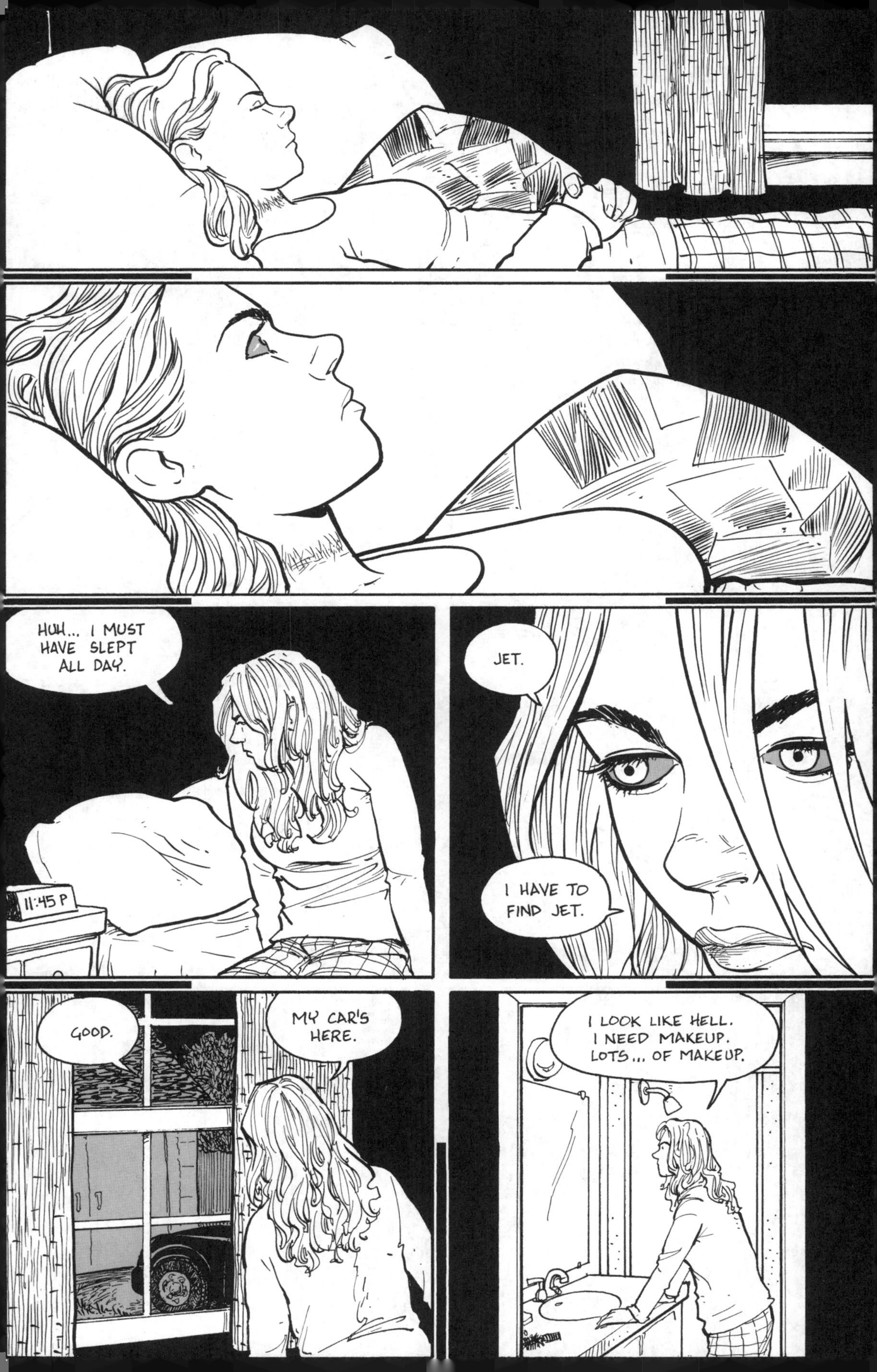
HUH... I MUST HAVE SLEPT ALL DAY.
11:45 P
JET.
I HAVE TO FIND JET.
GOOD.
MY CAR'S HERE.
I LOOK LIKE HELL. I NEED MAKEUP. LOTS... OF MAKEUP.

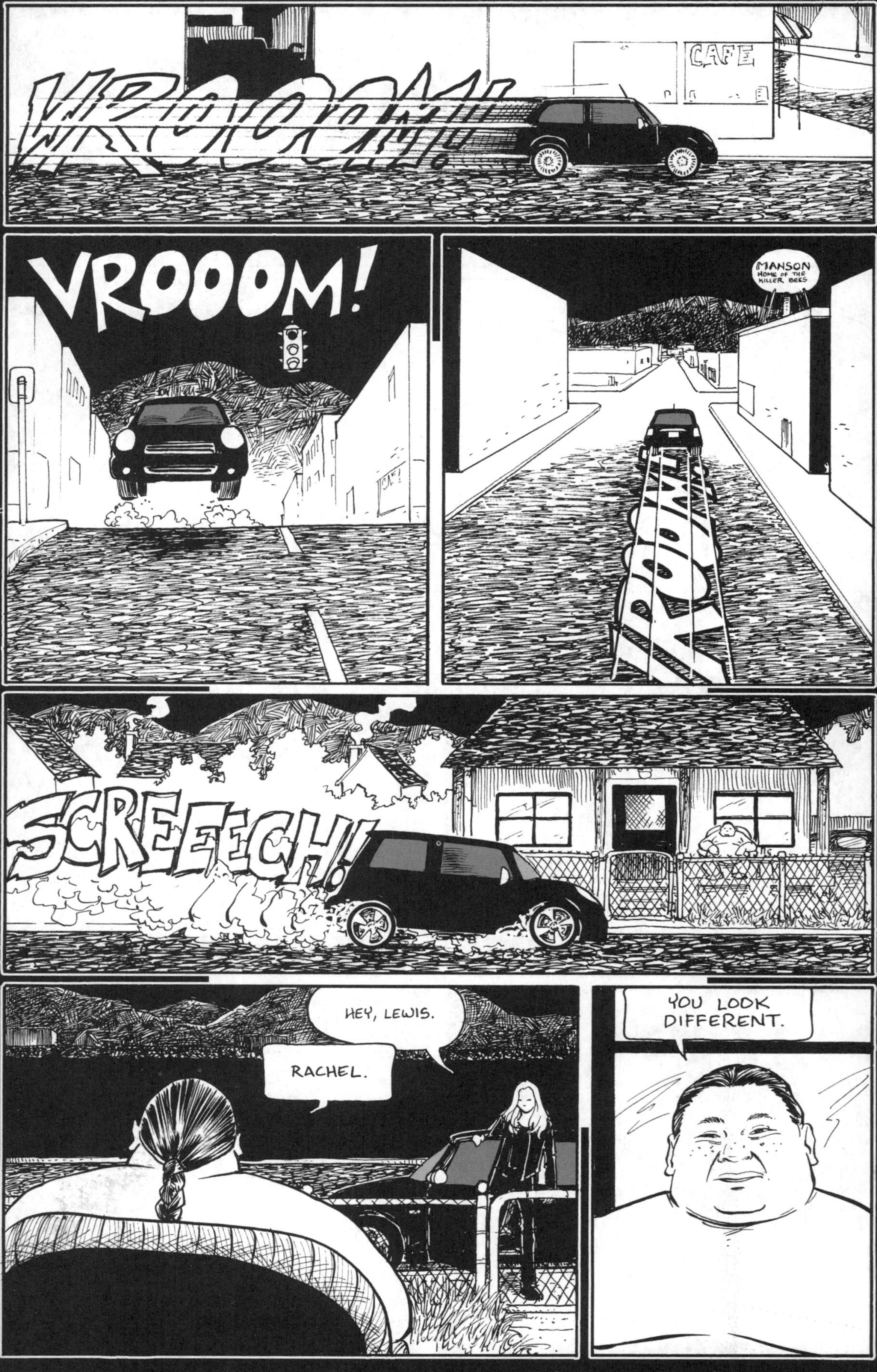
CAFE
VROOOM!
MANSON
HOME OF THE KILLER BEES
SCREEECH!
HEY, LEWIS.
RACHEL.
YOU LOOK DIFFERENT.

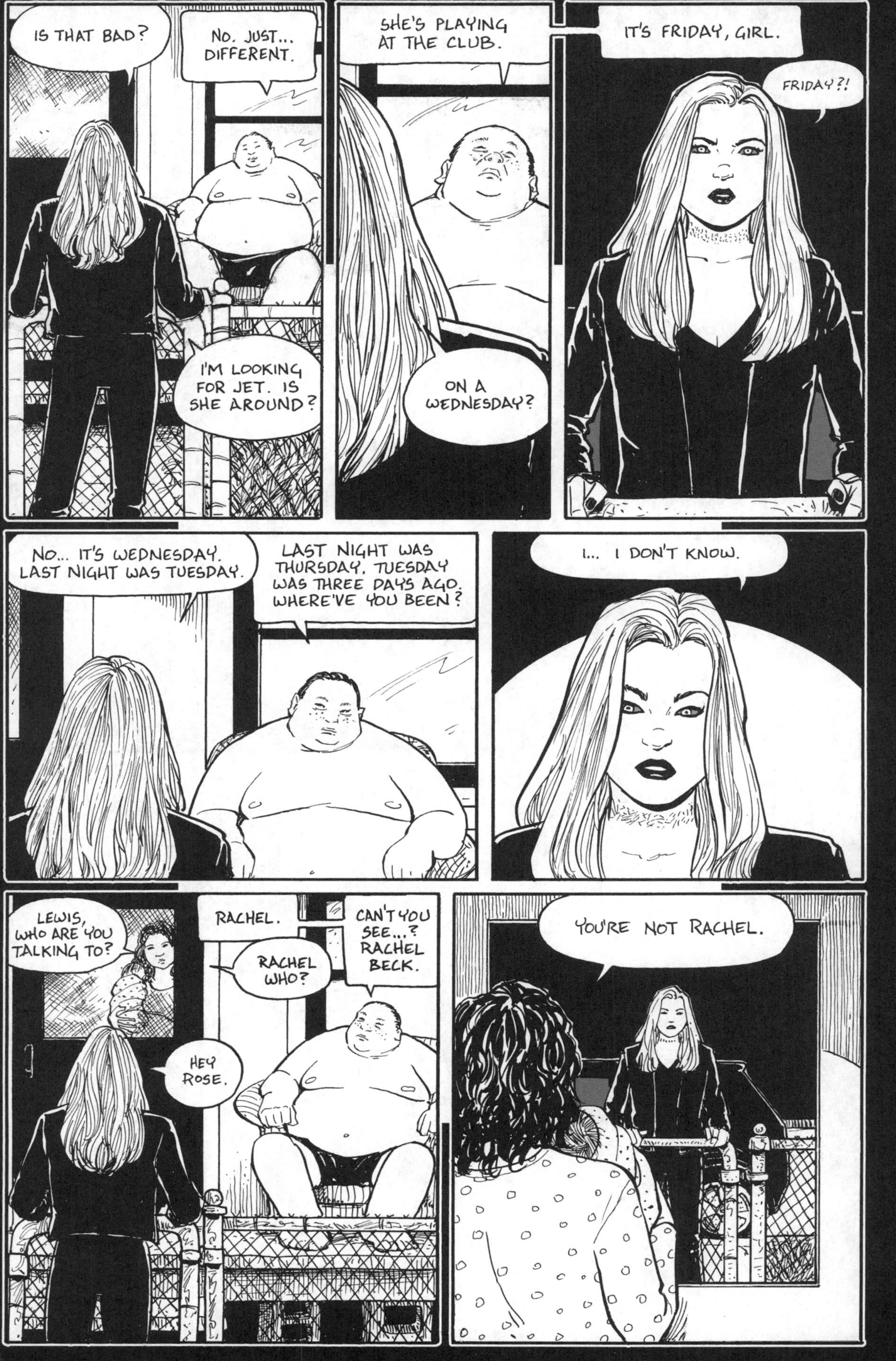
IS THAT BAD?
NO. JUST... DIFFERENT.
I'M LOOKING FOR JET. IS SHE AROUND?
SHE'S PLAYING AT THE CLUB.
ON A WEDNESDAY?
IT'S FRIDAY, GIRL.
FRIDAY?!
NO... IT'S WEDNESDAY. LAST NIGHT WAS TUESDAY.
LAST NIGHT WAS THURSDAY. TUESDAY WAS THREE DAYS AGO. WHERE'VE YOU BEEN?
I... I DON'T KNOW.
LEWIS, WHO ARE YOU TALKING TO?
HEY ROSE.
RACHEL.
RACHEL WHO?
CAN'T YOU SEE...? RACHEL BECK.
YOU'RE NOT RACHEL.

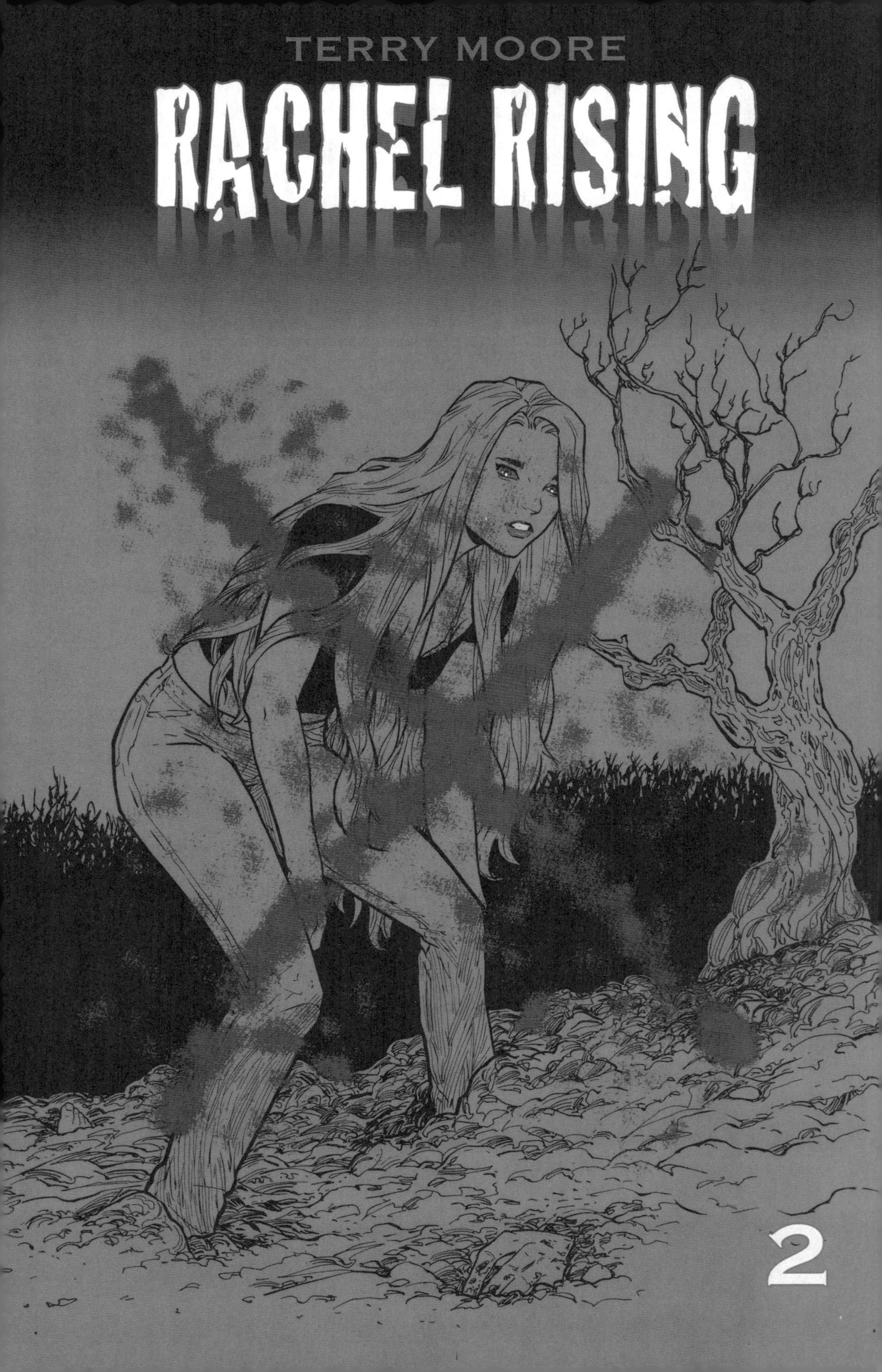
TERRY MOORE
RACHEL RISING
2

FROM MY ROTTING BODY, FLOWERS
SHALL GROW AND I AM IN THEM
AND THAT IS ETERNITY.
—EDWARD MUNCH

SCREEECH!

AUTHORIZED PERSONELL ONLY

BZZt!

WHO IS IT?

IT'S ME, RACHEL.

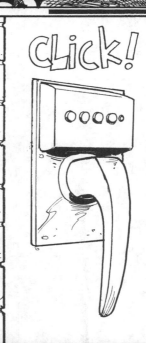

CLICK!

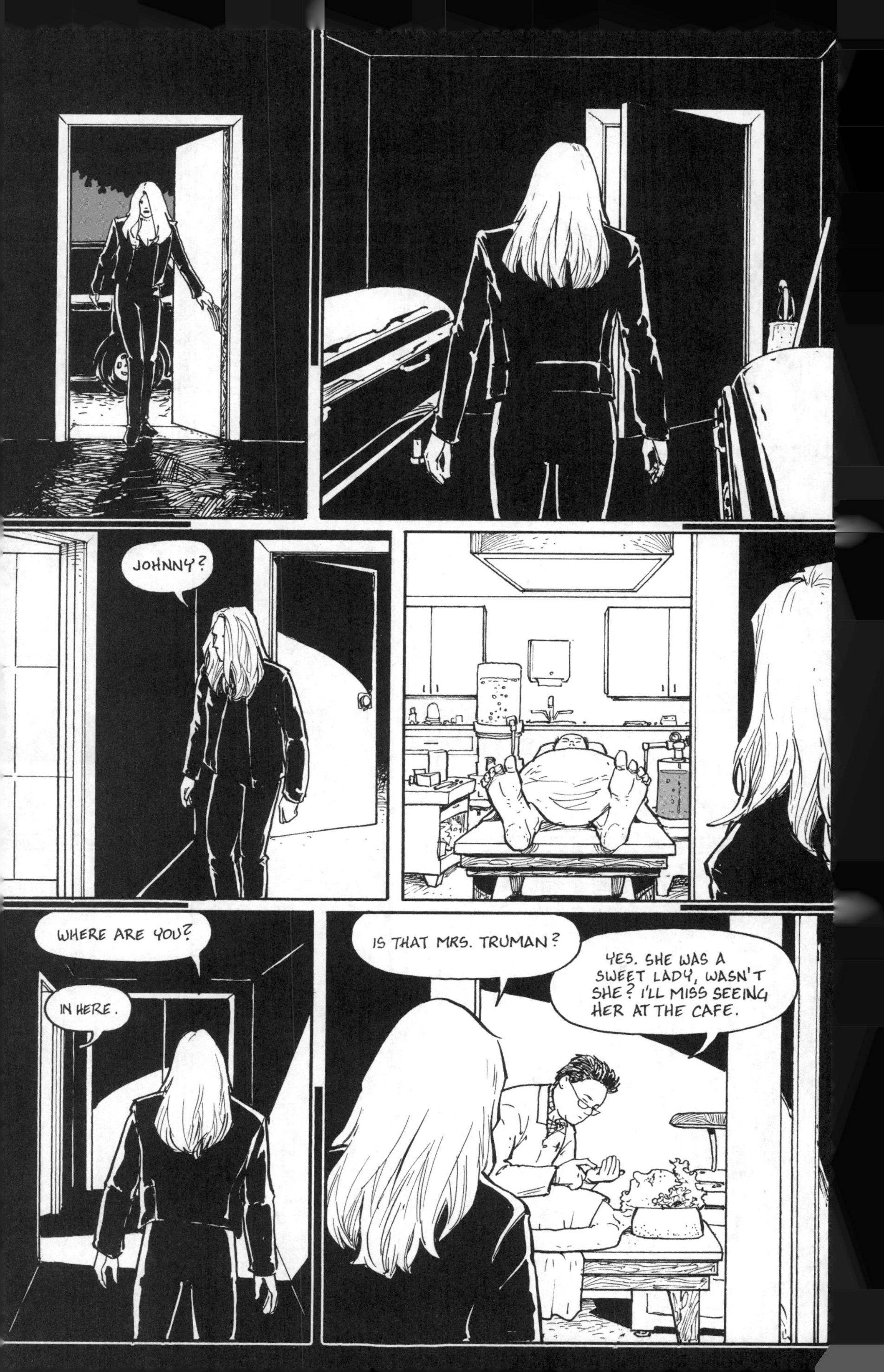
JOHNNY?
WHERE ARE YOU?
IN HERE.
IS THAT MRS. TRUMAN?
YES. SHE WAS A SWEET LADY, WASN'T SHE? I'LL MISS SEEING HER AT THE CAFE.

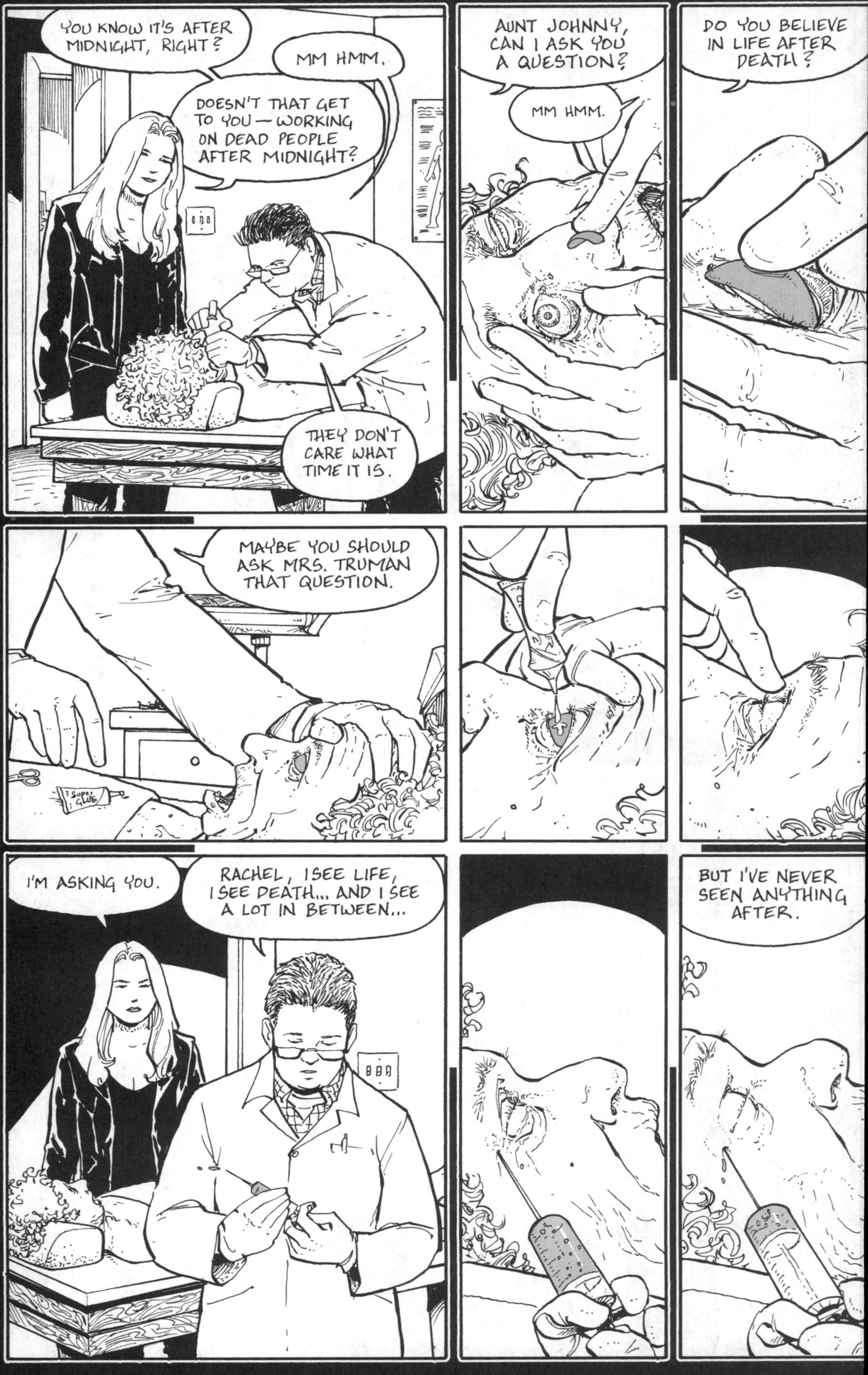
YOU KNOW IT'S AFTER MIDNIGHT, RIGHT?
MM HMM.
DOESN'T THAT GET TO YOU — WORKING ON DEAD PEOPLE AFTER MIDNIGHT?
THEY DON'T CARE WHAT TIME IT IS.
AUNT JOHNNY, CAN I ASK YOU A QUESTION?
MM HMM.
DO YOU BELIEVE IN LIFE AFTER DEATH?
MAYBE YOU SHOULD ASK MRS. TRUMAN THAT QUESTION.
SUPER GLUE
I'M ASKING YOU.
RACHEL, I SEE LIFE, I SEE DEATH... AND I SEE A LOT IN BETWEEN...
BUT I'VE NEVER SEEN ANYTHING AFTER.

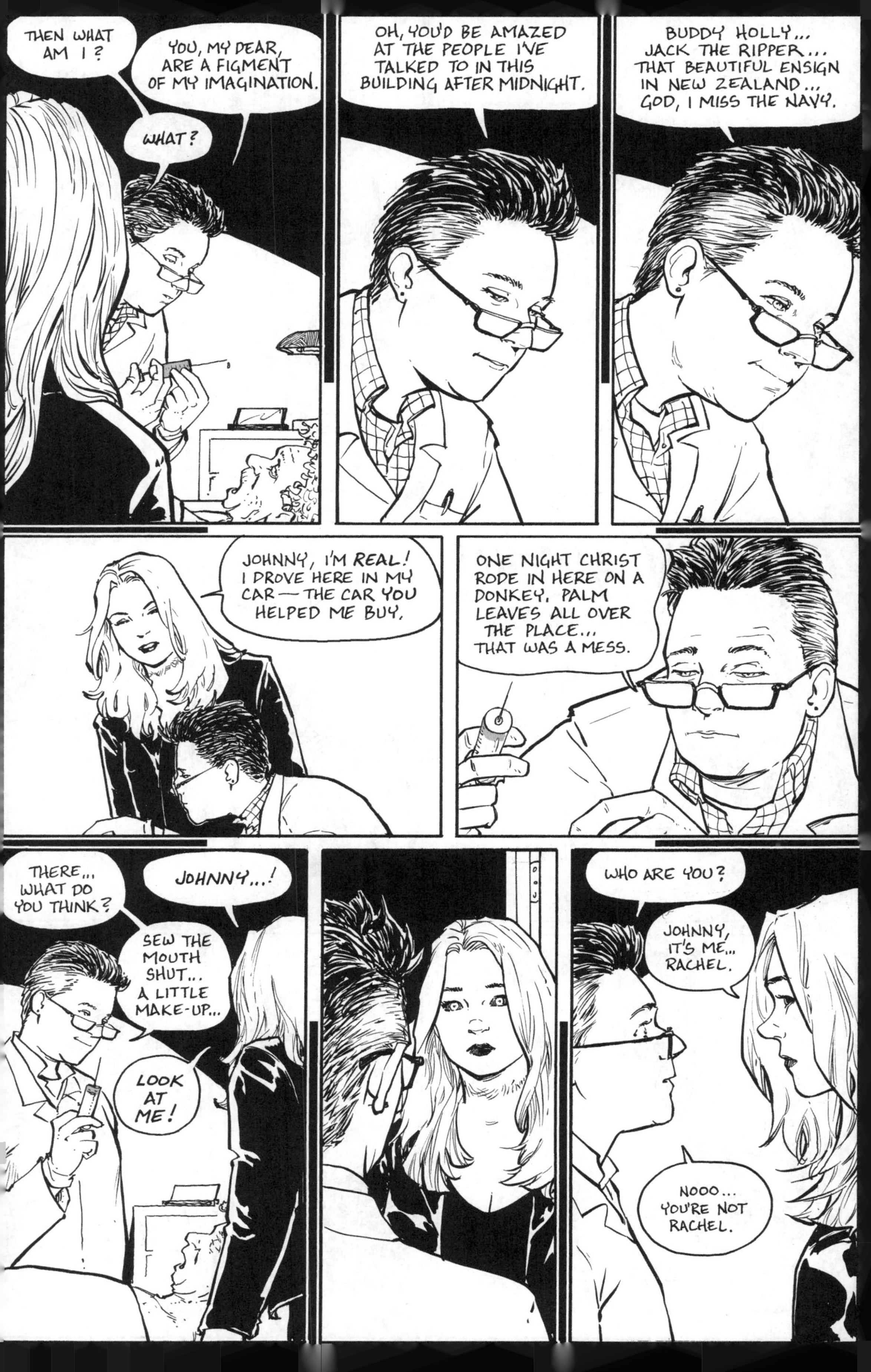
THEN WHAT AM I?
YOU, MY DEAR, ARE A FIGMENT OF MY IMAGINATION.
WHAT?
OH, YOU'D BE AMAZED AT THE PEOPLE I'VE TALKED TO IN THIS BUILDING AFTER MIDNIGHT.
BUDDY HOLLY... JACK THE RIPPER... THAT BEAUTIFUL ENSIGN IN NEW ZEALAND... GOD, I MISS THE NAVY.
JOHNNY, I'M REAL! I DROVE HERE IN MY CAR — THE CAR YOU HELPED ME BUY.
ONE NIGHT CHRIST RODE IN HERE ON A DONKEY, PALM LEAVES ALL OVER THE PLACE... THAT WAS A MESS.
THERE... WHAT DO YOU THINK?
JOHNNY...!
SEW THE MOUTH SHUT... A LITTLE MAKE-UP...
LOOK AT ME!
WHO ARE YOU?
JOHNNY, IT'S ME... RACHEL.
NOOO... YOU'RE NOT RACHEL.

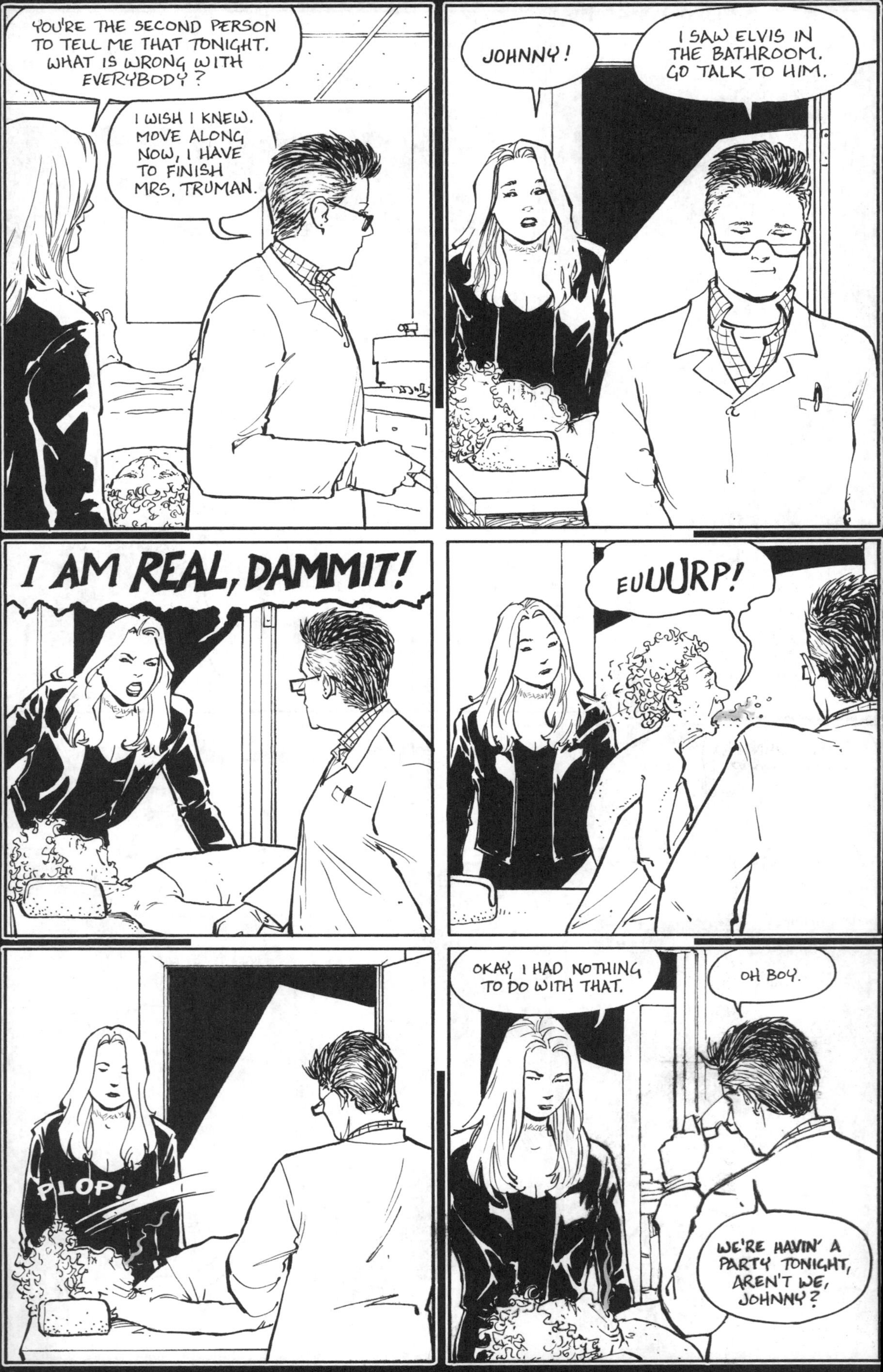
YOU'RE THE SECOND PERSON TO TELL ME THAT TONIGHT. WHAT IS WRONG WITH EVERYBODY?
I WISH I KNEW. MOVE ALONG NOW, I HAVE TO FINISH MRS. TRUMAN.
JOHNNY!
I SAW ELVIS IN THE BATHROOM. GO TALK TO HIM.
I AM REAL, DAMMIT!
EUUURP!
PLOP!
OKAY, I HAD NOTHING TO DO WITH THAT.
OH BOY.
WE'RE HAVIN' A PARTY TONIGHT, AREN'T WE, JOHNNY?

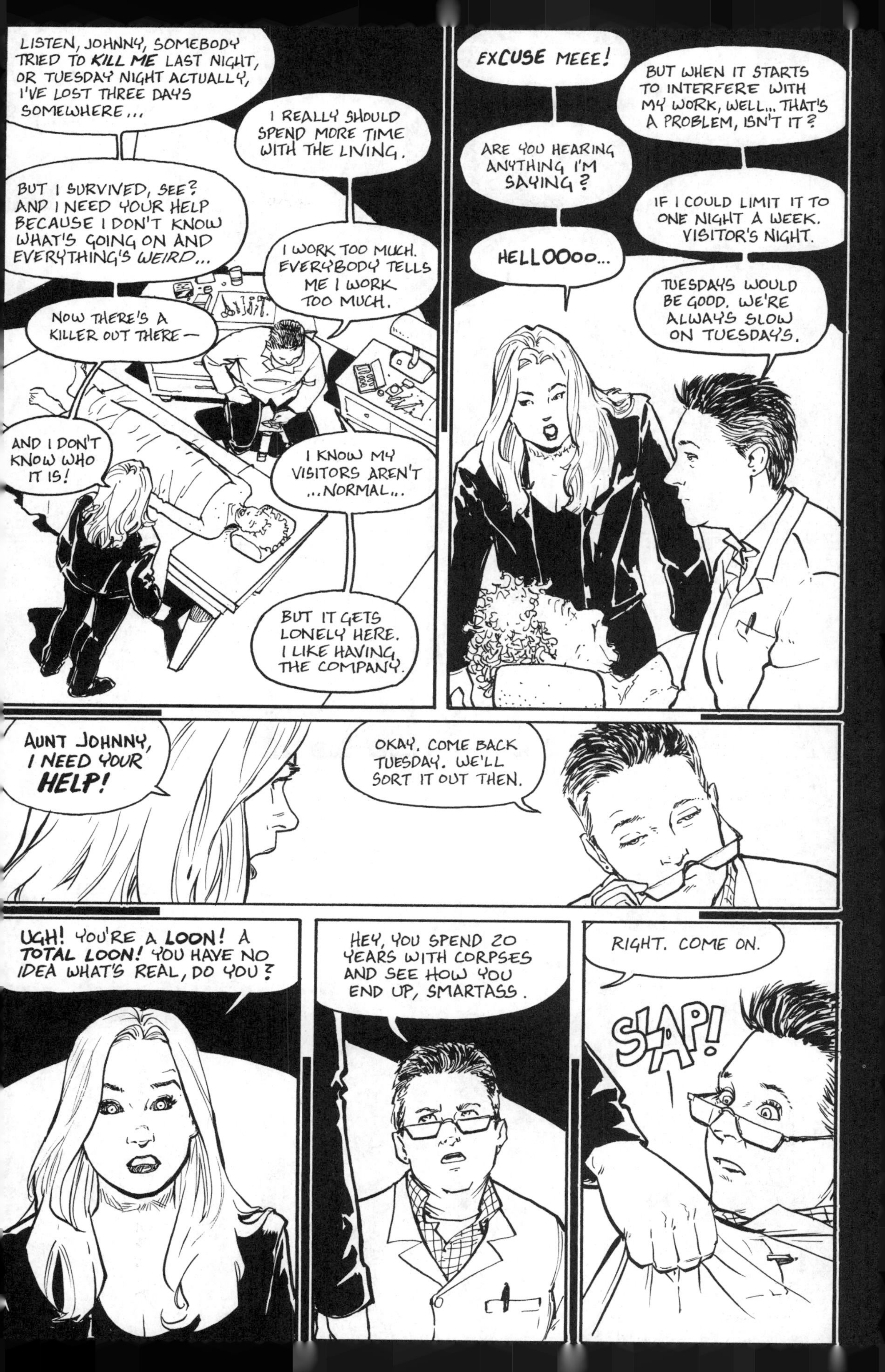
LISTEN, JOHNNY, SOMEBODY TRIED TO KILL ME LAST NIGHT, OR TUESDAY NIGHT ACTUALLY, I'VE LOST THREE DAYS SOMEWHERE...
I REALLY SHOULD SPEND MORE TIME WITH THE LIVING.
BUT I SURVIVED, SEE? AND I NEED YOUR HELP BECAUSE I DON'T KNOW WHAT'S GOING ON AND EVERYTHING'S WEIRD...
I WORK TOO MUCH. EVERYBODY TELLS ME I WORK TOO MUCH.
NOW THERE'S A KILLER OUT THERE—
AND I DON'T KNOW WHO IT IS!
I KNOW MY VISITORS AREN'T ...NORMAL...
BUT IT GETS LONELY HERE. I LIKE HAVING THE COMPANY.
EXCUSE MEEE!
BUT WHEN IT STARTS TO INTERFERE WITH MY WORK, WELL... THAT'S A PROBLEM, ISN'T IT?
ARE YOU HEARING ANYTHING I'M SAYING?
IF I COULD LIMIT IT TO ONE NIGHT A WEEK. VISITOR'S NIGHT.
HELLOOoo...
TUESDAYS WOULD BE GOOD. WE'RE ALWAYS SLOW ON TUESDAYS.
AUNT JOHNNY, I NEED YOUR HELP!
OKAY. COME BACK TUESDAY. WE'LL SORT IT OUT THEN.
UGH! YOU'RE A LOON! A TOTAL LOON! YOU HAVE NO IDEA WHAT'S REAL, DO YOU?
HEY, YOU SPEND 20 YEARS WITH CORPSES AND SEE HOW YOU END UP, SMARTASS.
RIGHT. COME ON.
SLAP!

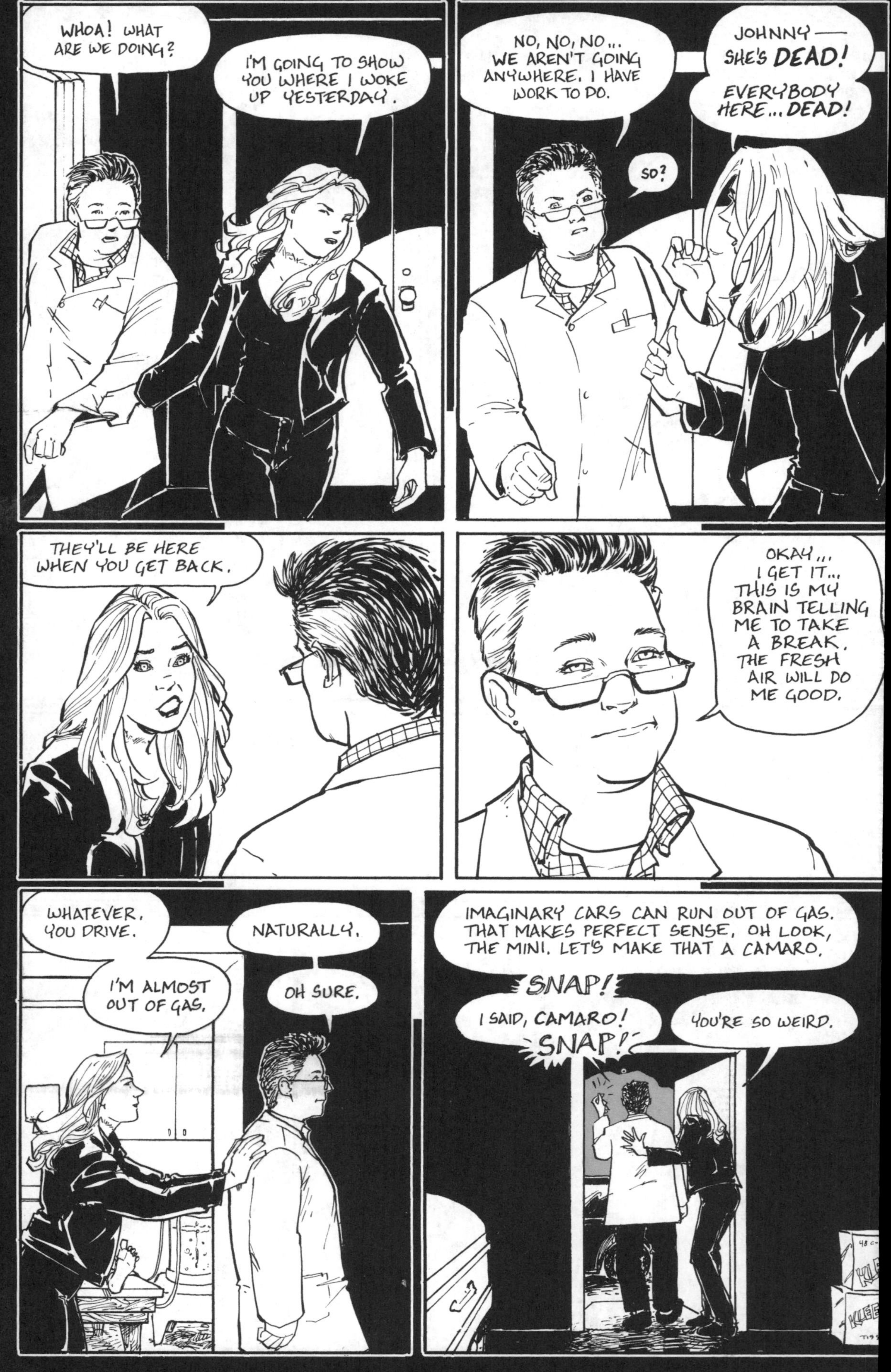

WHOA! WHAT ARE WE DOING?
I'M GOING TO SHOW YOU WHERE I WOKE UP YESTERDAY.
NO, NO, NO... WE AREN'T GOING ANYWHERE. I HAVE WORK TO DO.
JOHNNY — SHE'S DEAD!
EVERYBODY HERE... DEAD!
SO?
THEY'LL BE HERE WHEN YOU GET BACK.
OKAY... I GET IT... THIS IS MY BRAIN TELLING ME TO TAKE A BREAK. THE FRESH AIR WILL DO ME GOOD.
WHATEVER. YOU DRIVE.
NATURALLY.
I'M ALMOST OUT OF GAS.
OH SURE.
IMAGINARY CARS CAN RUN OUT OF GAS. THAT MAKES PERFECT SENSE, OH LOOK, THE MINI. LET'S MAKE THAT A CAMARO.
SNAP!
I SAID, CAMARO!
SNAP!
YOU'RE SO WEIRD.

VAROOOM!

BLAPBLAP!

I LOVE THIS CAR.

YOU SAY THAT EVERY TIME,

I LOVE IT EVERY TIME,

SINCE YOU WERE A CHILD,

YEP. FLOOR IT.

BRAAAUGH!

SCREEECH!

LOVE

IT!

BRAAAUGGHH! SCREEEECH!

UNDERWOOD MORTUARY

WHERE TO?

STRAIGHT. FIREHILL.

FIREHILL? I DON'T HAVE TIME TO GO WAY UP THERE.

BRRAAAAAUUUGHH!

DRIVE.

LEAVING MANSON COME BACK SOON

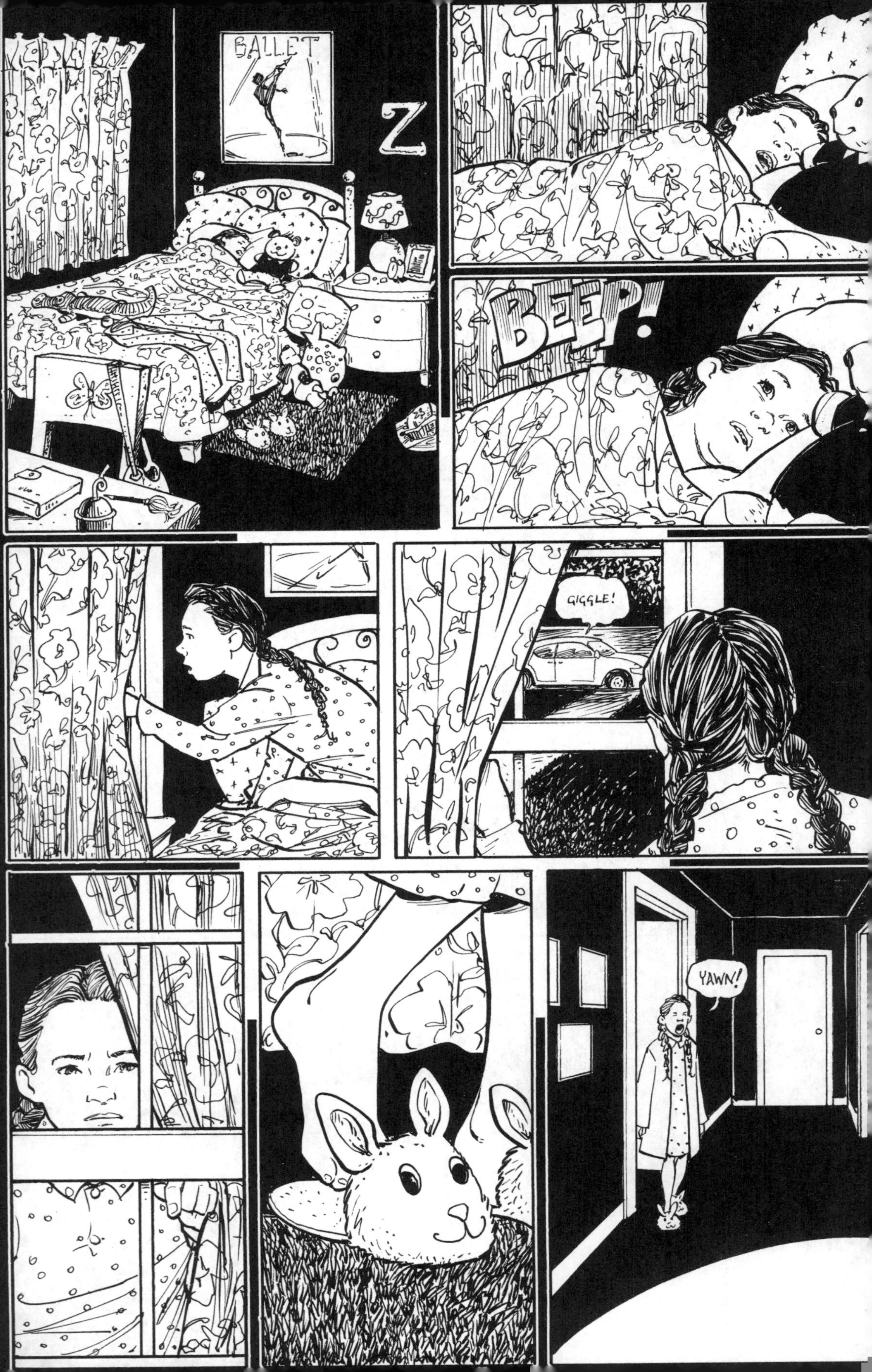
BALLET
Z
BEEP!
GIGGLE!
YAWN!

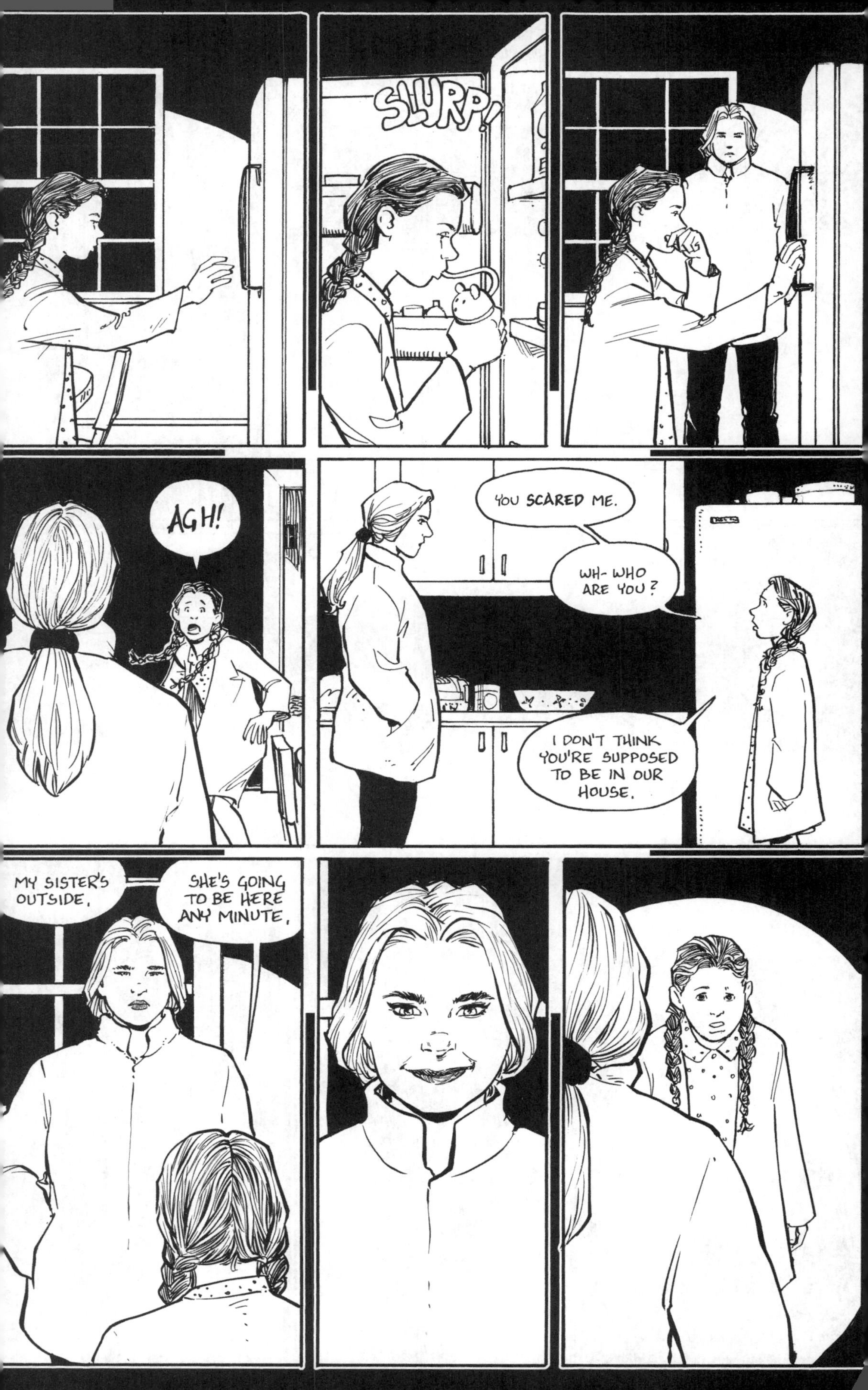
SLURP!
AGH!
YOU SCARED ME.
WH- WHO ARE YOU?
I DON'T THINK YOU'RE SUPPOSED TO BE IN OUR HOUSE.
MY SISTER'S OUTSIDE.
SHE'S GOING TO BE HERE ANY MINUTE.

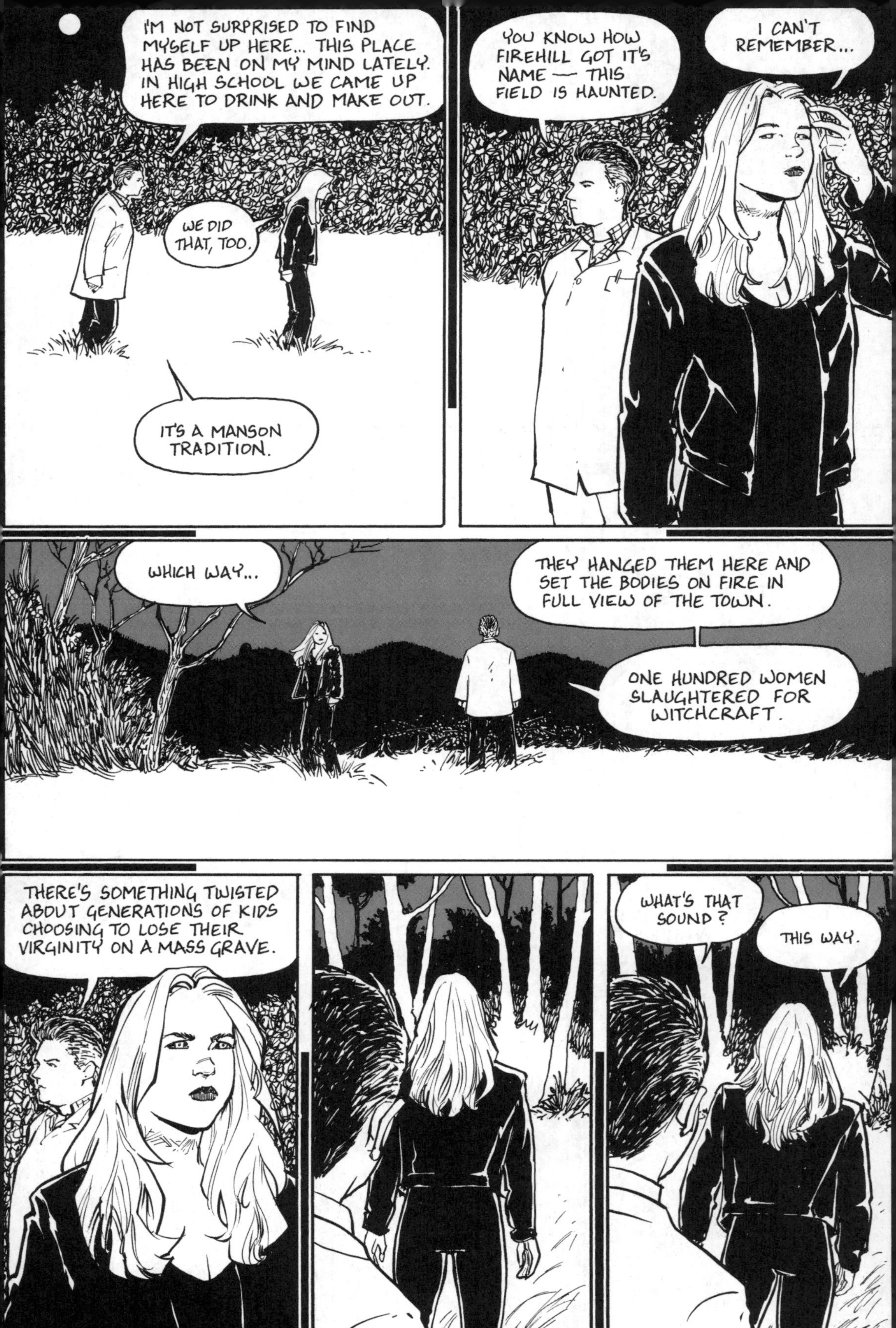
I'M NOT SURPRISED TO FIND MYSELF UP HERE... THIS PLACE HAS BEEN ON MY MIND LATELY. IN HIGH SCHOOL WE CAME UP HERE TO DRINK AND MAKE OUT.
WE DID THAT, TOO.
IT'S A MANSON TRADITION.
YOU KNOW HOW FIREHILL GOT IT'S NAME — THIS FIELD IS HAUNTED.
I CAN'T REMEMBER...
WHICH WAY...
THEY HANGED THEM HERE AND SET THE BODIES ON FIRE IN FULL VIEW OF THE TOWN.
ONE HUNDRED WOMEN SLAUGHTERED FOR WITCHCRAFT.
THERE'S SOMETHING TWISTED ABOUT GENERATIONS OF KIDS CHOOSING TO LOSE THEIR VIRGINITY ON A MASS GRAVE.
WHAT'S THAT SOUND?
THIS WAY.

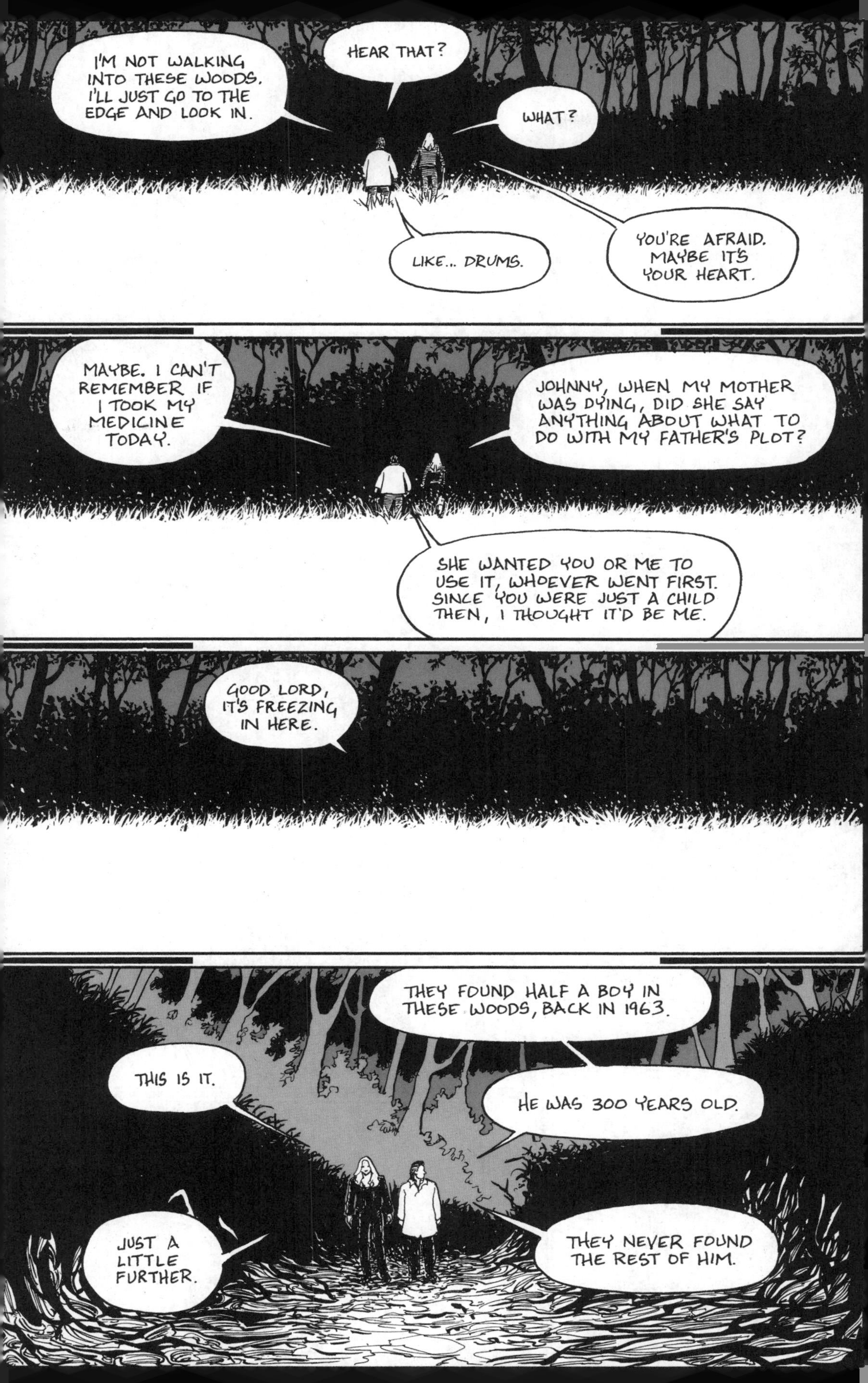
I'M NOT WALKING INTO THESE WOODS. I'LL JUST GO TO THE EDGE AND LOOK IN.
HEAR THAT?
WHAT?
LIKE... DRUMS.
YOU'RE AFRAID. MAYBE IT'S YOUR HEART.
MAYBE. I CAN'T REMEMBER IF I TOOK MY MEDICINE TODAY.
JOHNNY, WHEN MY MOTHER WAS DYING, DID SHE SAY ANYTHING ABOUT WHAT TO DO WITH MY FATHER'S PLOT?
SHE WANTED YOU OR ME TO USE IT, WHOEVER WENT FIRST. SINCE YOU WERE JUST A CHILD THEN, I THOUGHT IT'D BE ME.
GOOD LORD, IT'S FREEZING IN HERE.
THEY FOUND HALF A BOY IN THESE WOODS, BACK IN 1963.
THIS IS IT.
HE WAS 300 YEARS OLD.
JUST A LITTLE FURTHER.
THEY NEVER FOUND THE REST OF HIM.

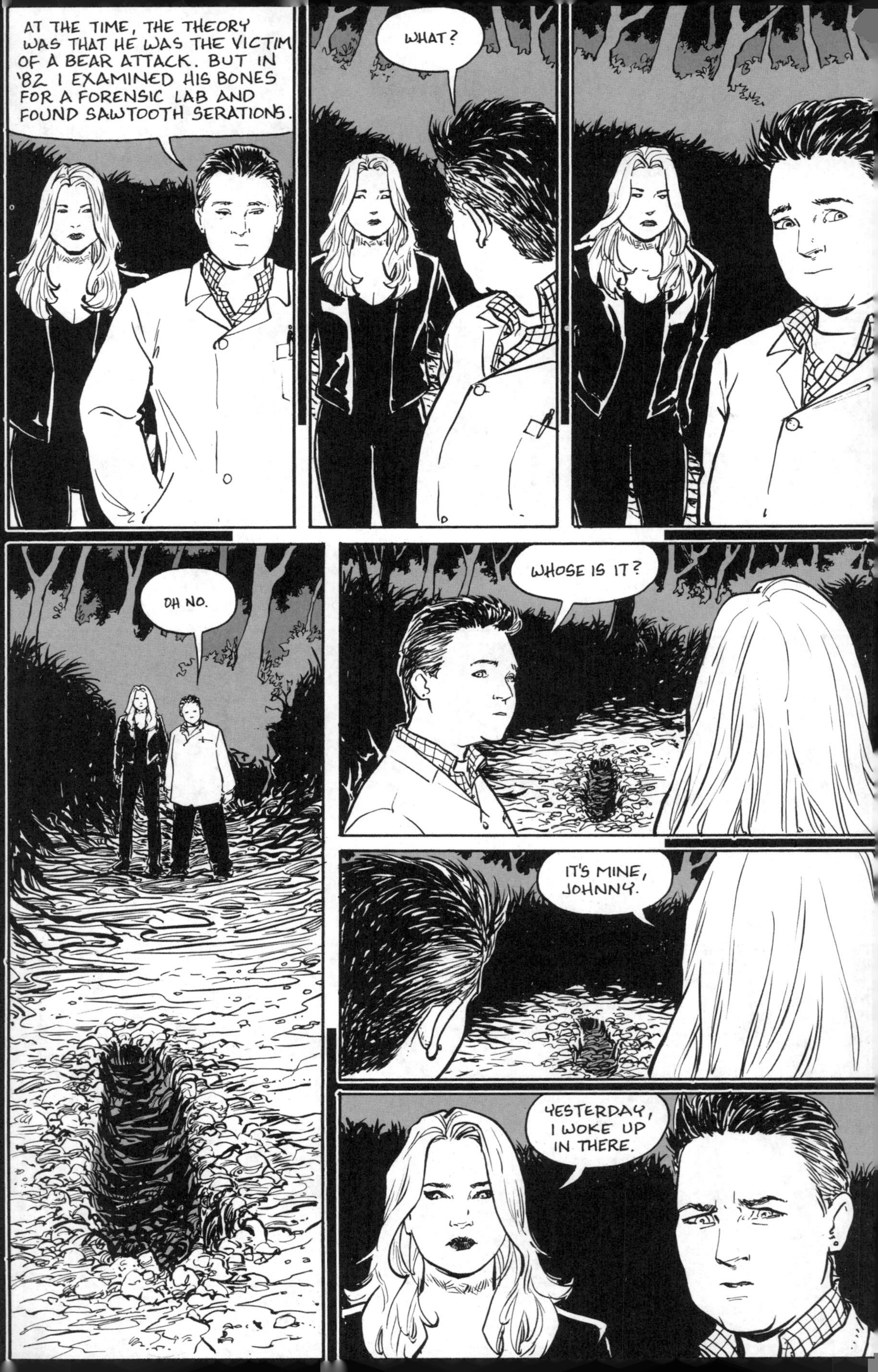
AT THE TIME, THE THEORY WAS THAT HE WAS THE VICTIM OF A BEAR ATTACK. BUT IN '82 I EXAMINED HIS BONES FOR A FORENSIC LAB AND FOUND SAWTOOTH SERATIONS.
WHAT?
OH NO.
WHOSE IS IT?
IT'S MINE, JOHNNY.
YESTERDAY, I WOKE UP IN THERE.

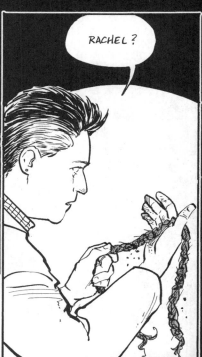

RACHEL?

NO, NO, NO!

RACHEL!

JOHNNY, I'M HERE.

WHERE'S THE BODY?
WHERE'S *YOUR* BODY?

JOHNNY, I'M
NOT A GHOST,
I'M NOT DEAD.

NOT...?
>PANT<
>PANT<

Oh God,
Look at me...

I'm losing
my mind.

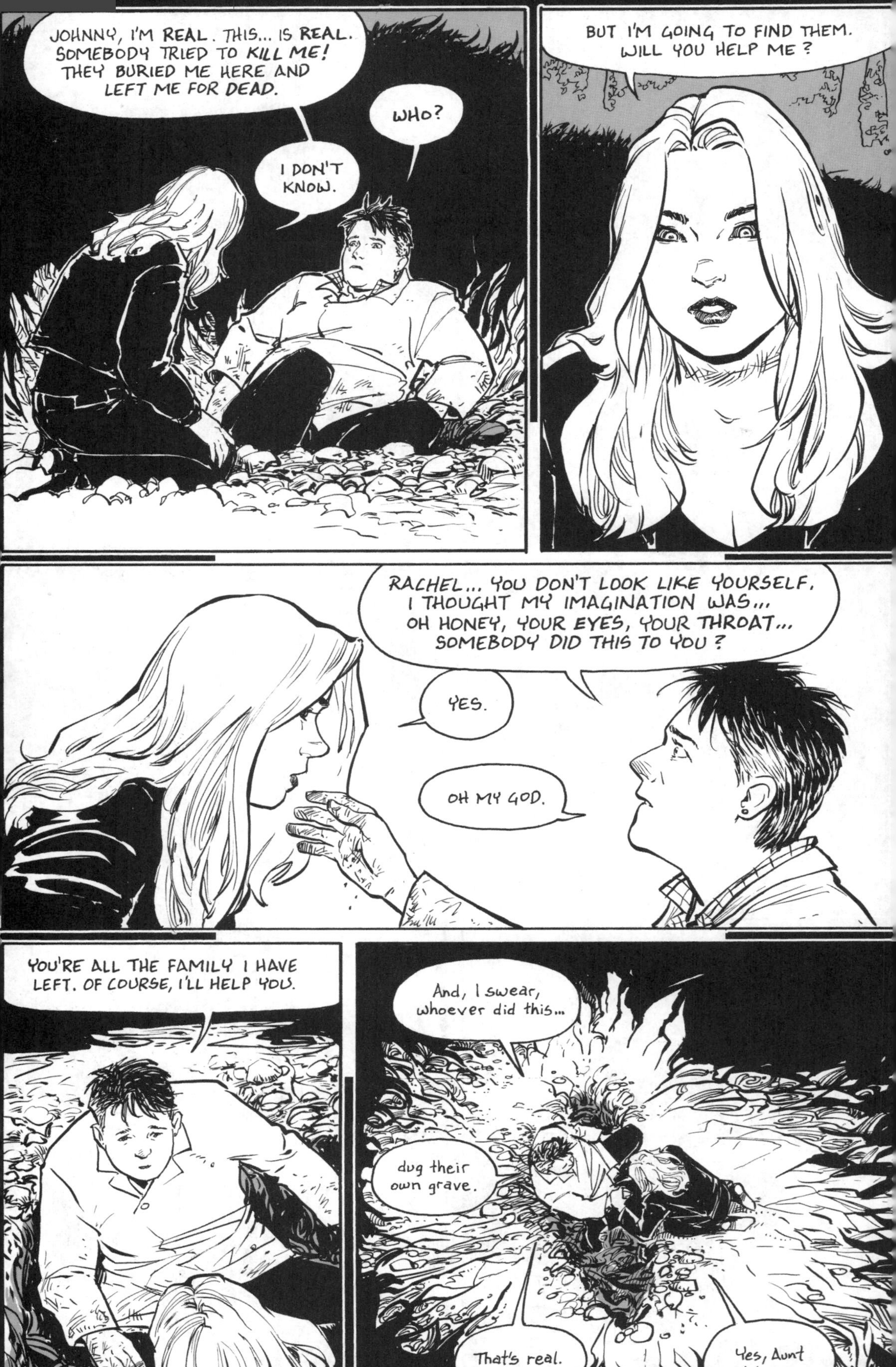
JOHNNY, I'M REAL. THIS... IS REAL. SOMEBODY TRIED TO KILL ME! THEY BURIED ME HERE AND LEFT ME FOR DEAD.
WHO?
I DON'T KNOW.
BUT I'M GOING TO FIND THEM. WILL YOU HELP ME?
RACHEL... YOU DON'T LOOK LIKE YOURSELF. I THOUGHT MY IMAGINATION WAS... OH HONEY, YOUR EYES, YOUR THROAT... SOMEBODY DID THIS TO YOU?
YES.
OH MY GOD.
YOU'RE ALL THE FAMILY I HAVE LEFT. OF COURSE, I'LL HELP YOU.
And, I swear, whoever did this...
dug their own grave.
That's real.
Yes, Aunt Johnny.

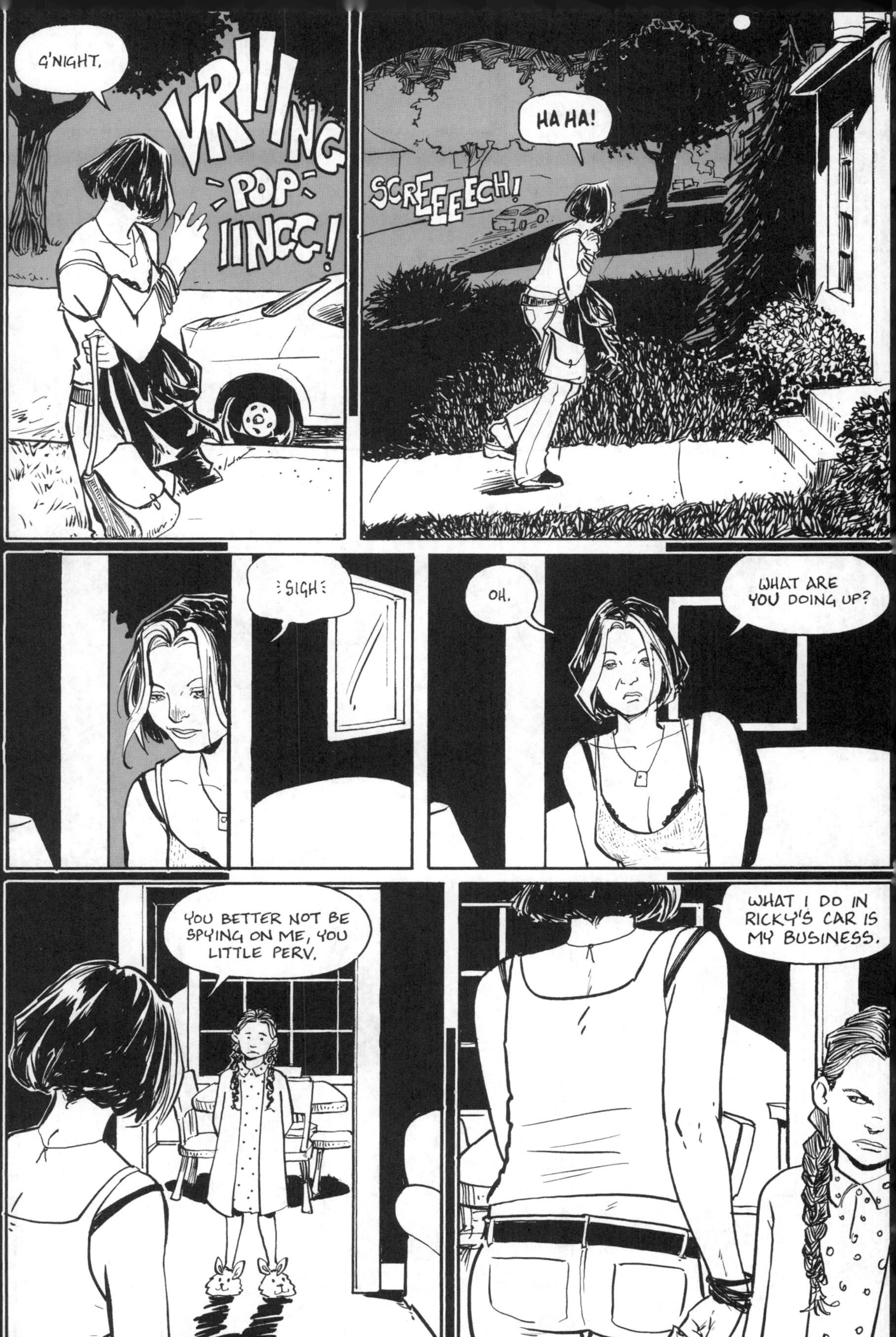
G'NIGHT.
VRIIING
-POP-
IINGG!
HA HA!
SCREEEEECH!
SIGH
OH.
WHAT ARE YOU DOING UP?
YOU BETTER NOT BE SPYING ON ME, YOU LITTLE PERV.
WHAT I DO IN RICKY'S CAR IS MY BUSINESS.

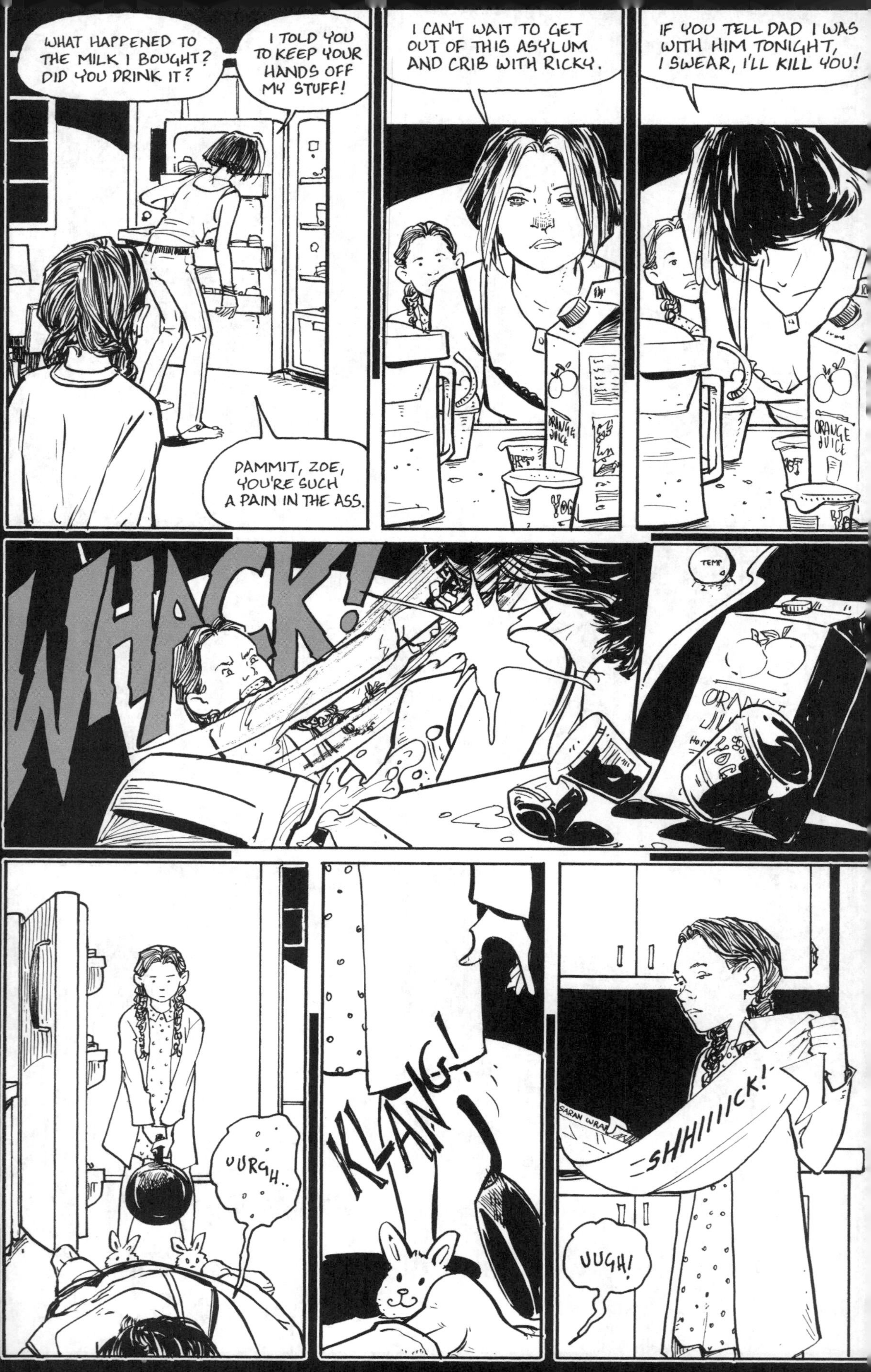
WHAT HAPPENED TO THE MILK I BOUGHT? DID YOU DRINK IT?
I TOLD YOU TO KEEP YOUR HANDS OFF MY STUFF!
DAMMIT, ZOE, YOU'RE SUCH A PAIN IN THE ASS.
I CAN'T WAIT TO GET OUT OF THIS ASYLUM AND CRIB WITH RICKY.
IF YOU TELL DAD I WAS WITH HIM TONIGHT, I SWEAR, I'LL KILL YOU!
WHACK!
UURGH..
KLANG!
SHHIIIICK!
UUGH!

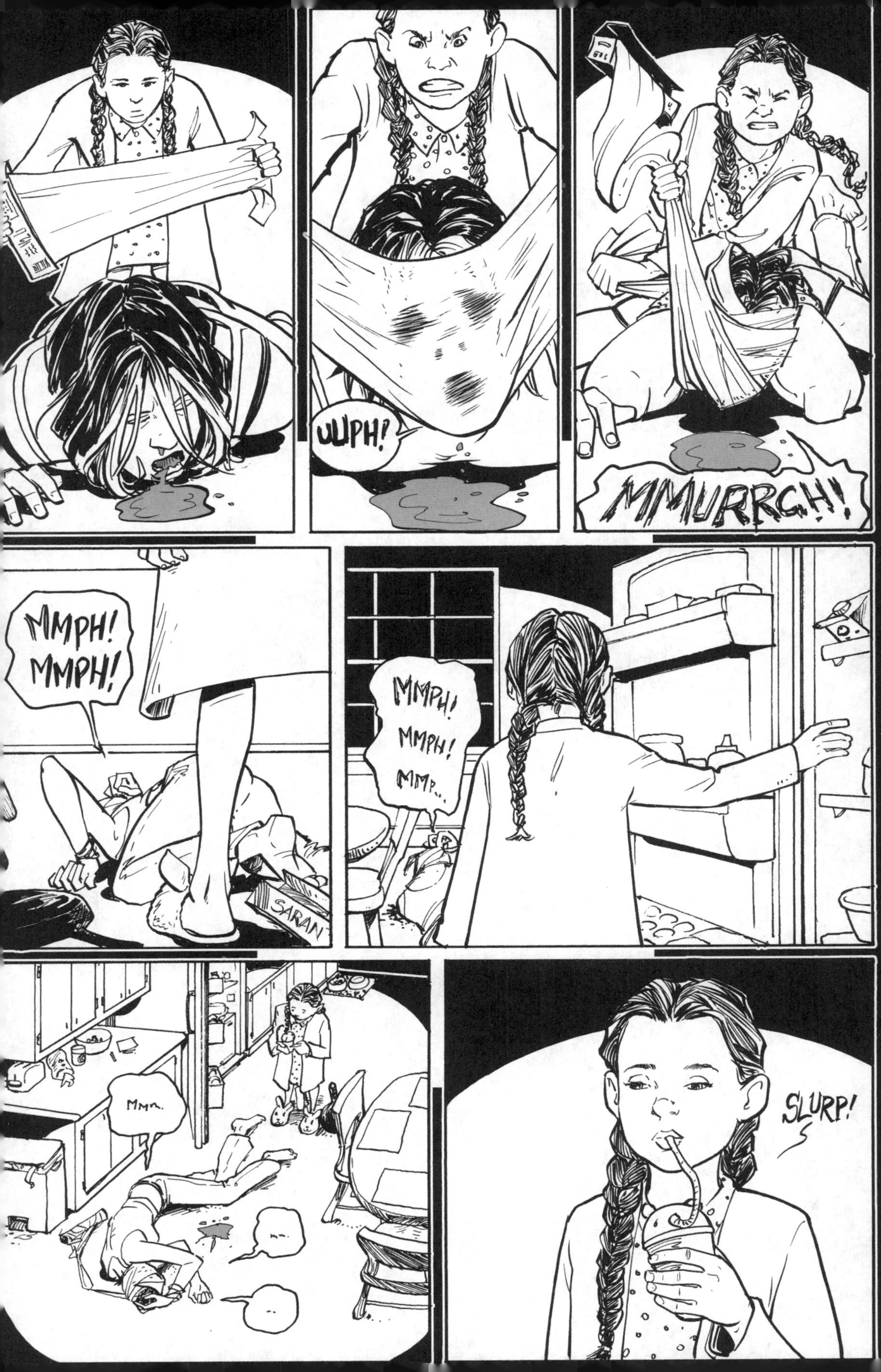
UUPH!
MMURRGH!
MMPH! MMPH!
MMPH! MMPH! MMP...
SARAN
Mmn.
mn.
..
SLURP!

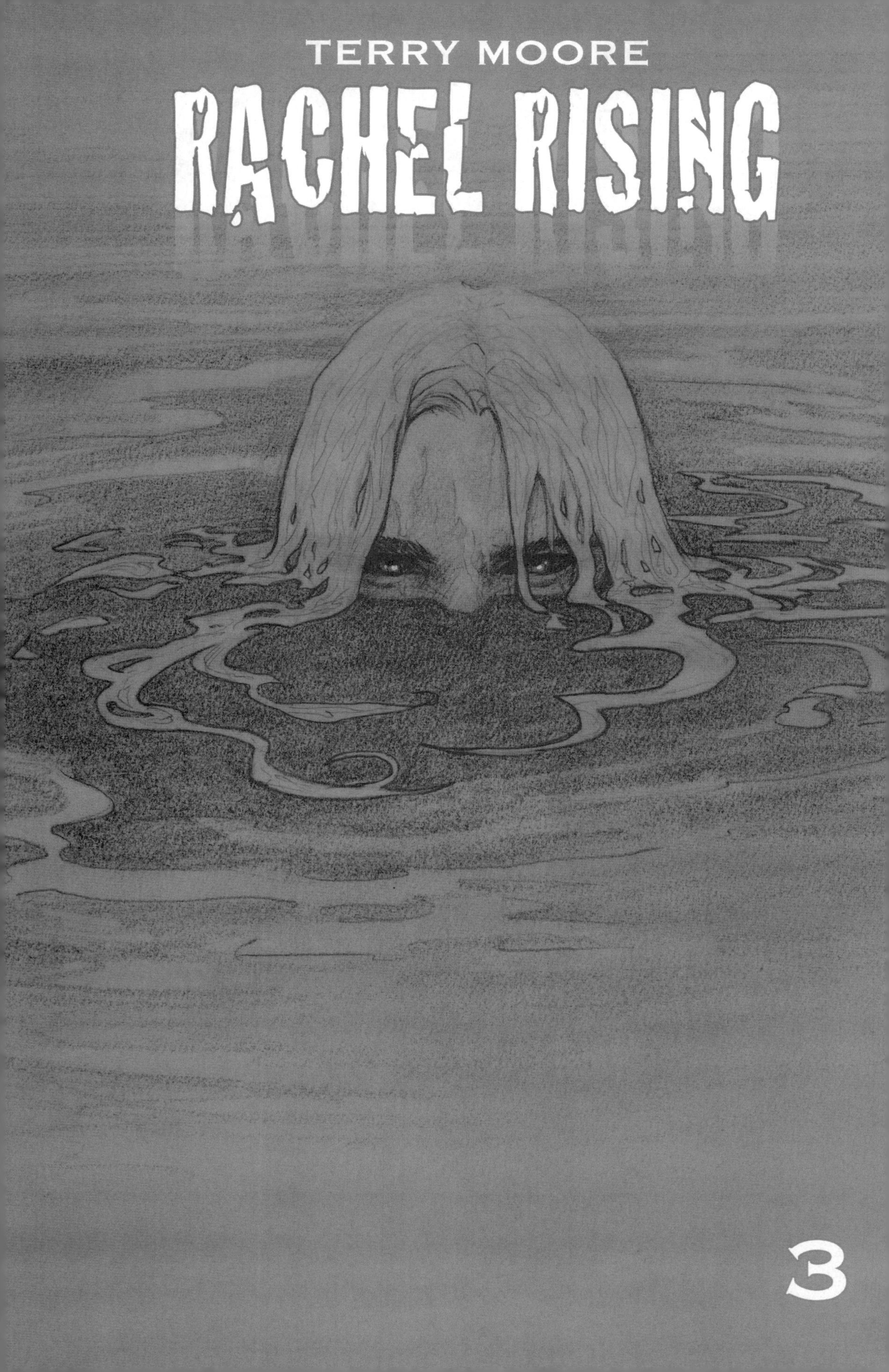
TERRY MOORE
RACHEL RISING
3

IT IS EXTREME EVIL TO DEPART FROM THE
COMPANY OF THE LIVING BEFORE YOU DIE.
—SENECA

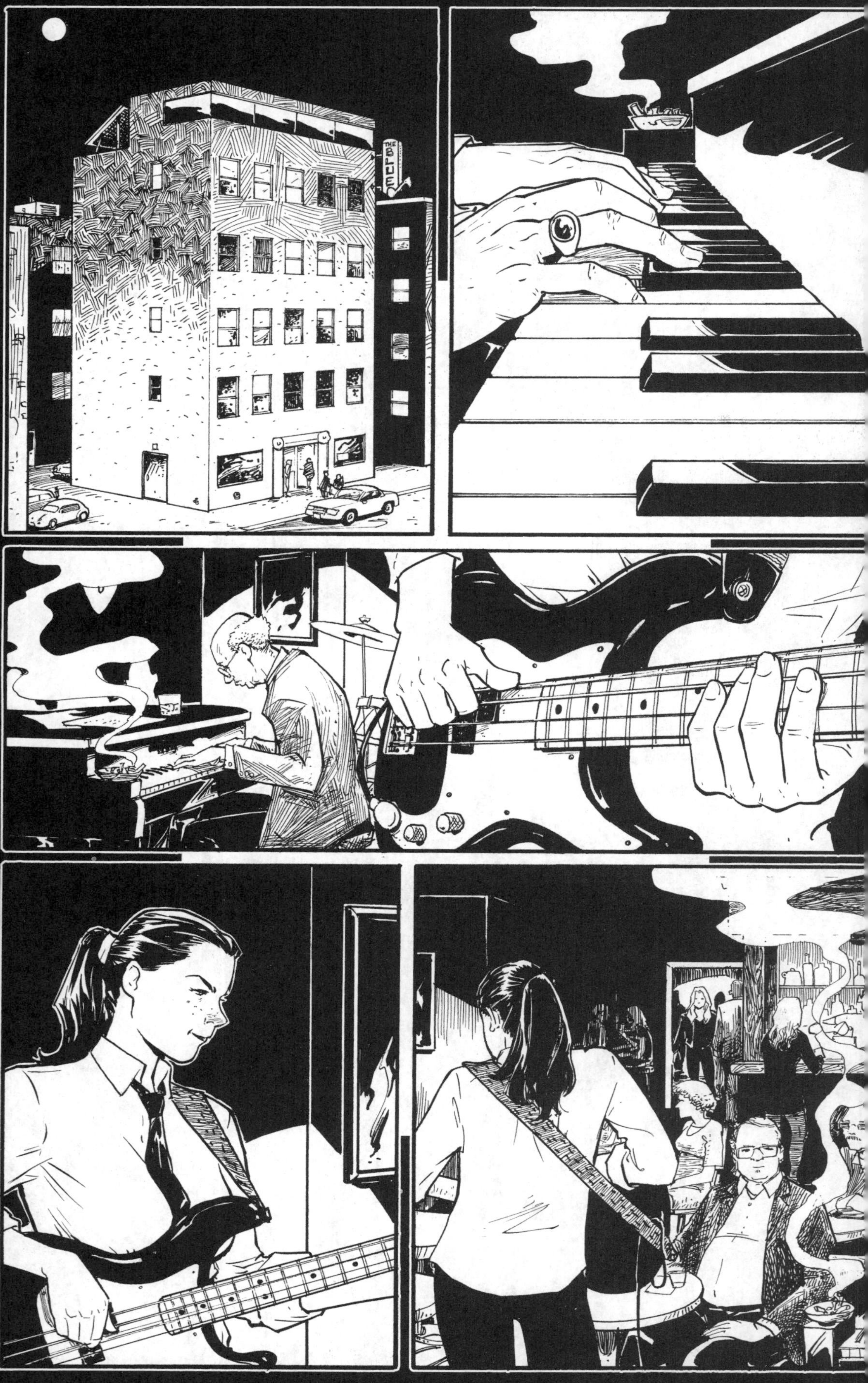
THE BLUE

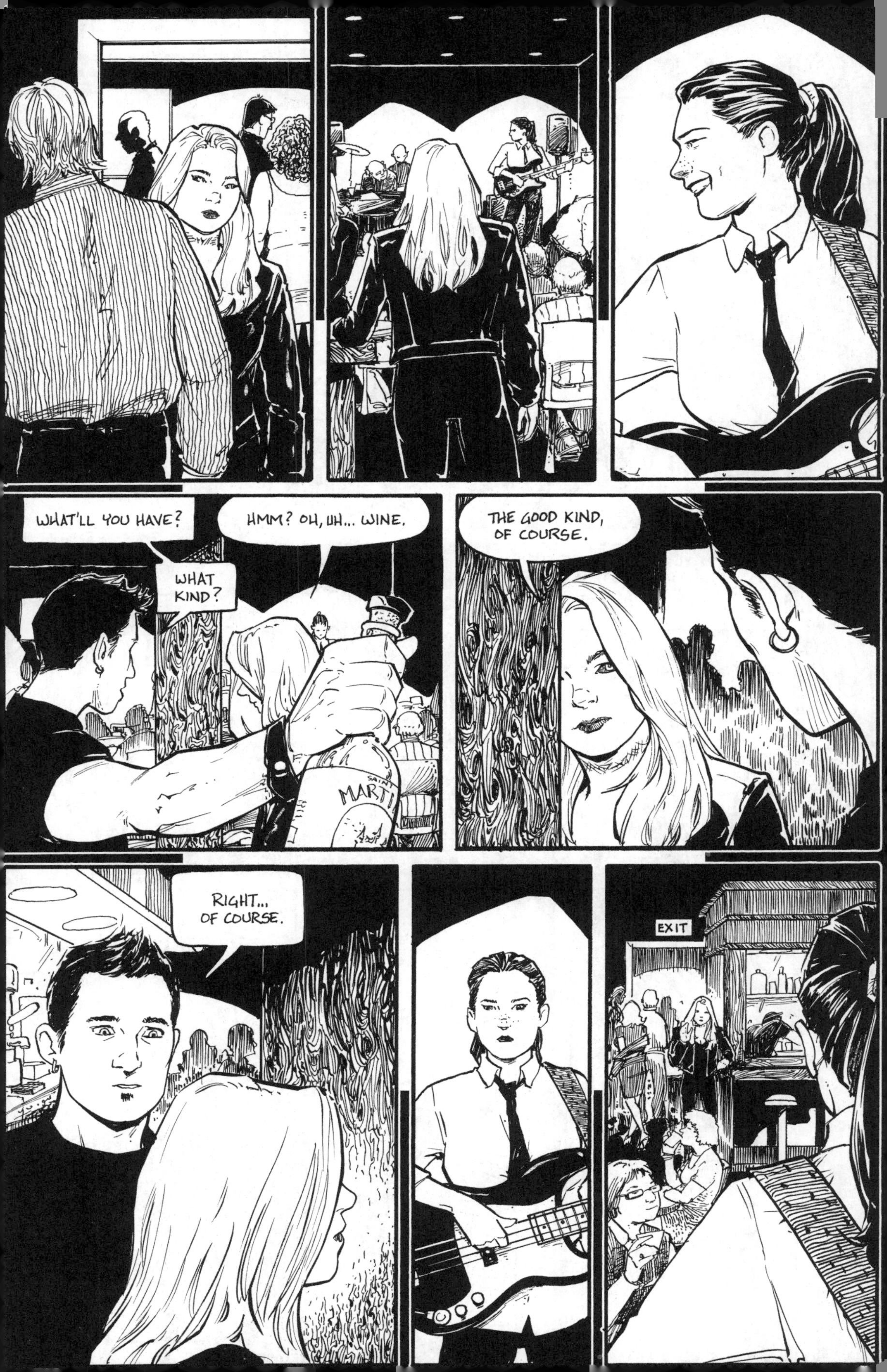

WHAT'LL YOU HAVE?
HMM? OH, UH... WINE.
WHAT KIND?
SAINT MARTI
THE GOOD KIND, OF COURSE.
RIGHT... OF COURSE.
EXIT

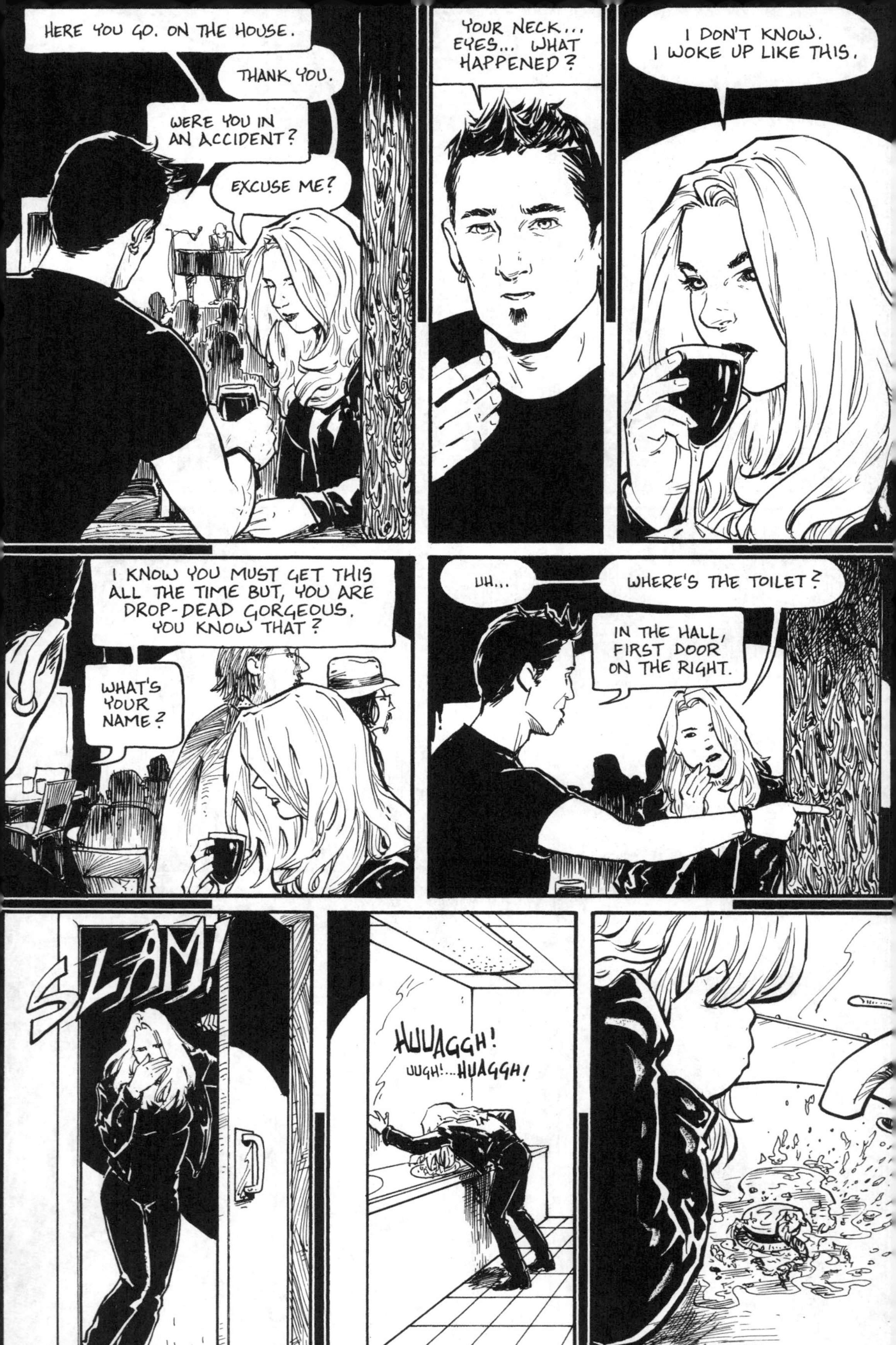
HERE YOU GO. ON THE HOUSE.
THANK YOU.
WERE YOU IN AN ACCIDENT?
EXCUSE ME?
YOUR NECK... EYES... WHAT HAPPENED?
I DON'T KNOW. I WOKE UP LIKE THIS.
I KNOW YOU MUST GET THIS ALL THE TIME BUT, YOU ARE DROP-DEAD GORGEOUS. YOU KNOW THAT?
WHAT'S YOUR NAME?
UH...
WHERE'S THE TOILET?
IN THE HALL, FIRST DOOR ON THE RIGHT.
SLAM!
HUUAGGH!
UUGH!...HUAGGH!

WHAT THE HELL?

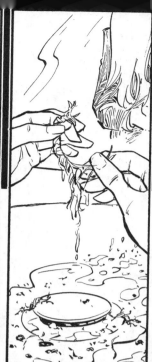

ROPE?!

BAM!

EXCUSE ME, WOULD YOU MIND?

Panel 1:
IT'S A BEAUTIFUL NECKLACE.

THANK YOU. MY FIANCE JUST GAVE IT TO ME. WE'RE GETTING MARRIED ON SUNDAY.

Panel 2:
NO... YOU'RE NOT.

Panel 3:
EXCUSE ME?

I—I'M SORRY. I DON'T KNOW WHY I SAID THAT. IT JUST HIT ME.

Panel 4:
WHAT A TERRIBLE THING TO SAY.

I KNOW. I'M SORRY.

I...

Panel 5:
HEY! GET YOUR HAND OFF ME!

Panel 6:
YOU... YOU'LL BE DEAD SOON—

I CAN FEEL IT!

Panel 7:
YOUR WEDDING BED WILL BE A SHALLOW GRAVE... YOUR LUNGS FULL OF MUD.

Panel 8:
SOMETHING OLD WILL VIOLATE YOU AND YOU WILL FEEL IT... MAKING ITS HOME IN YOU.

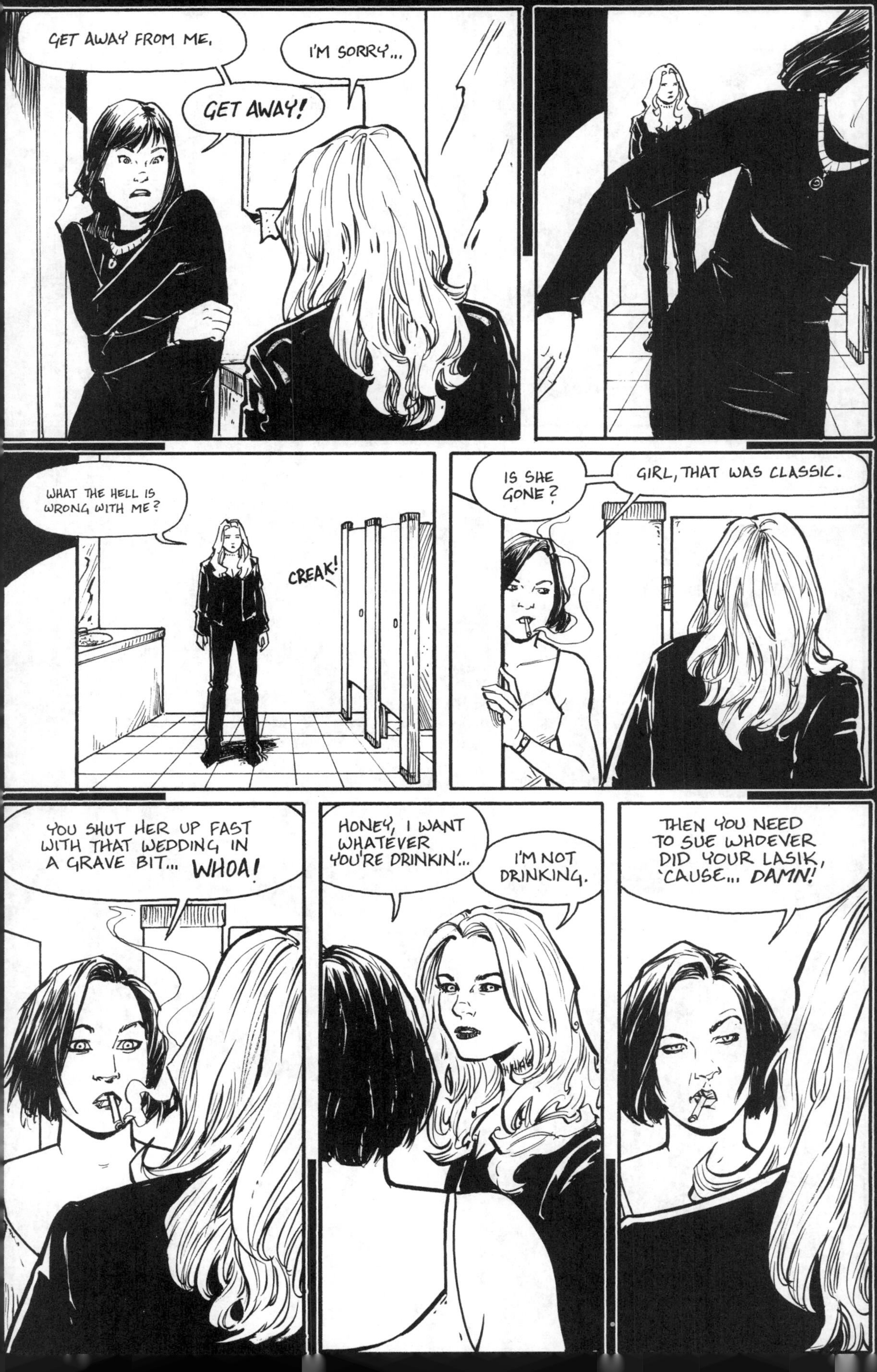
GET AWAY FROM ME,
GET AWAY!
I'M SORRY...
WHAT THE HELL IS WRONG WITH ME?
CREAK!
IS SHE GONE?
GIRL, THAT WAS CLASSIC.
YOU SHUT HER UP FAST WITH THAT WEDDING IN A GRAVE BIT... WHOA!
HONEY, I WANT WHATEVER YOU'RE DRINKIN'...
I'M NOT DRINKING.
THEN YOU NEED TO SUE WHOEVER DID YOUR LASIK, 'CAUSE... DAMN!

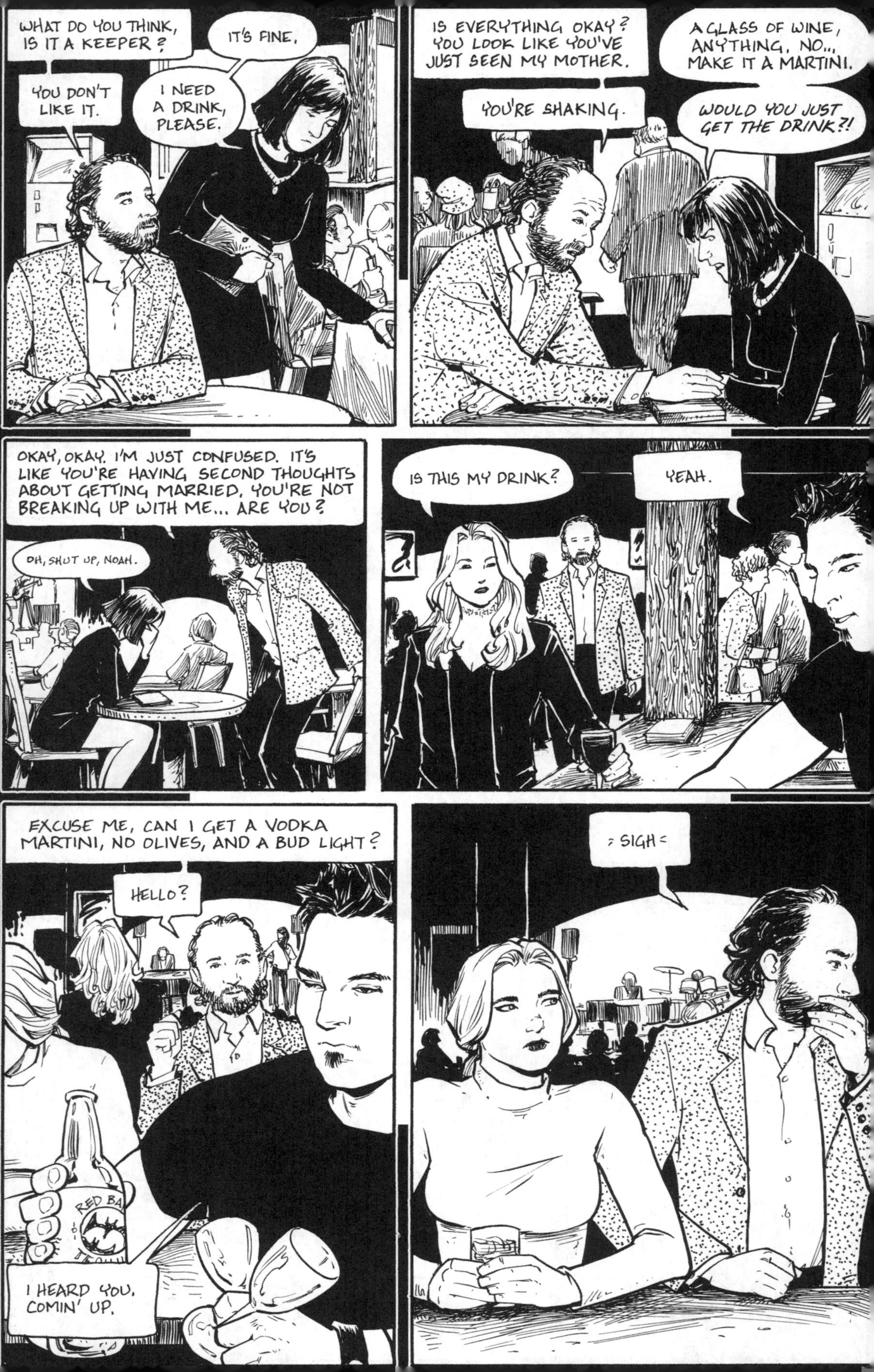
WHAT DO YOU THINK, IS IT A KEEPER?
IT'S FINE.
YOU DON'T LIKE IT.
I NEED A DRINK, PLEASE.
IS EVERYTHING OKAY? YOU LOOK LIKE YOU'VE JUST SEEN MY MOTHER.
A GLASS OF WINE, ANYTHING, NO... MAKE IT A MARTINI.
YOU'RE SHAKING.
WOULD YOU JUST GET THE DRINK?!
OKAY, OKAY. I'M JUST CONFUSED. IT'S LIKE YOU'RE HAVING SECOND THOUGHTS ABOUT GETTING MARRIED. YOU'RE NOT BREAKING UP WITH ME... ARE YOU?
OH, SHUT UP, NOAH.
IS THIS MY DRINK?
YEAH.
EXCUSE ME, CAN I GET A VODKA MARTINI, NO OLIVES, AND A BUD LIGHT?
HELLO?
RED BA
I HEARD YOU, COMIN' UP.
= SIGH =

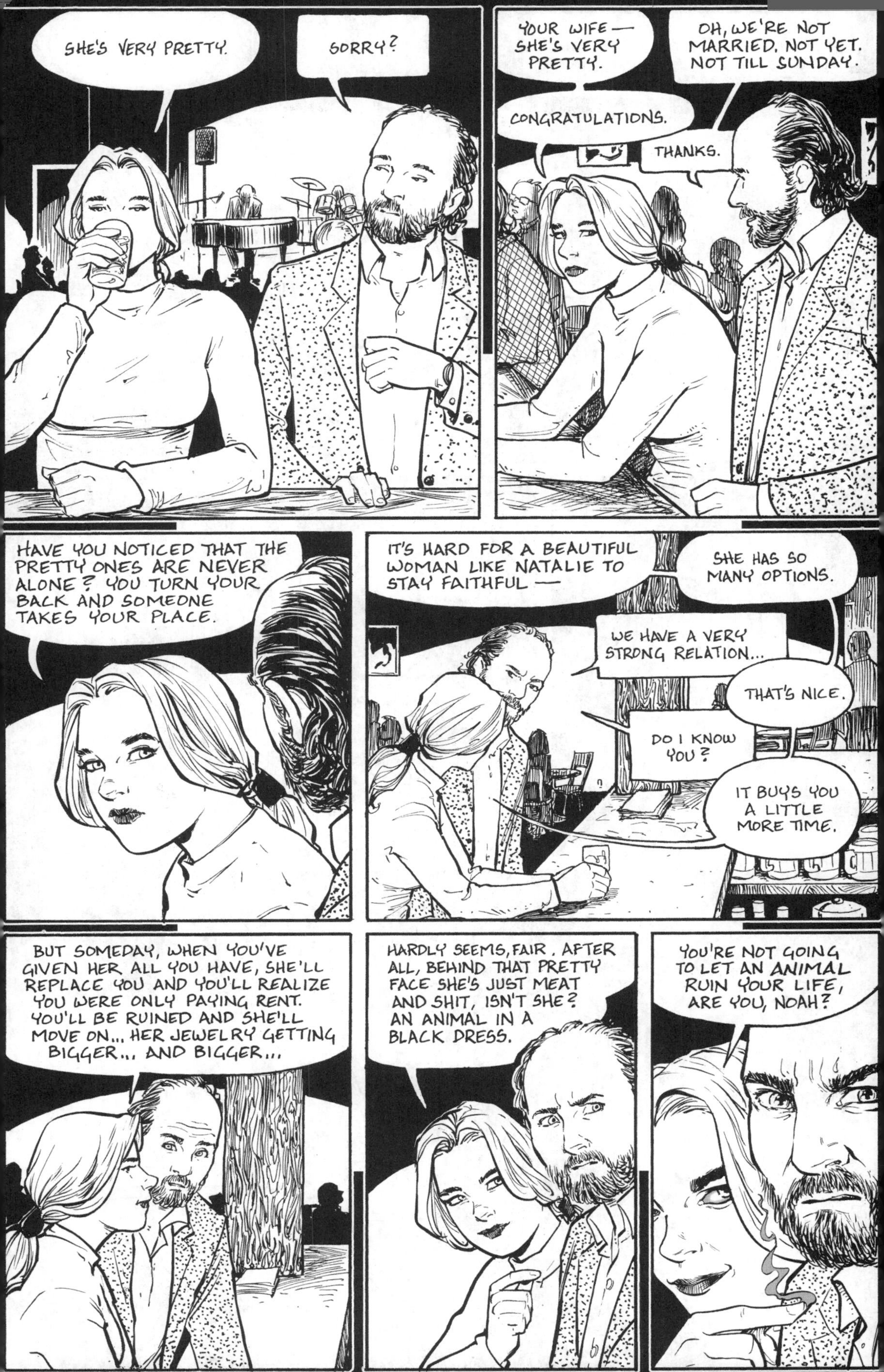
SHE'S VERY PRETTY.
SORRY?
YOUR WIFE — SHE'S VERY PRETTY.
OH, WE'RE NOT MARRIED. NOT YET. NOT TILL SUNDAY.
CONGRATULATIONS.
THANKS.
HAVE YOU NOTICED THAT THE PRETTY ONES ARE NEVER ALONE? YOU TURN YOUR BACK AND SOMEONE TAKES YOUR PLACE.
IT'S HARD FOR A BEAUTIFUL WOMAN LIKE NATALIE TO STAY FAITHFUL —
SHE HAS SO MANY OPTIONS.
WE HAVE A VERY STRONG RELATION...
THAT'S NICE.
DO I KNOW YOU?
IT BUYS YOU A LITTLE MORE TIME.
BUT SOMEDAY, WHEN YOU'VE GIVEN HER ALL YOU HAVE, SHE'LL REPLACE YOU AND YOU'LL REALIZE YOU WERE ONLY PAYING RENT. YOU'LL BE RUINED AND SHE'LL MOVE ON... HER JEWELRY GETTING BIGGER... AND BIGGER...
HARDLY SEEMS, FAIR, AFTER ALL, BEHIND THAT PRETTY FACE SHE'S JUST MEAT AND SHIT, ISN'T SHE? AN ANIMAL IN A BLACK DRESS.
YOU'RE NOT GOING TO LET AN ANIMAL RUIN YOUR LIFE, ARE YOU, NOAH?

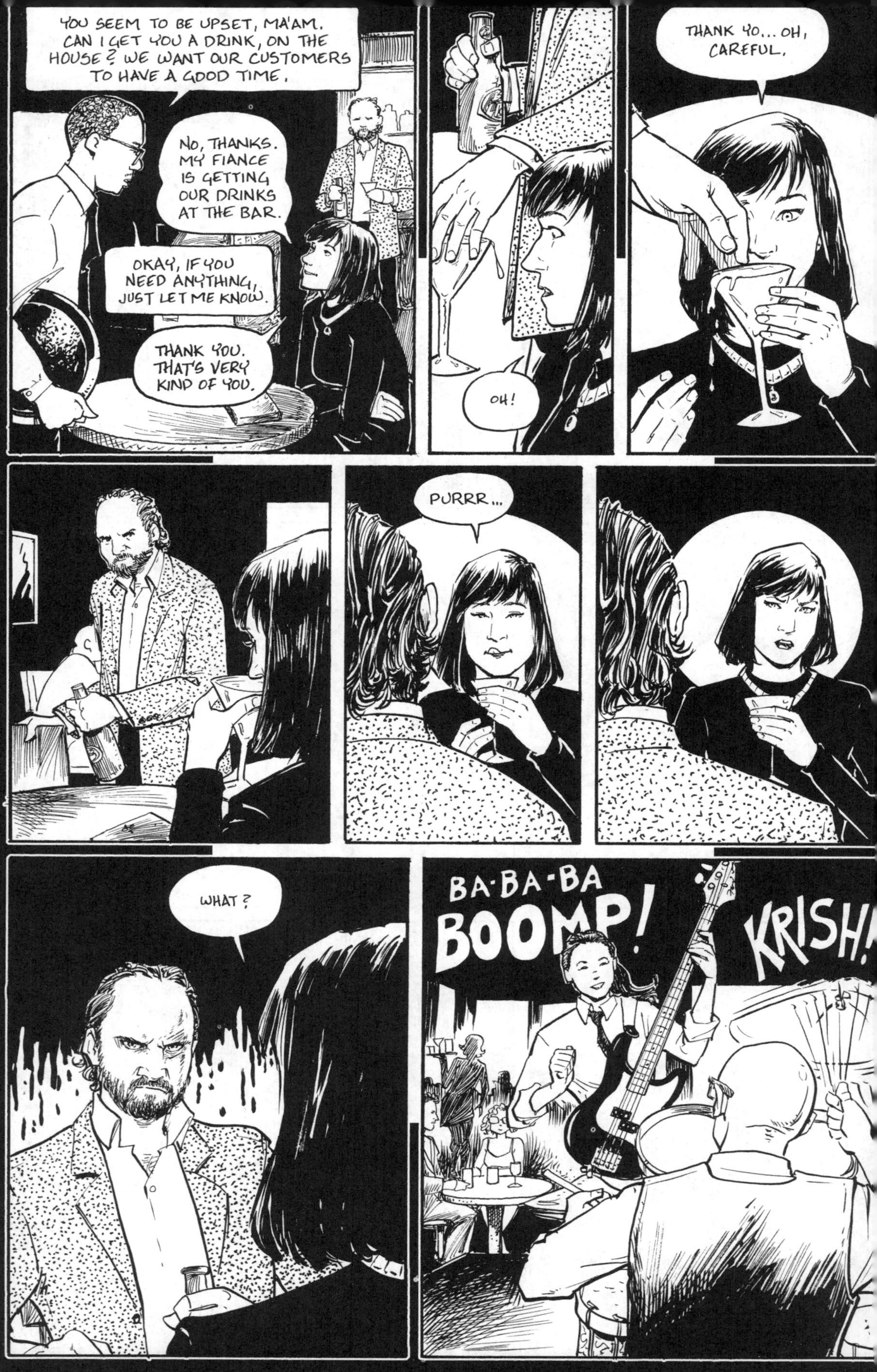
YOU SEEM TO BE UPSET, MA'AM. CAN I GET YOU A DRINK, ON THE HOUSE? WE WANT OUR CUSTOMERS TO HAVE A GOOD TIME.
NO, THANKS. MY FIANCE IS GETTING OUR DRINKS AT THE BAR.
OKAY, IF YOU NEED ANYTHING, JUST LET ME KNOW.
THANK YOU. THAT'S VERY KIND OF YOU.
OH!
THANK YO... OH, CAREFUL.
PURRR...
WHAT?
BA-BA-BA BOOMP!
KRISH!

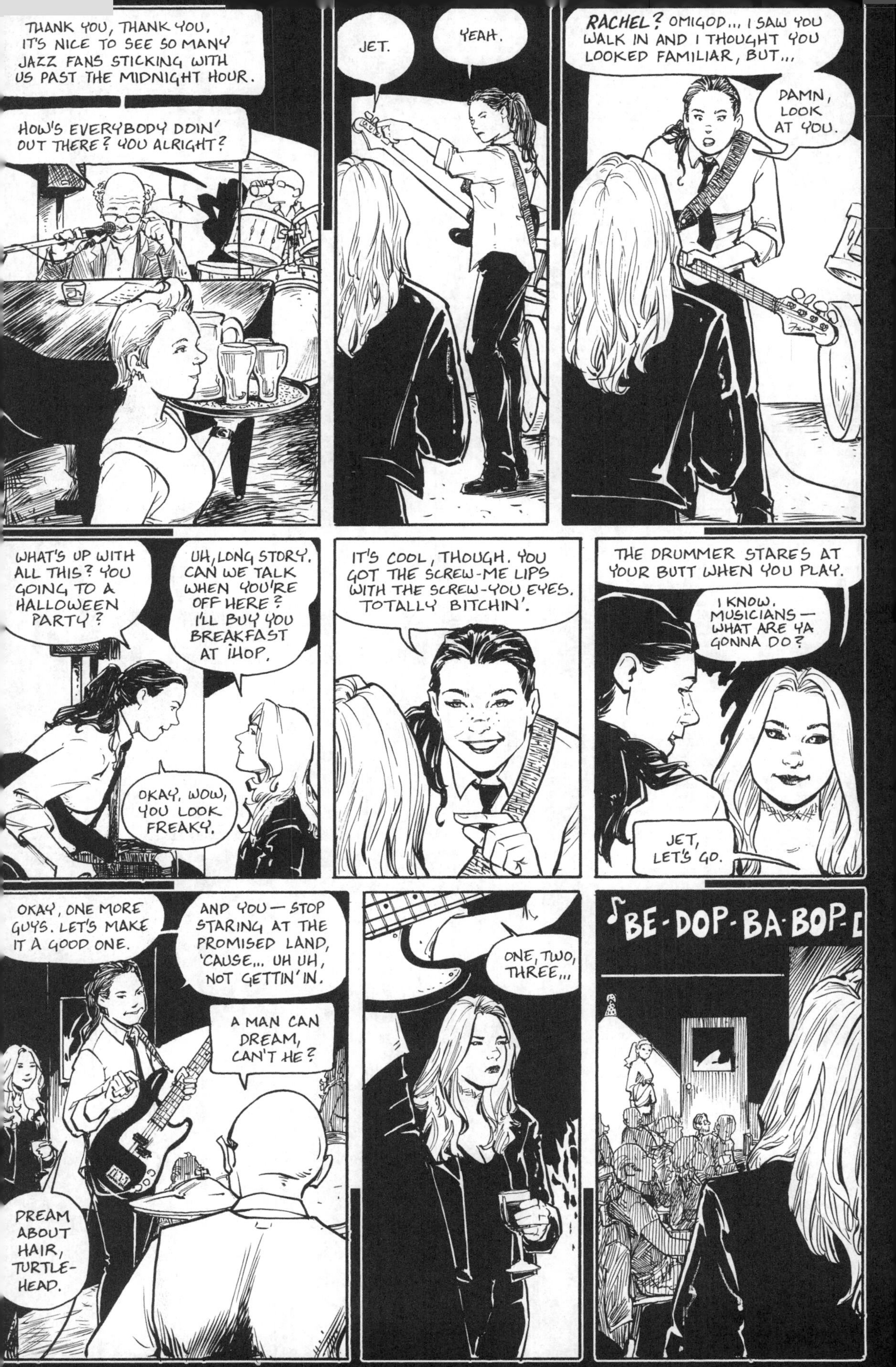
THANK YOU, THANK YOU, IT'S NICE TO SEE SO MANY JAZZ FANS STICKING WITH US PAST THE MIDNIGHT HOUR.
HOW'S EVERYBODY DOIN' OUT THERE? YOU ALRIGHT?
JET.
YEAH.
RACHEL? OMIGOD... I SAW YOU WALK IN AND I THOUGHT YOU LOOKED FAMILIAR, BUT...
DAMN, LOOK AT YOU.
WHAT'S UP WITH ALL THIS? YOU GOING TO A HALLOWEEN PARTY?
UH, LONG STORY. CAN WE TALK WHEN YOU'RE OFF HERE? I'LL BUY YOU BREAKFAST AT IHOP.
OKAY, WOW, YOU LOOK FREAKY.
IT'S COOL, THOUGH. YOU GOT THE SCREW-ME LIPS WITH THE SCREW-YOU EYES. TOTALLY BITCHIN'.
THE DRUMMER STARES AT YOUR BUTT WHEN YOU PLAY.
I KNOW. MUSICIANS— WHAT ARE YA GONNA DO?
JET, LET'S GO.
OKAY, ONE MORE GUYS. LET'S MAKE IT A GOOD ONE.
AND YOU— STOP STARING AT THE PROMISED LAND, 'CAUSE... UH UH, NOT GETTIN' IN.
A MAN CAN DREAM, CAN'T HE?
DREAM ABOUT HAIR, TURTLE-HEAD.
ONE, TWO, THREE...
BE-DOP-BA-BOP-

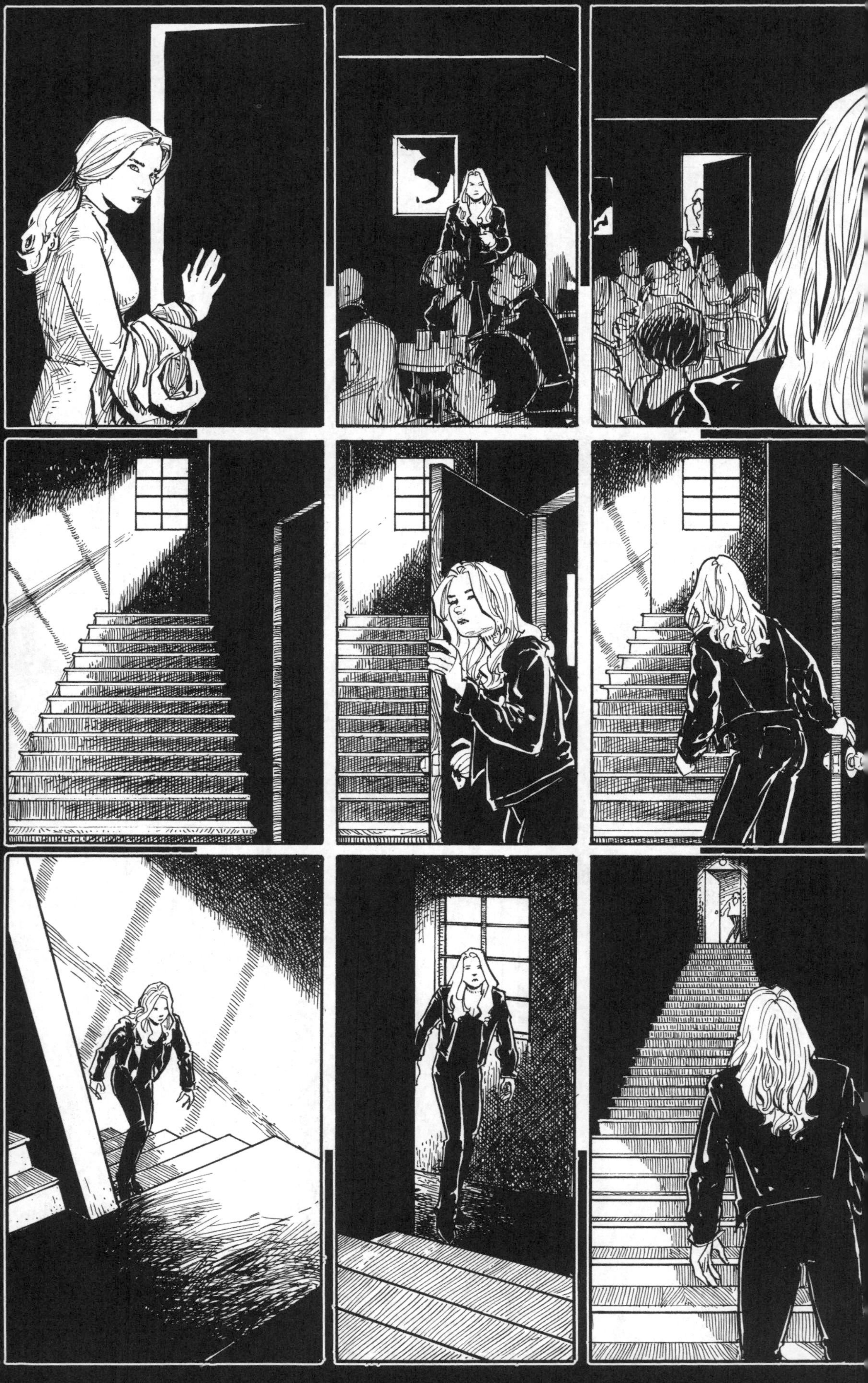

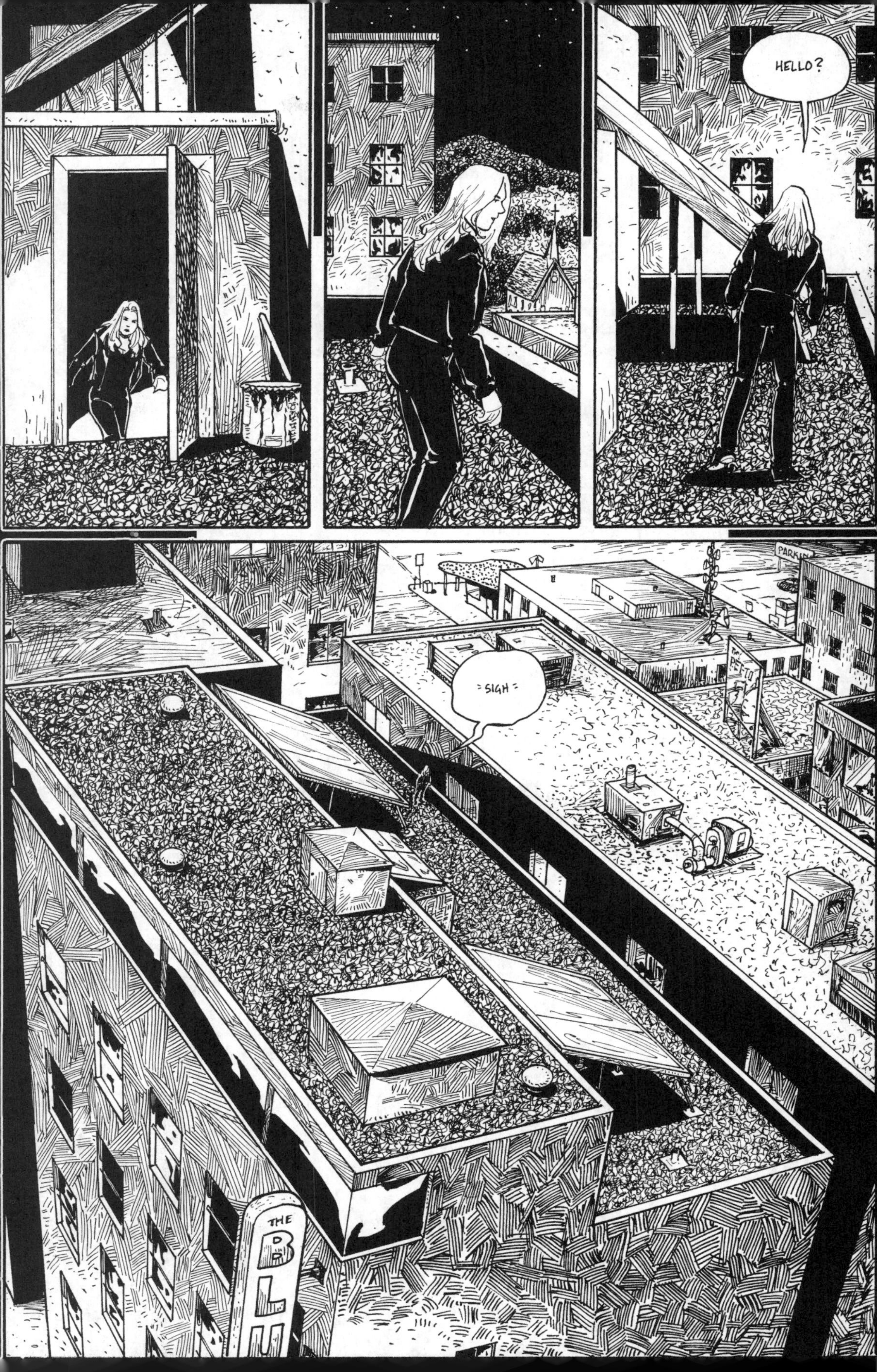
HELLO?
= SIGH =

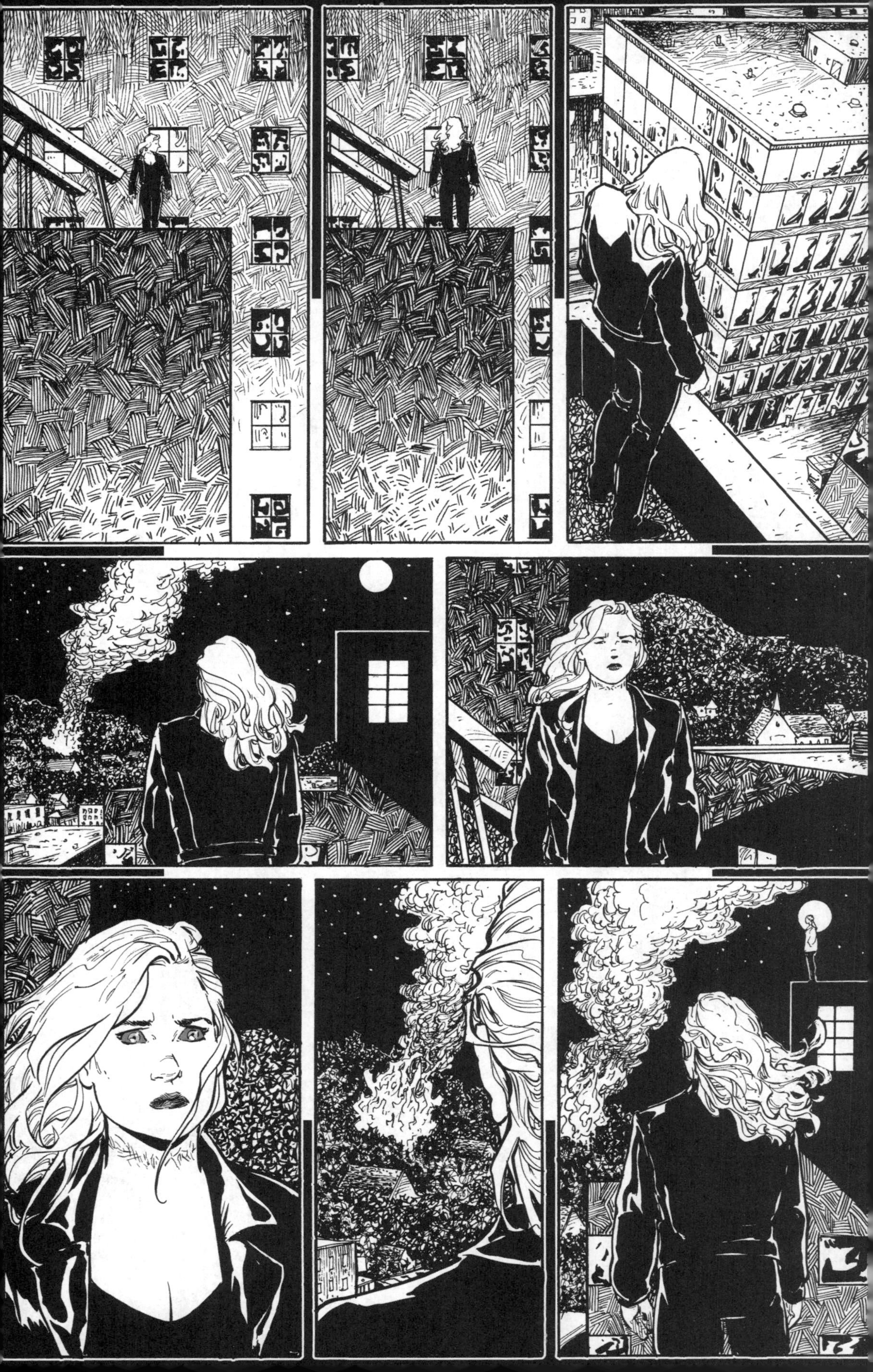

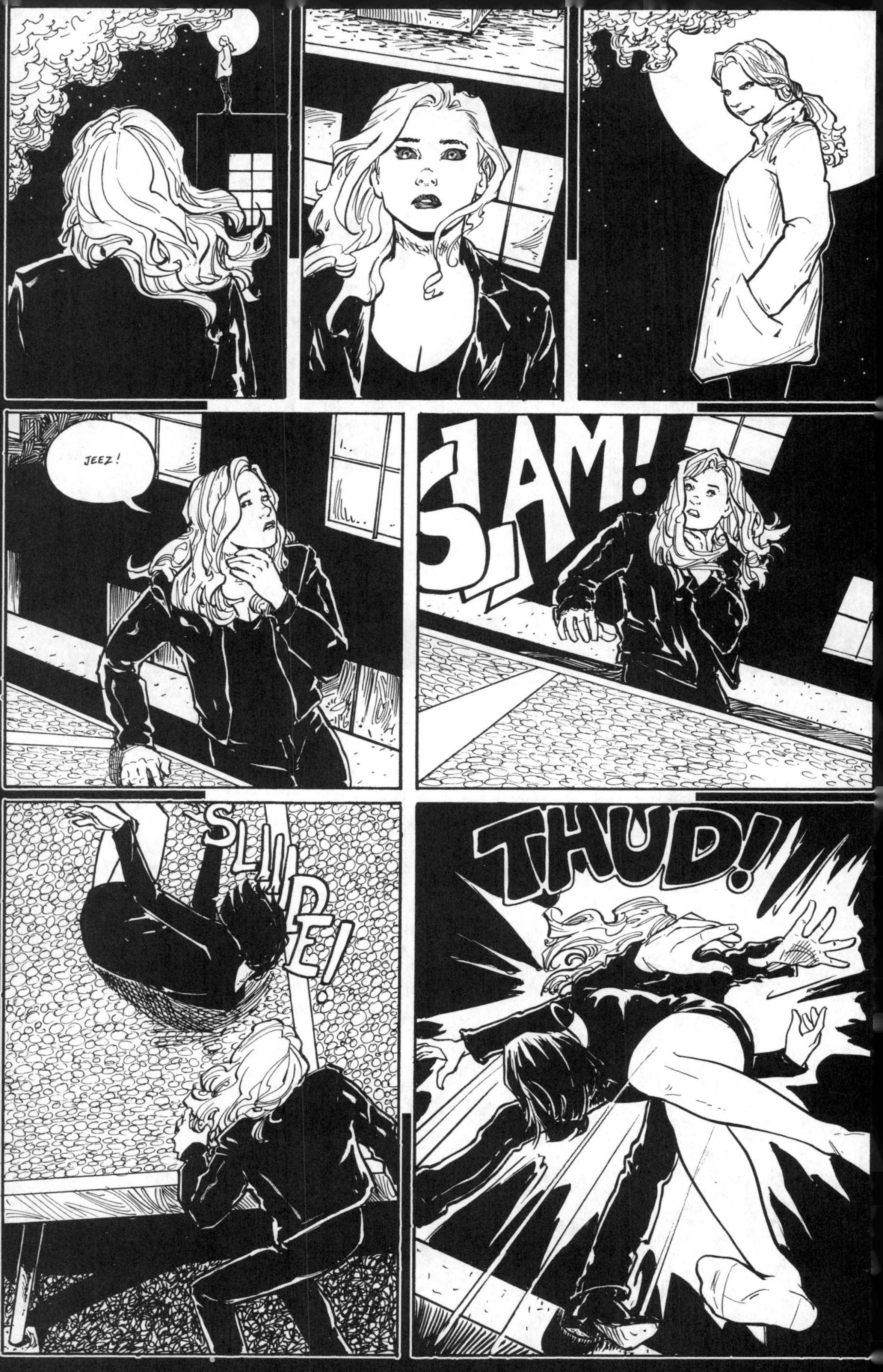

JEEZ!
SLAM!
SLIIDE!
THUD!

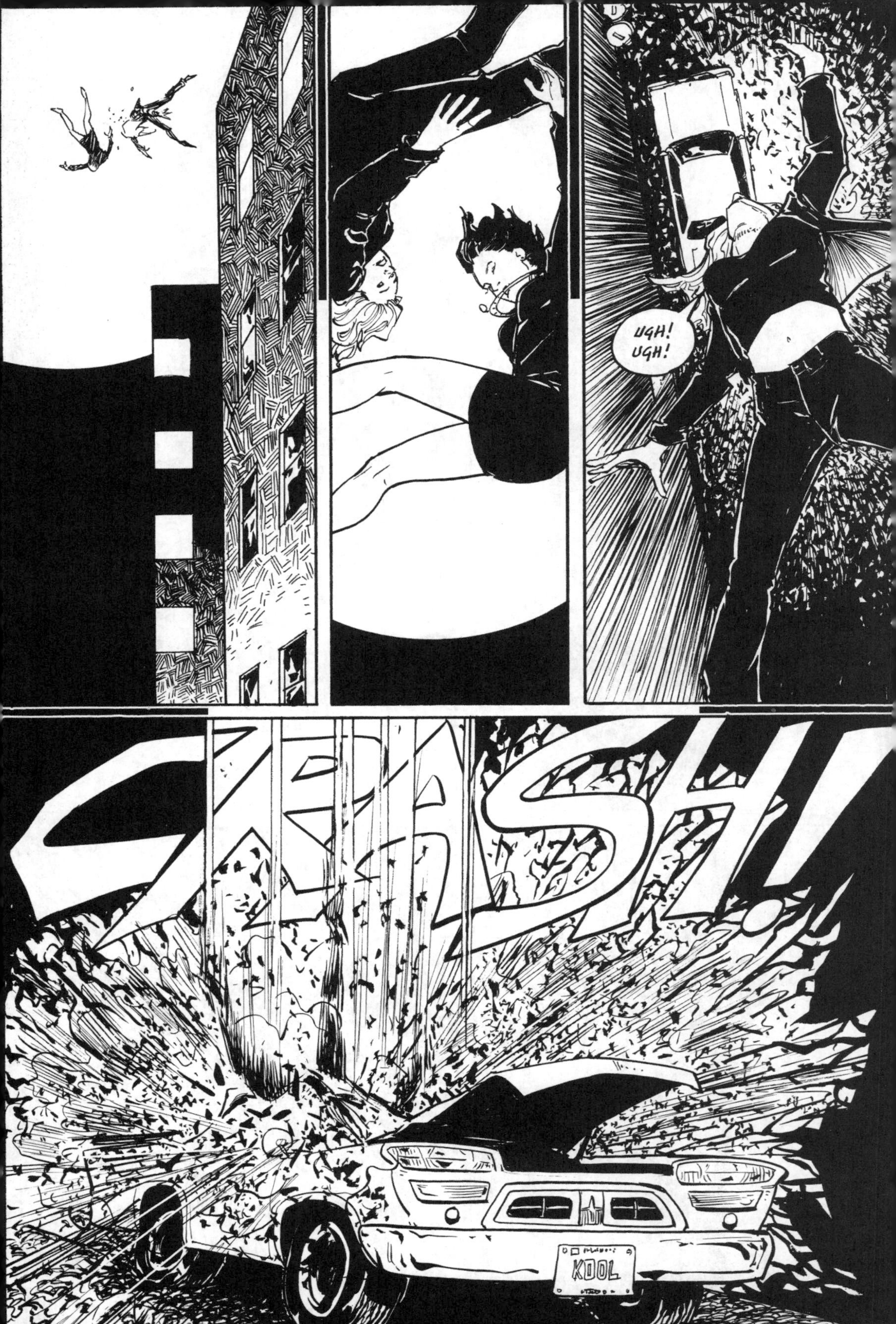
UGH! UGH!
CRASH!
KOOL

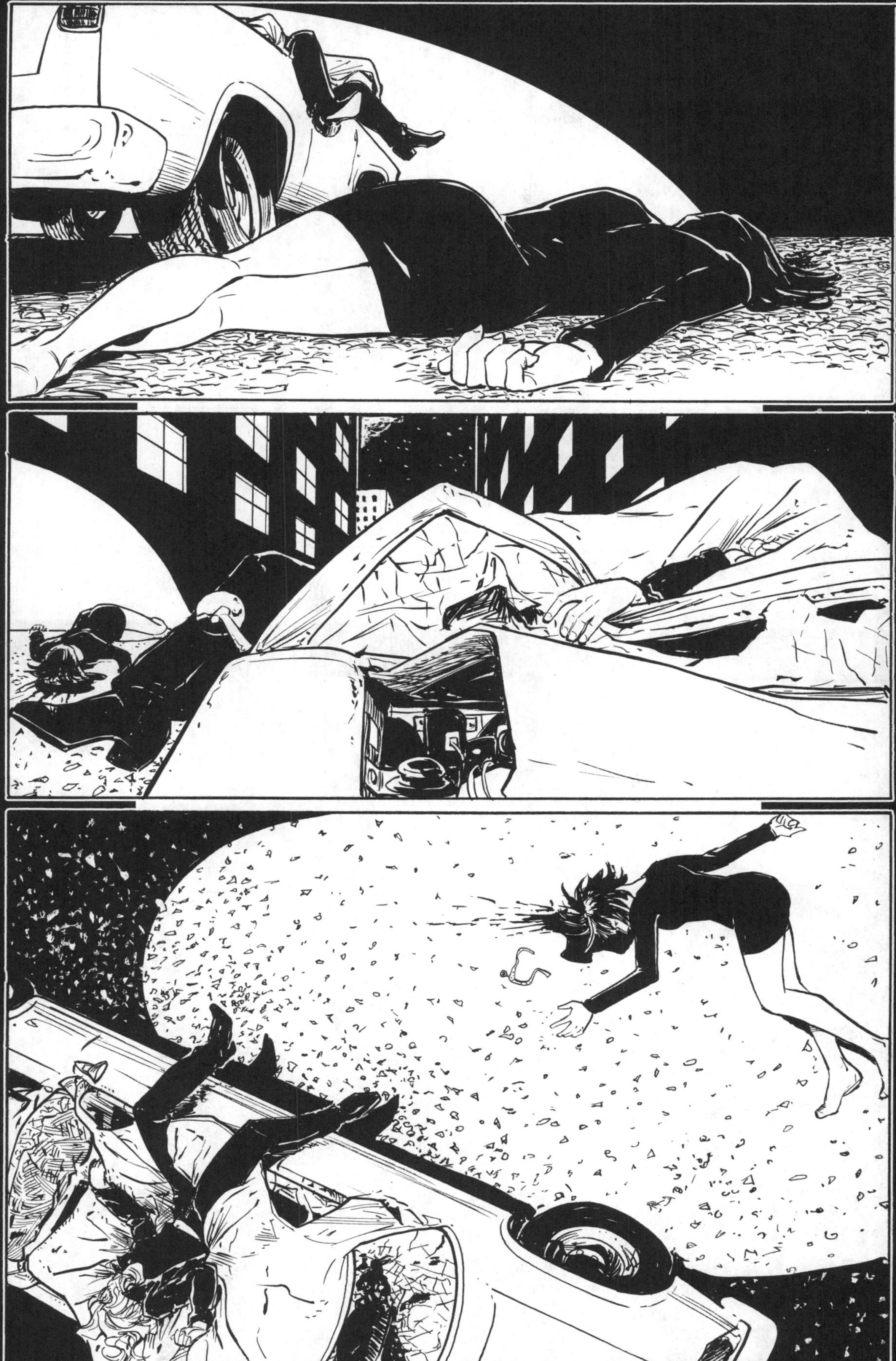

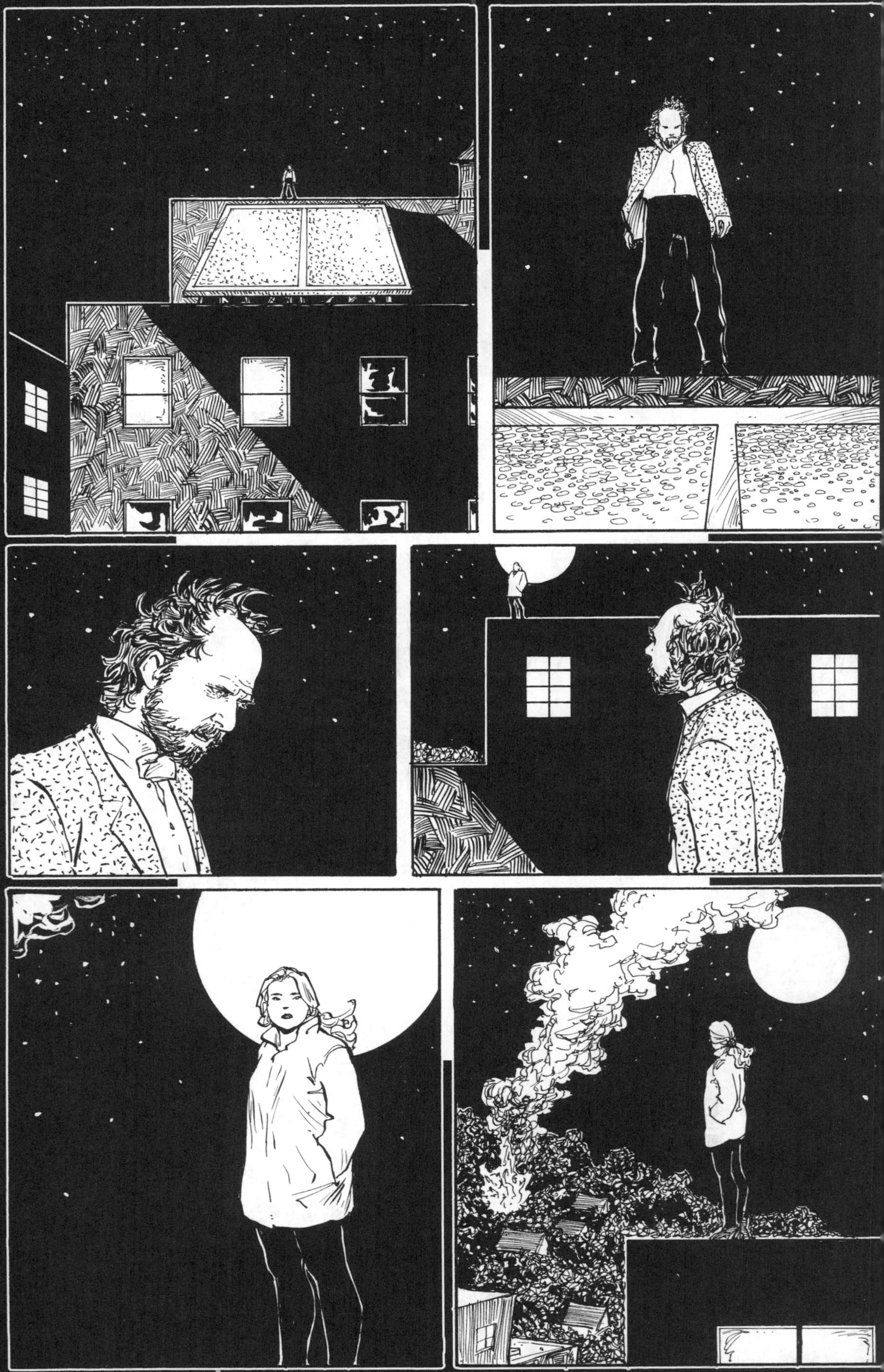

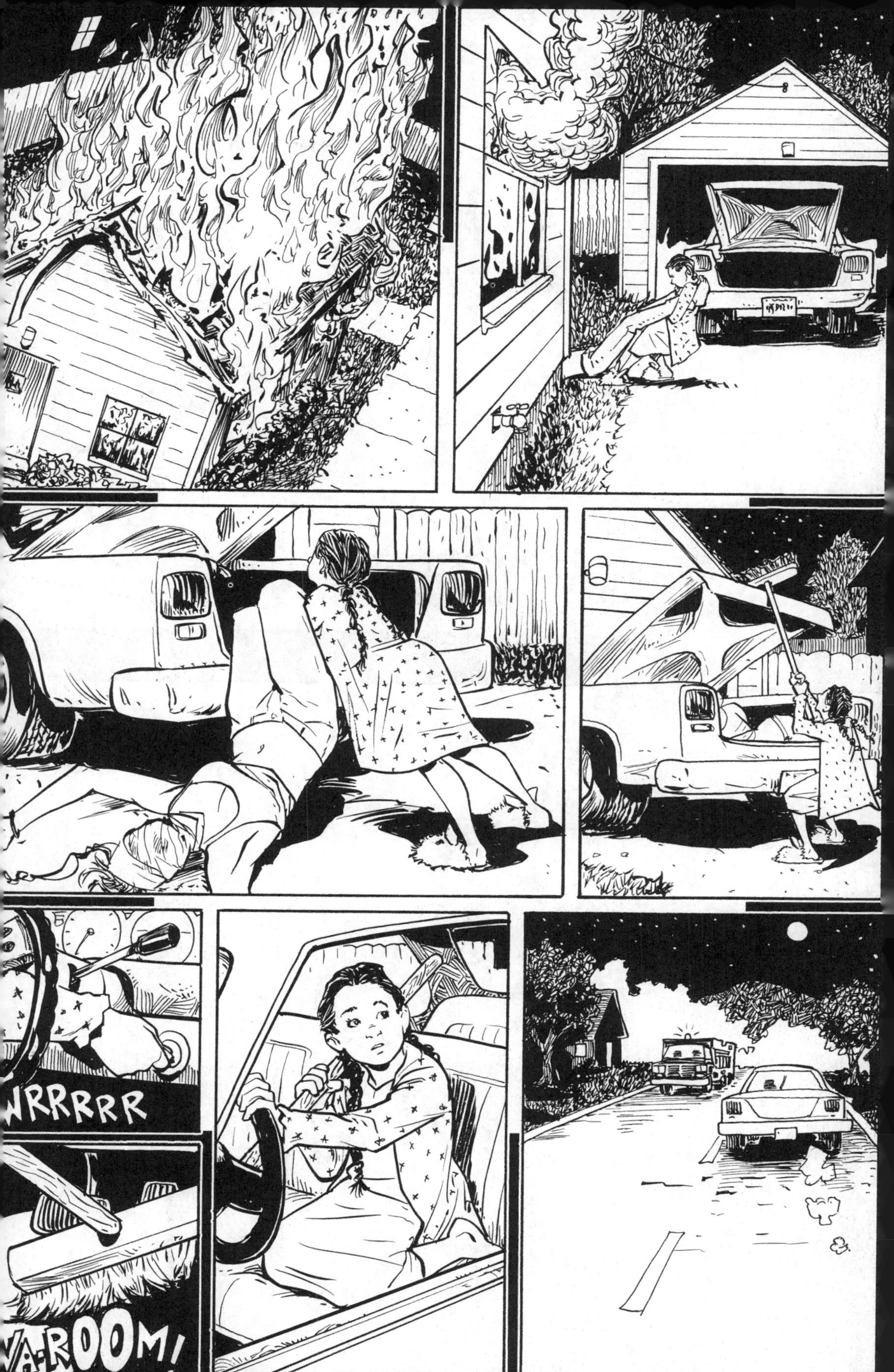
WRRRRR
VA-ROOM!

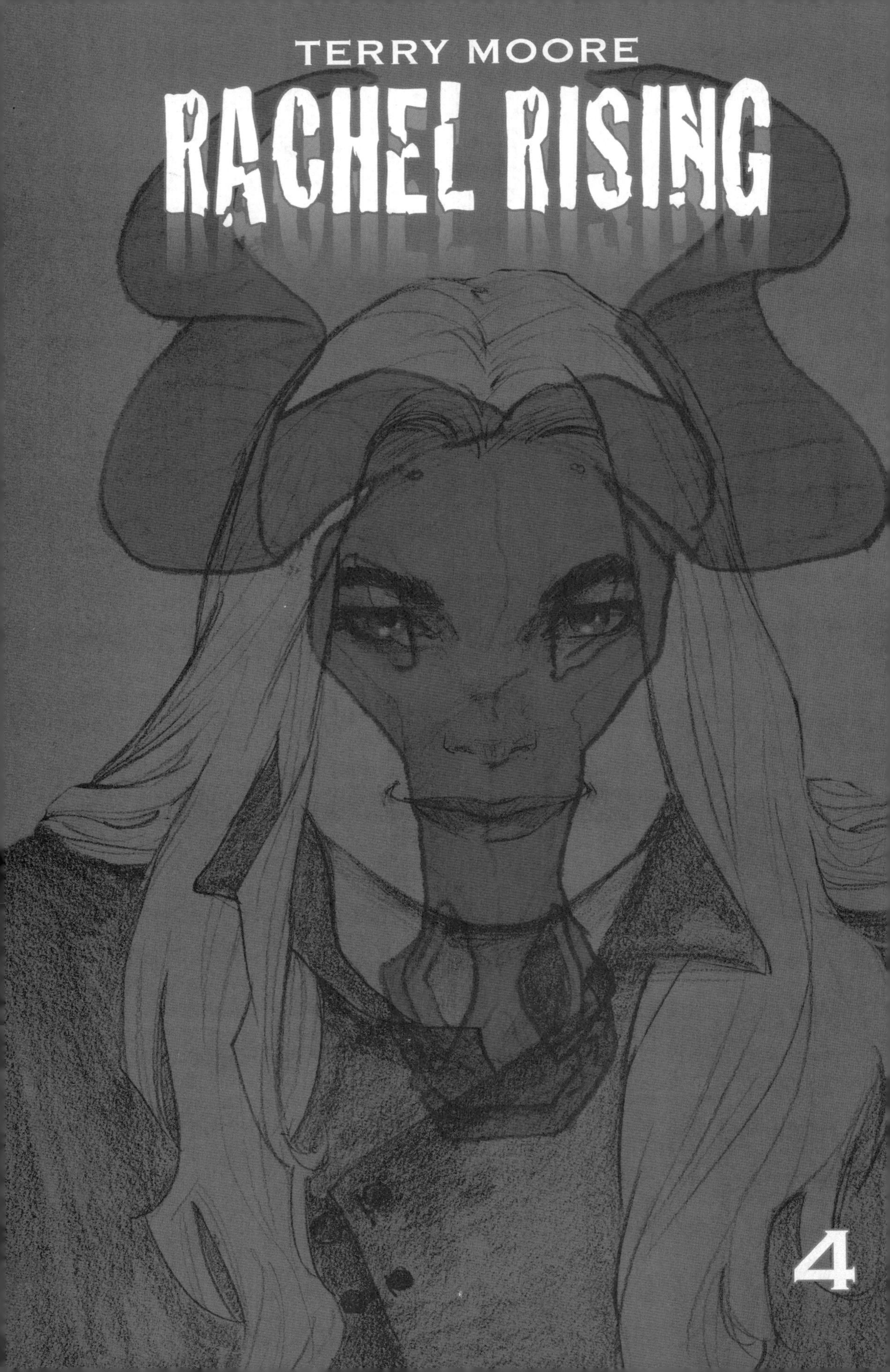
TERRY MOORE
RACHEL RISING
4

YEA, THO' I WALK THROUGH THE
VALLEY OF THE SHADOW OF DEATH...
—DAVID

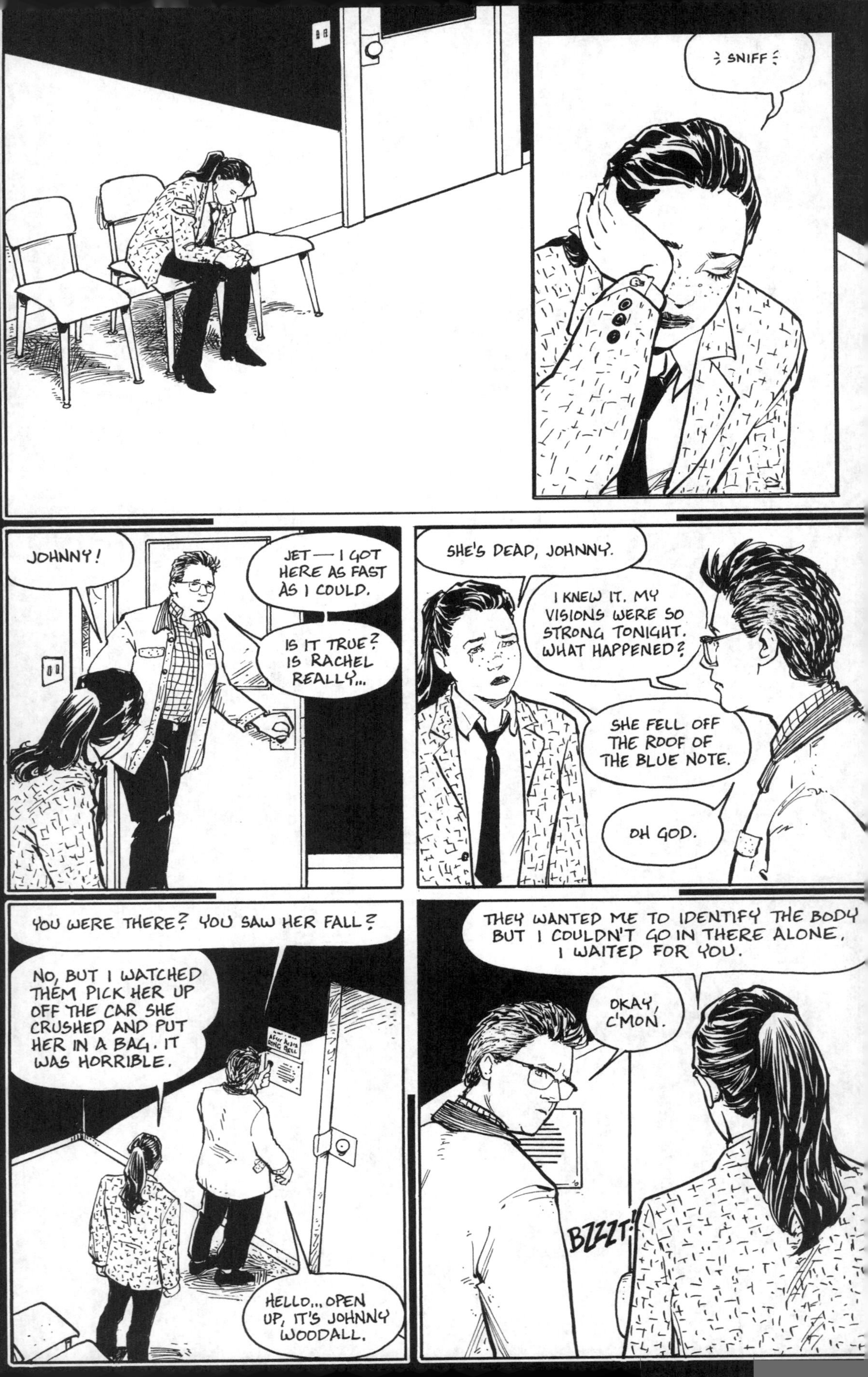
SNIFF
JOHNNY!
JET — I GOT HERE AS FAST AS I COULD.
IS IT TRUE? IS RACHEL REALLY...
SHE'S DEAD, JOHNNY.
I KNEW IT. MY VISIONS WERE SO STRONG TONIGHT. WHAT HAPPENED?
SHE FELL OFF THE ROOF OF THE BLUE NOTE.
OH GOD.
YOU WERE THERE? YOU SAW HER FALL?
NO, BUT I WATCHED THEM PICK HER UP OFF THE CAR SHE CRUSHED AND PUT HER IN A BAG. IT WAS HORRIBLE.
HELLO... OPEN UP, IT'S JOHNNY WOODALL.
THEY WANTED ME TO IDENTIFY THE BODY BUT I COULDN'T GO IN THERE ALONE, I WAITED FOR YOU.
OKAY, C'MON.
BZZZT!

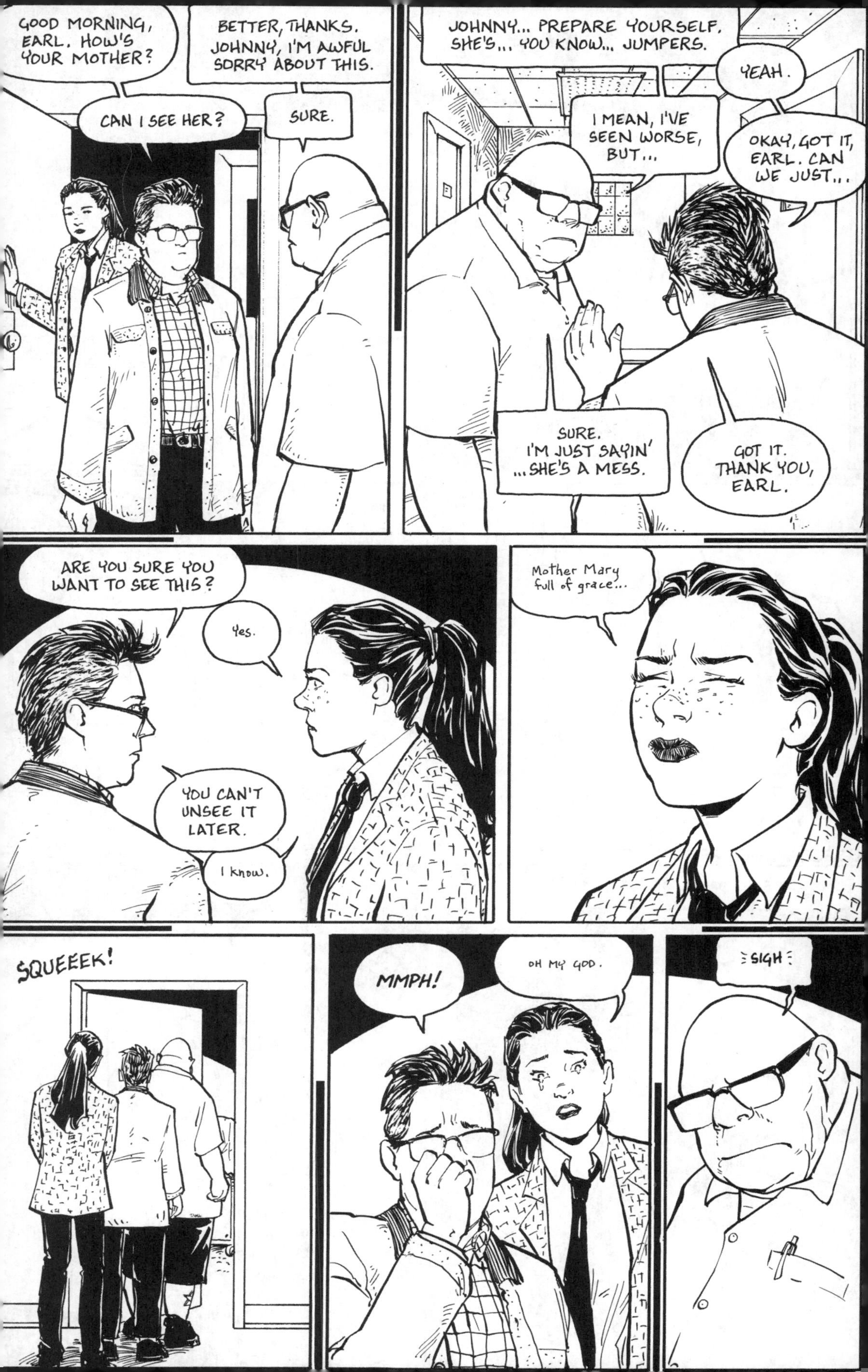
GOOD MORNING, EARL. HOW'S YOUR MOTHER?
BETTER, THANKS. JOHNNY, I'M AWFUL SORRY ABOUT THIS.
CAN I SEE HER?
SURE.
JOHNNY... PREPARE YOURSELF. SHE'S... YOU KNOW... JUMPERS.
YEAH.
I MEAN, I'VE SEEN WORSE, BUT...
OKAY, GOT IT, EARL. CAN WE JUST...
SURE. I'M JUST SAYIN' ...SHE'S A MESS.
GOT IT. THANK YOU, EARL.
ARE YOU SURE YOU WANT TO SEE THIS?
Yes.
YOU CAN'T UNSEE IT LATER.
I know.
Mother Mary full of grace...
SQUEEEK!
MMPH!
OH MY GOD.
SIGH

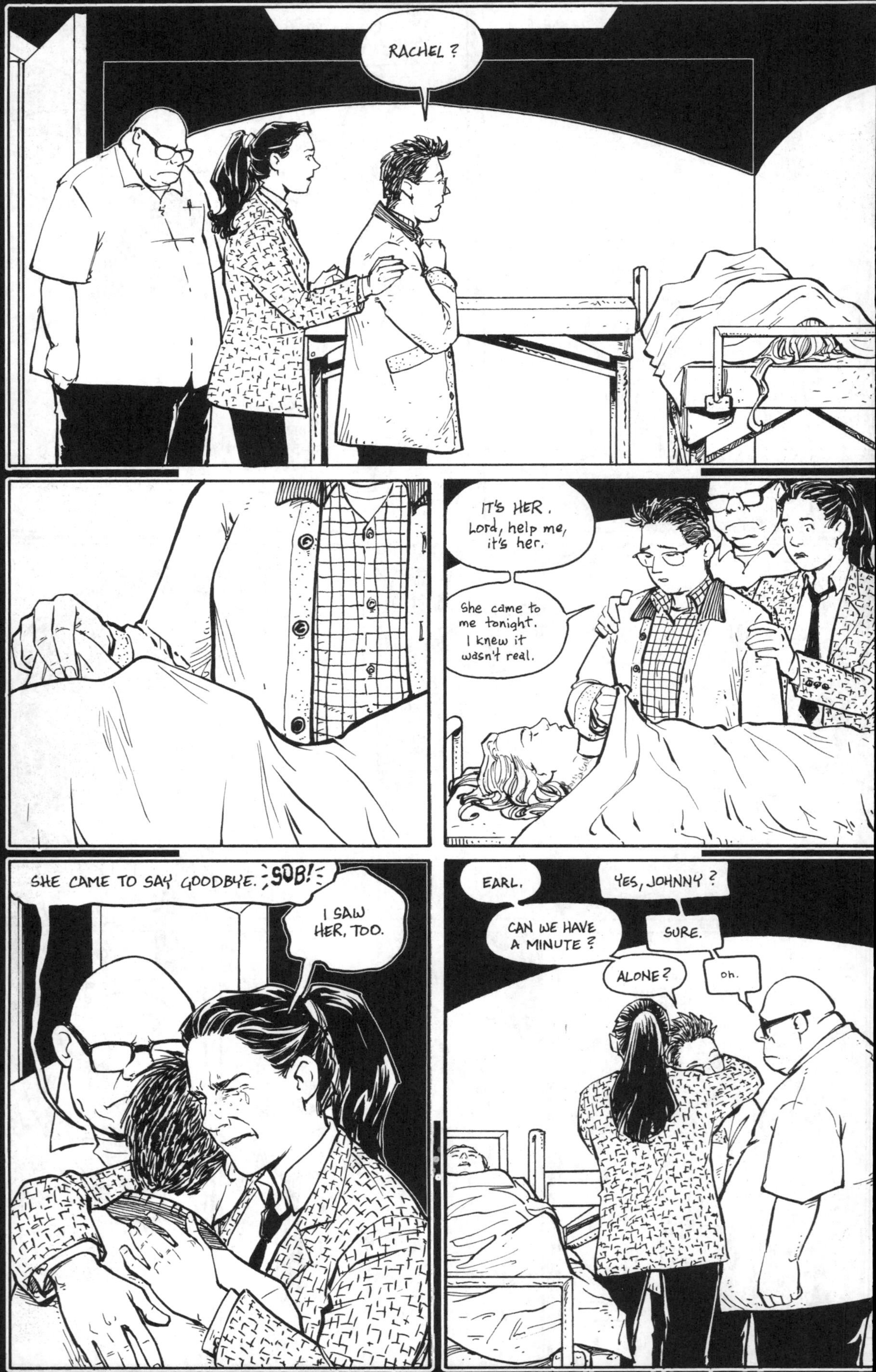
RACHEL ?
IT'S HER. Lord, help me, it's her.
She came to me tonight. I knew it wasn't real.
SHE CAME TO SAY GOODBYE. SOB!
I SAW HER, TOO.
EARL.
YES, JOHNNY ?
CAN WE HAVE A MINUTE ?
SURE.
ALONE ?
oh.

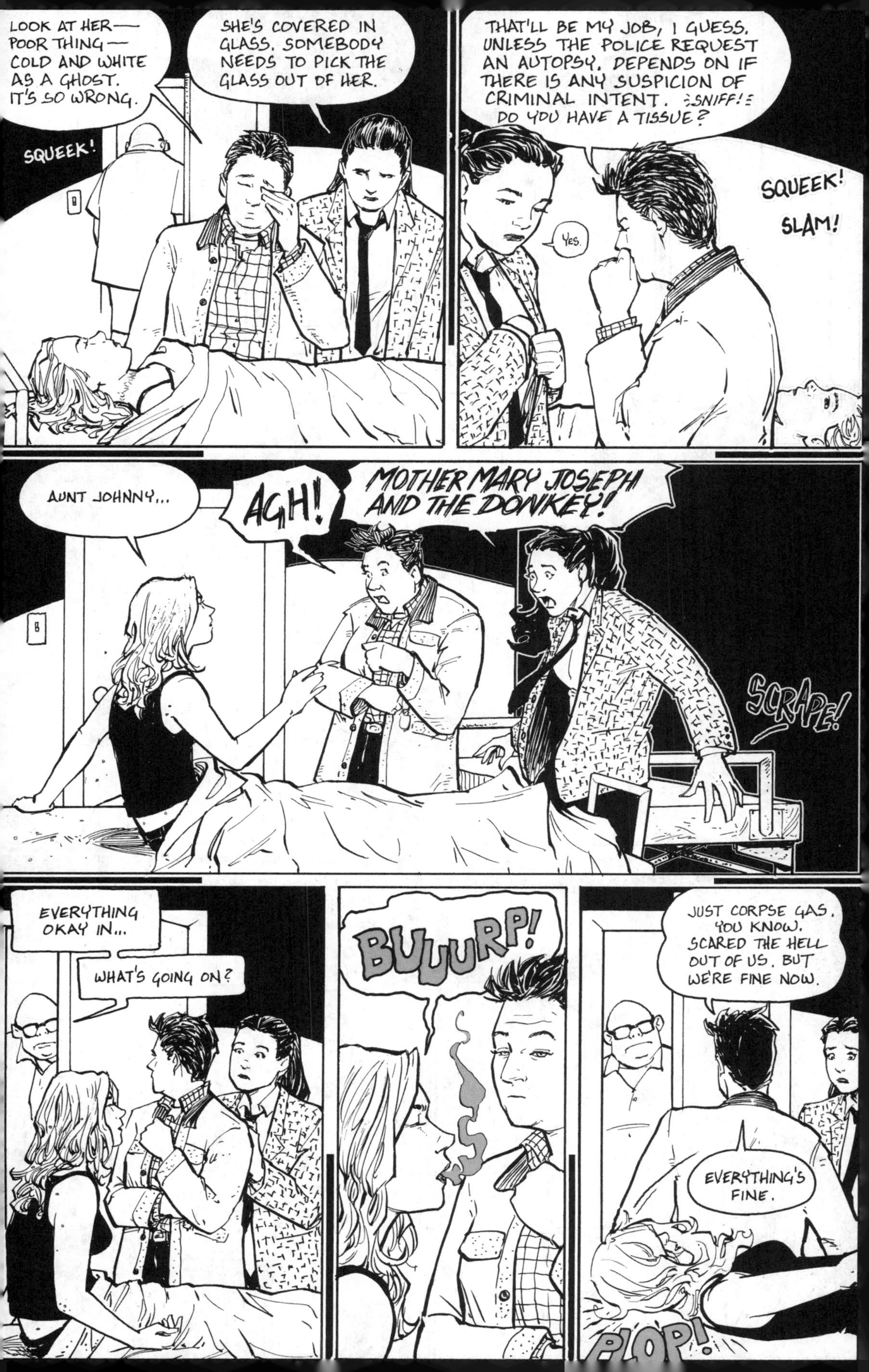

LOOK AT HER— POOR THING— COLD AND WHITE AS A GHOST. IT'S SO WRONG.
SHE'S COVERED IN GLASS. SOMEBODY NEEDS TO PICK THE GLASS OUT OF HER.
SQUEEK!
THAT'LL BE MY JOB, I GUESS, UNLESS THE POLICE REQUEST AN AUTOPSY. DEPENDS ON IF THERE IS ANY SUSPICION OF CRIMINAL INTENT. SNIFF! DO YOU HAVE A TISSUE?
YES.
SQUEEK!
SLAM!
AUNT JOHNNY...
AGH!
MOTHER MARY JOSEPH AND THE DONKEY!
SCRAPE!
EVERYTHING OKAY IN...
WHAT'S GOING ON?
BUUURP!
JUST CORPSE GAS. YOU KNOW. SCARED THE HELL OUT OF US. BUT WE'RE FINE NOW.
EVERYTHING'S FINE.
PLOP!

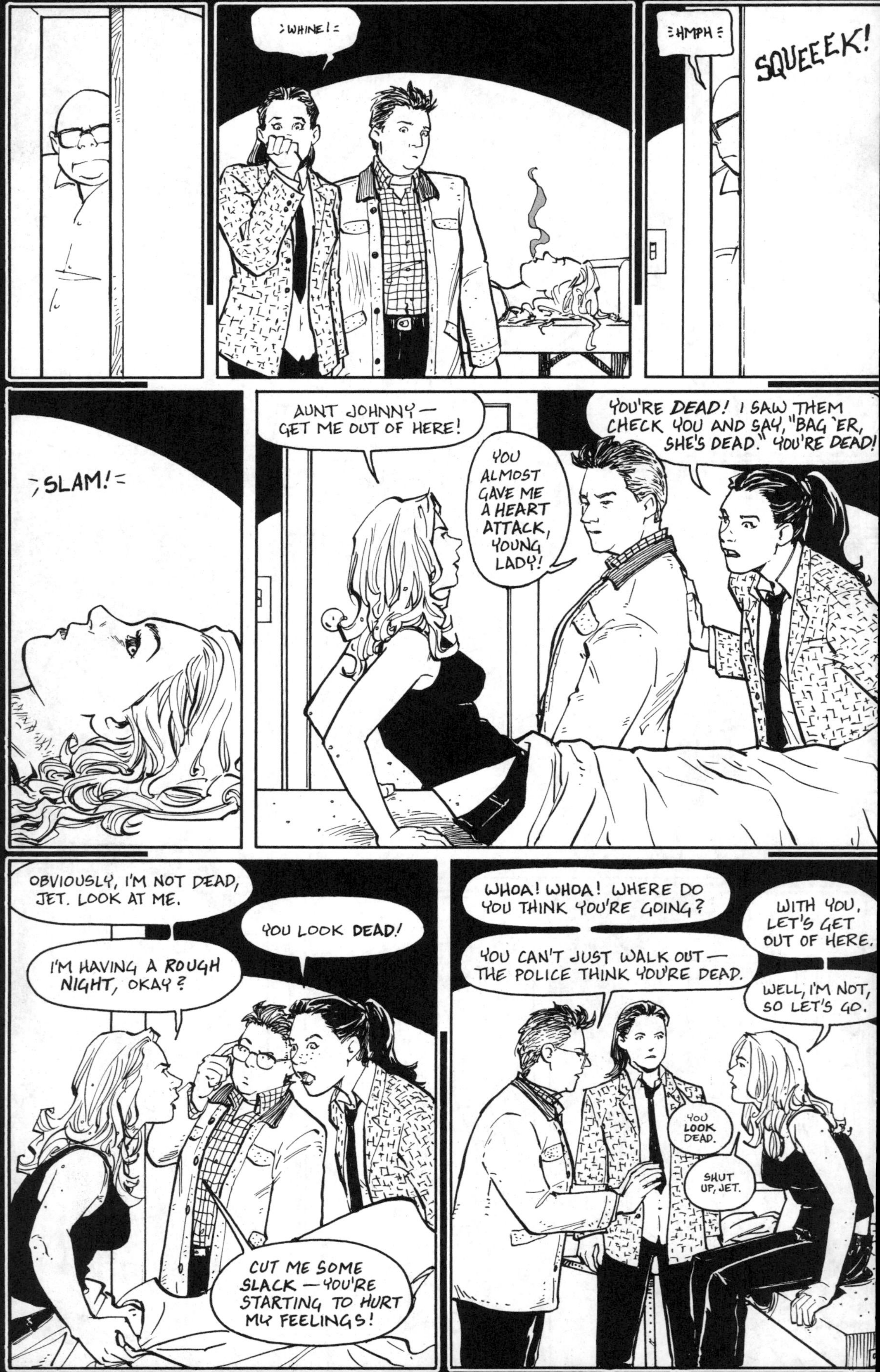

:WHINE!:
:HMPH:
SQUEEEK!
;SLAM!=
AUNT JOHNNY— GET ME OUT OF HERE!
YOU ALMOST GAVE ME A HEART ATTACK, YOUNG LADY!
YOU'RE DEAD! I SAW THEM CHECK YOU AND SAY, "BAG 'ER, SHE'S DEAD." YOU'RE DEAD!
OBVIOUSLY, I'M NOT DEAD, JET. LOOK AT ME.
I'M HAVING A ROUGH NIGHT, OKAY?
YOU LOOK DEAD!
CUT ME SOME SLACK — YOU'RE STARTING TO HURT MY FEELINGS!
WHOA! WHOA! WHERE DO YOU THINK YOU'RE GOING?
YOU CAN'T JUST WALK OUT— THE POLICE THINK YOU'RE DEAD.
WITH YOU, LET'S GET OUT OF HERE.
WELL, I'M NOT, SO LET'S GO.
YOU LOOK DEAD.
SHUT UP, JET.

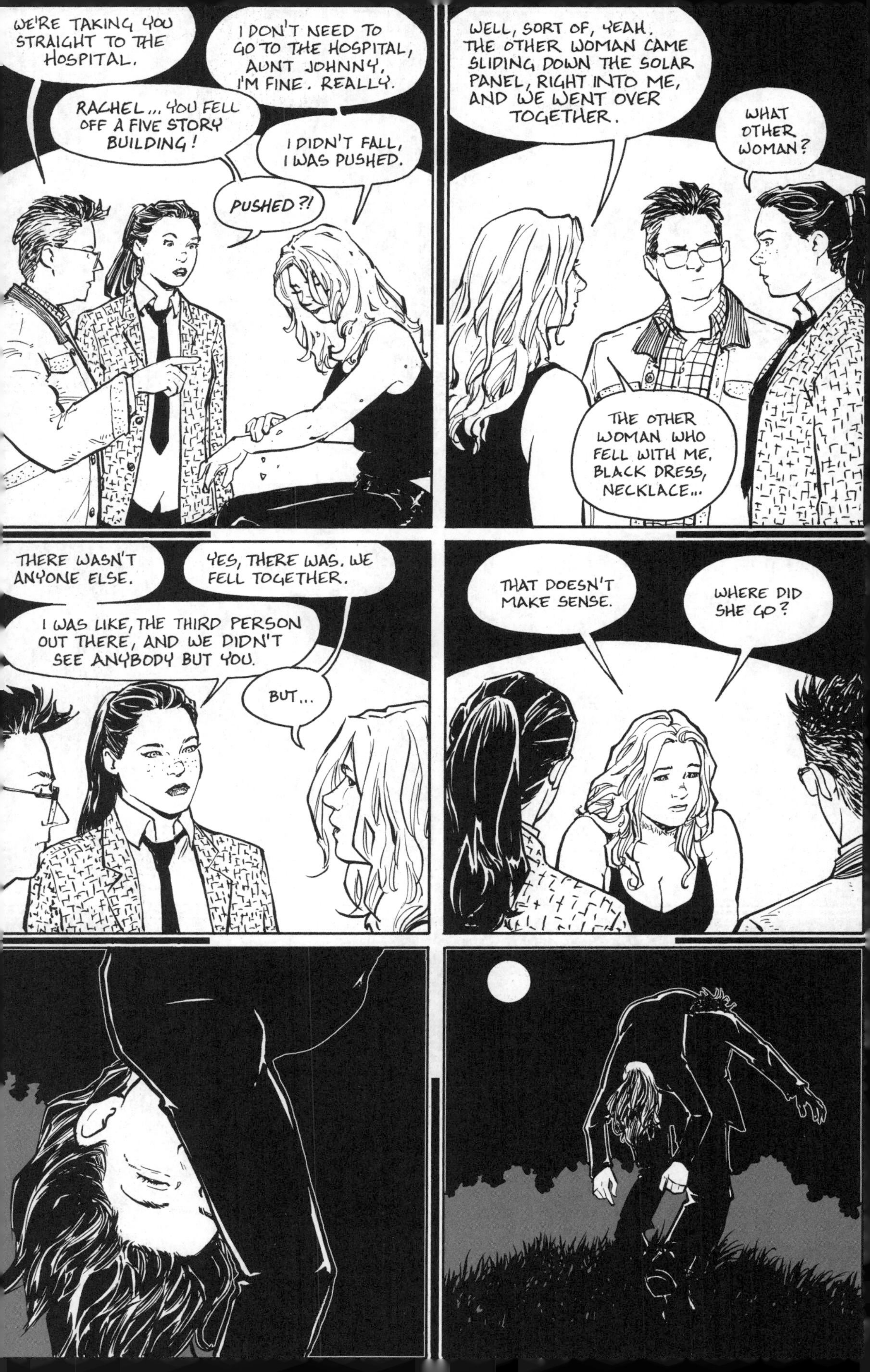
WE'RE TAKING YOU STRAIGHT TO THE HOSPITAL.
I DON'T NEED TO GO TO THE HOSPITAL, AUNT JOHNNY, I'M FINE. REALLY.
RACHEL... YOU FELL OFF A FIVE STORY BUILDING!
I DIDN'T FALL, I WAS PUSHED.
PUSHED?!
WELL, SORT OF, YEAH. THE OTHER WOMAN CAME SLIDING DOWN THE SOLAR PANEL, RIGHT INTO ME, AND WE WENT OVER TOGETHER.
WHAT OTHER WOMAN?
THE OTHER WOMAN WHO FELL WITH ME, BLACK DRESS, NECKLACE...
THERE WASN'T ANYONE ELSE.
YES, THERE WAS. WE FELL TOGETHER.
I WAS LIKE, THE THIRD PERSON OUT THERE, AND WE DIDN'T SEE ANYBODY BUT YOU.
BUT...
THAT DOESN'T MAKE SENSE.
WHERE DID SHE GO?

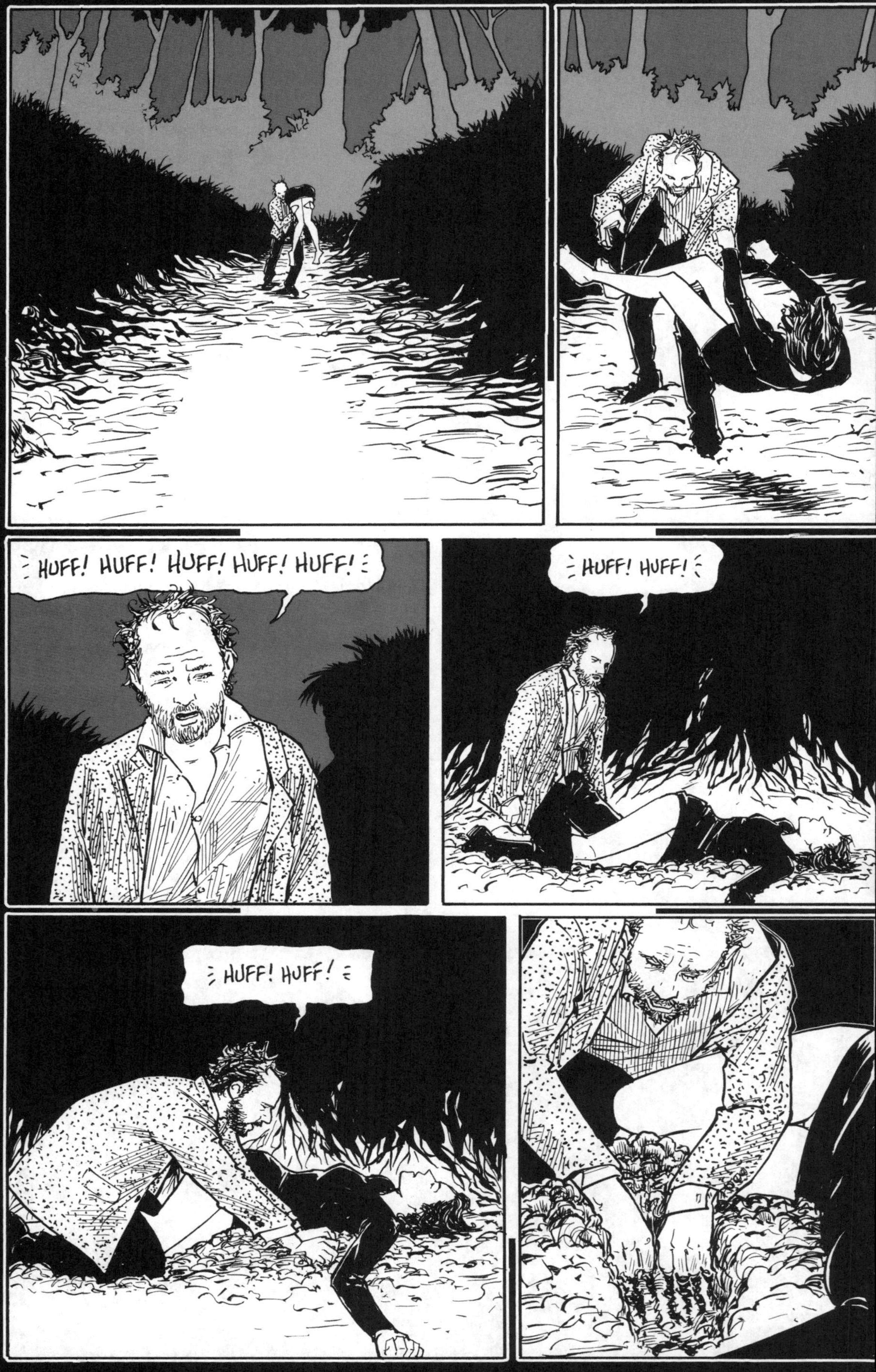
HUFF! HUFF! HUFF! HUFF! HUFF!
HUFF! HUFF!
HUFF! HUFF!

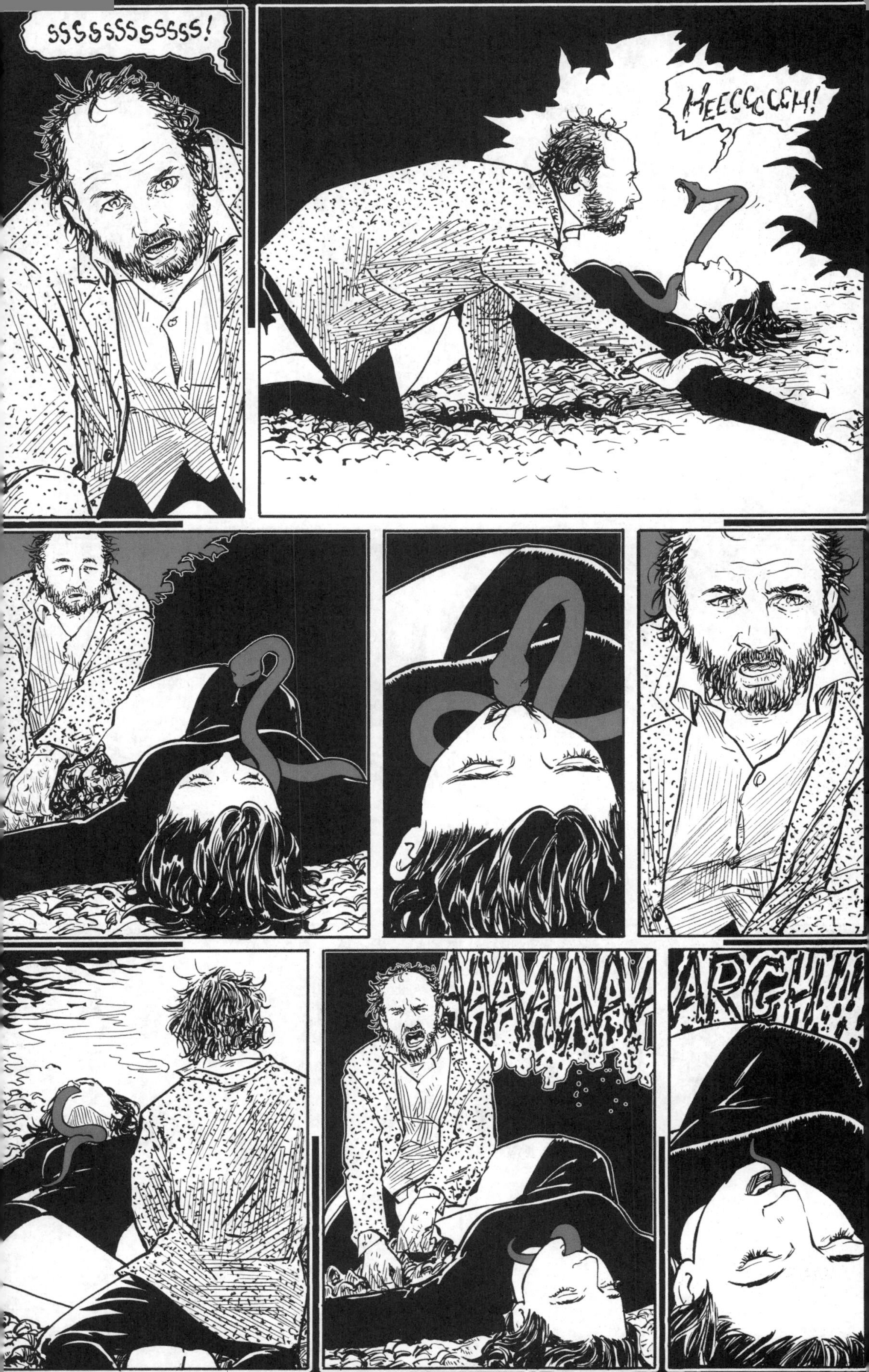
SSSSSSSSSSSSS!
HEECCCCCH!
AAAAAAAAH
ARGH!!

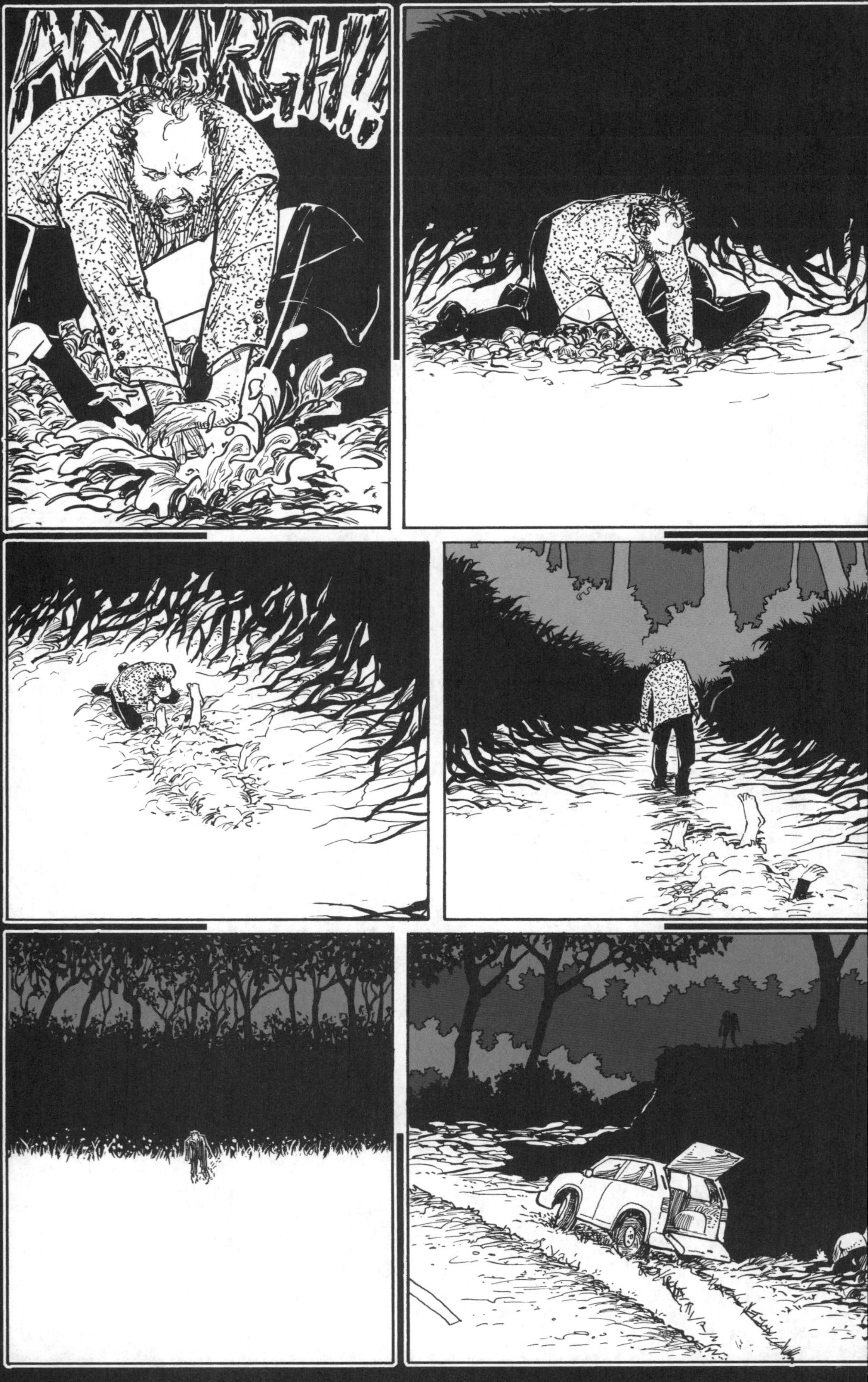
AAAARGH!!

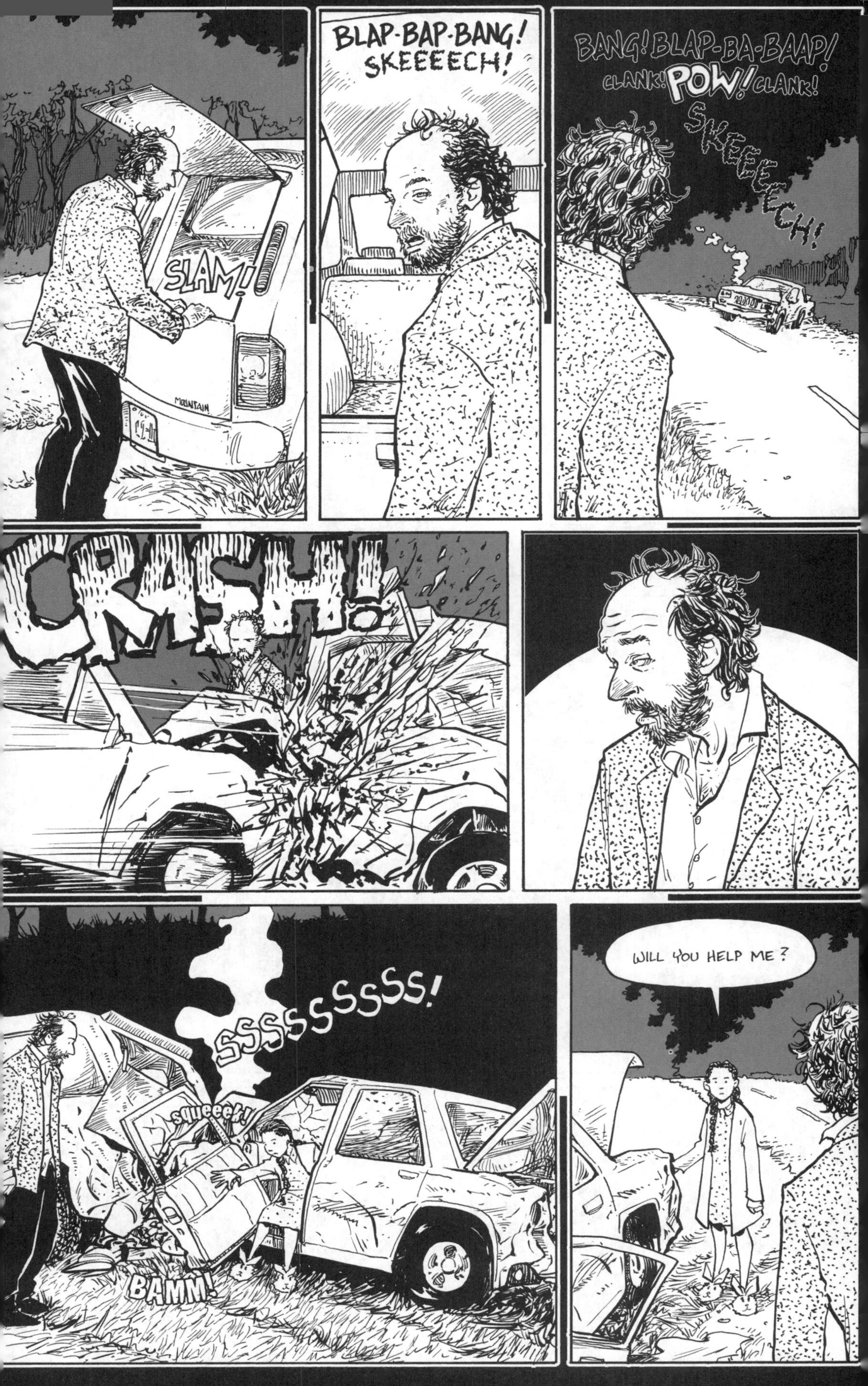
SLAM!
MOUNTAIN
BLAP-BAP-BANG!
SKEEEECH!
BANG! BLAP-BA-BAAP!
CLANK! POW! CLANK!
SKEEEECH!
CRASH!
SSSSSSSSS!
squeeek!
BAMM!
WILL YOU HELP ME?

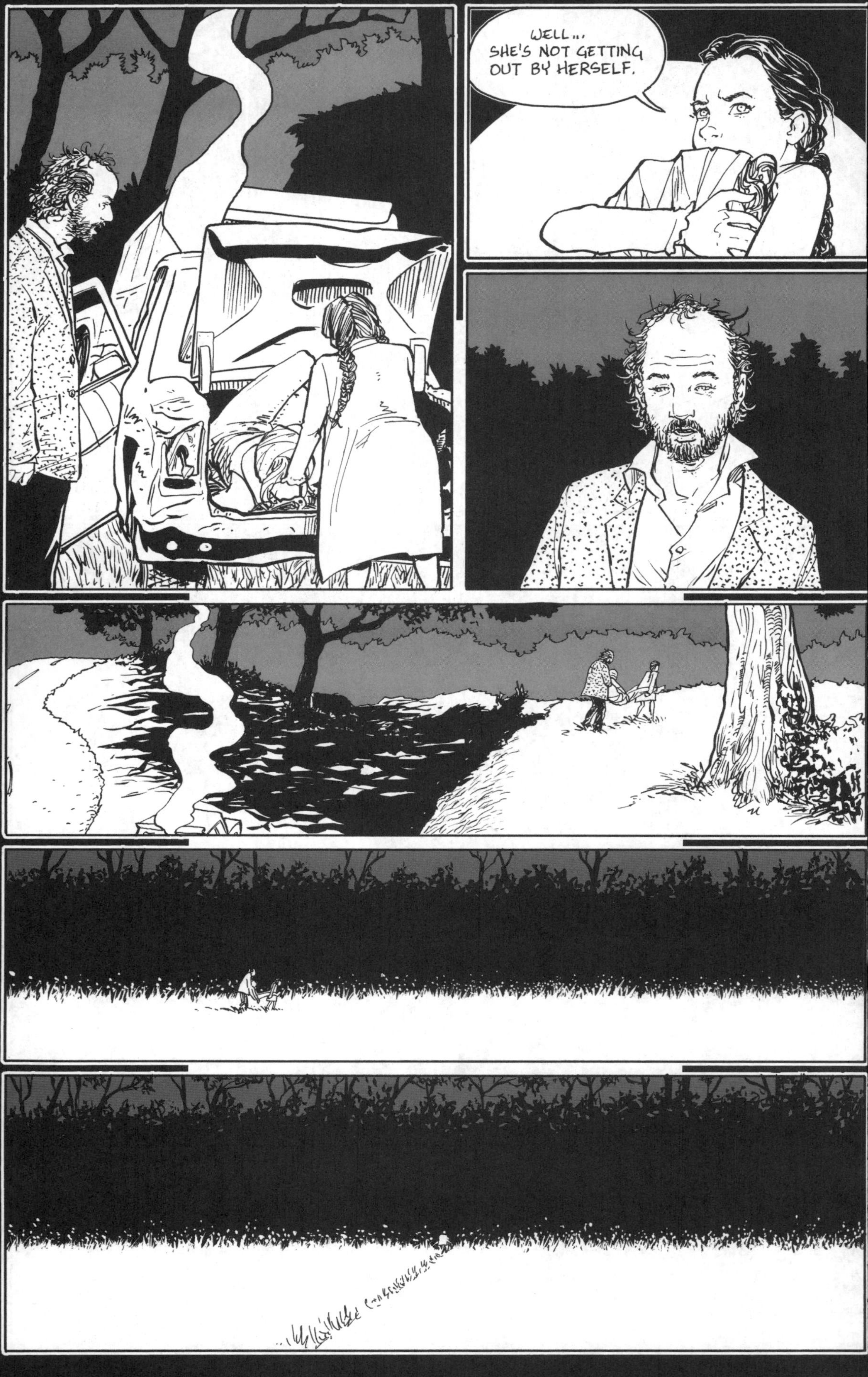
WELL... SHE'S NOT GETTING OUT BY HERSELF.

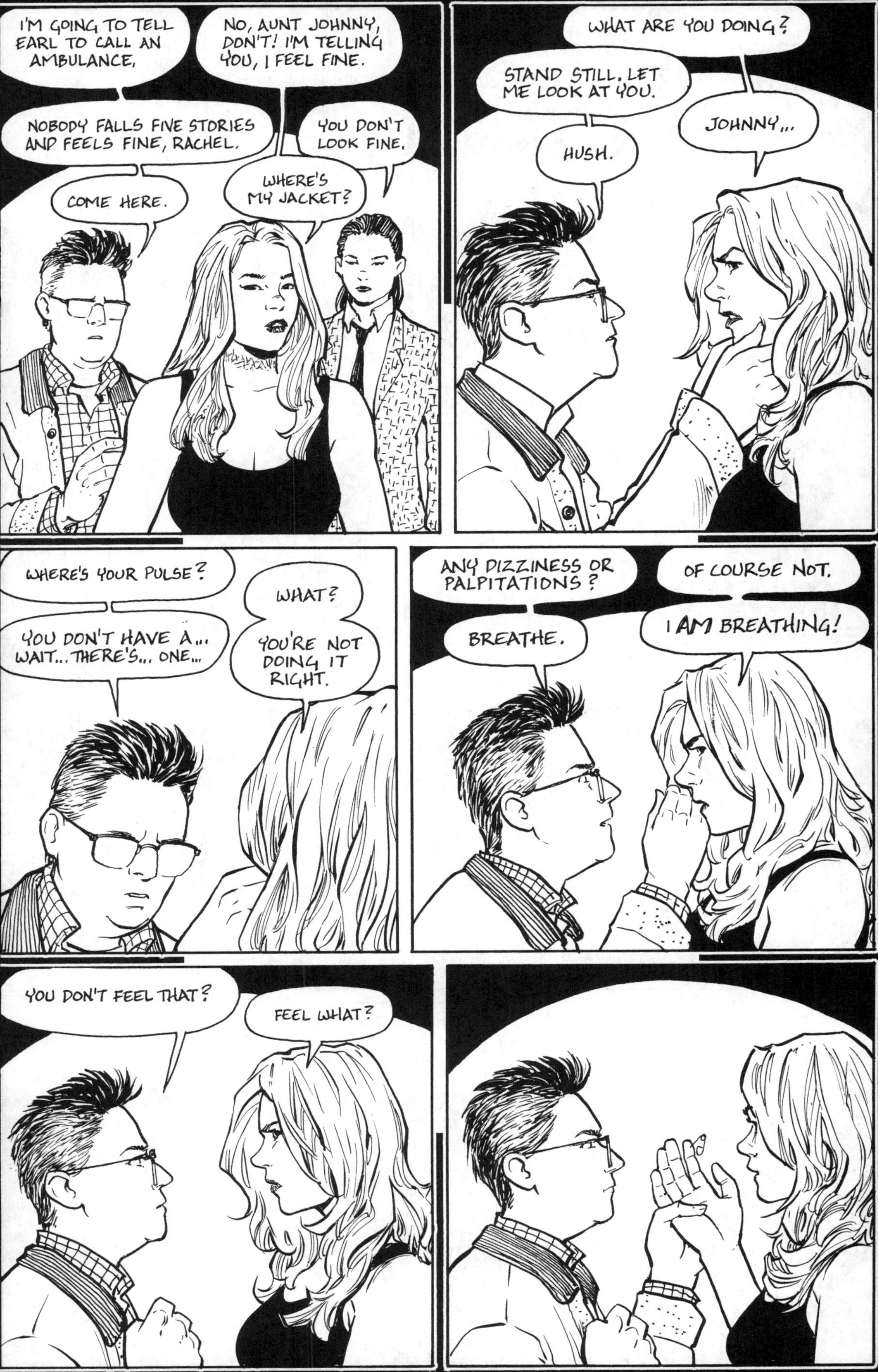
I'M GOING TO TELL EARL TO CALL AN AMBULANCE.
NO, AUNT JOHNNY, DON'T! I'M TELLING YOU, I FEEL FINE.
NOBODY FALLS FIVE STORIES AND FEELS FINE, RACHEL.
YOU DON'T LOOK FINE.
COME HERE.
WHERE'S MY JACKET?
WHAT ARE YOU DOING?
STAND STILL. LET ME LOOK AT YOU.
JOHNNY...
HUSH.
WHERE'S YOUR PULSE?
WHAT?
YOU DON'T HAVE A... WAIT... THERE'S... ONE...
YOU'RE NOT DOING IT RIGHT.
ANY DIZZINESS OR PALPITATIONS?
OF COURSE NOT.
BREATHE.
I AM BREATHING!
YOU DON'T FEEL THAT?
FEEL WHAT?

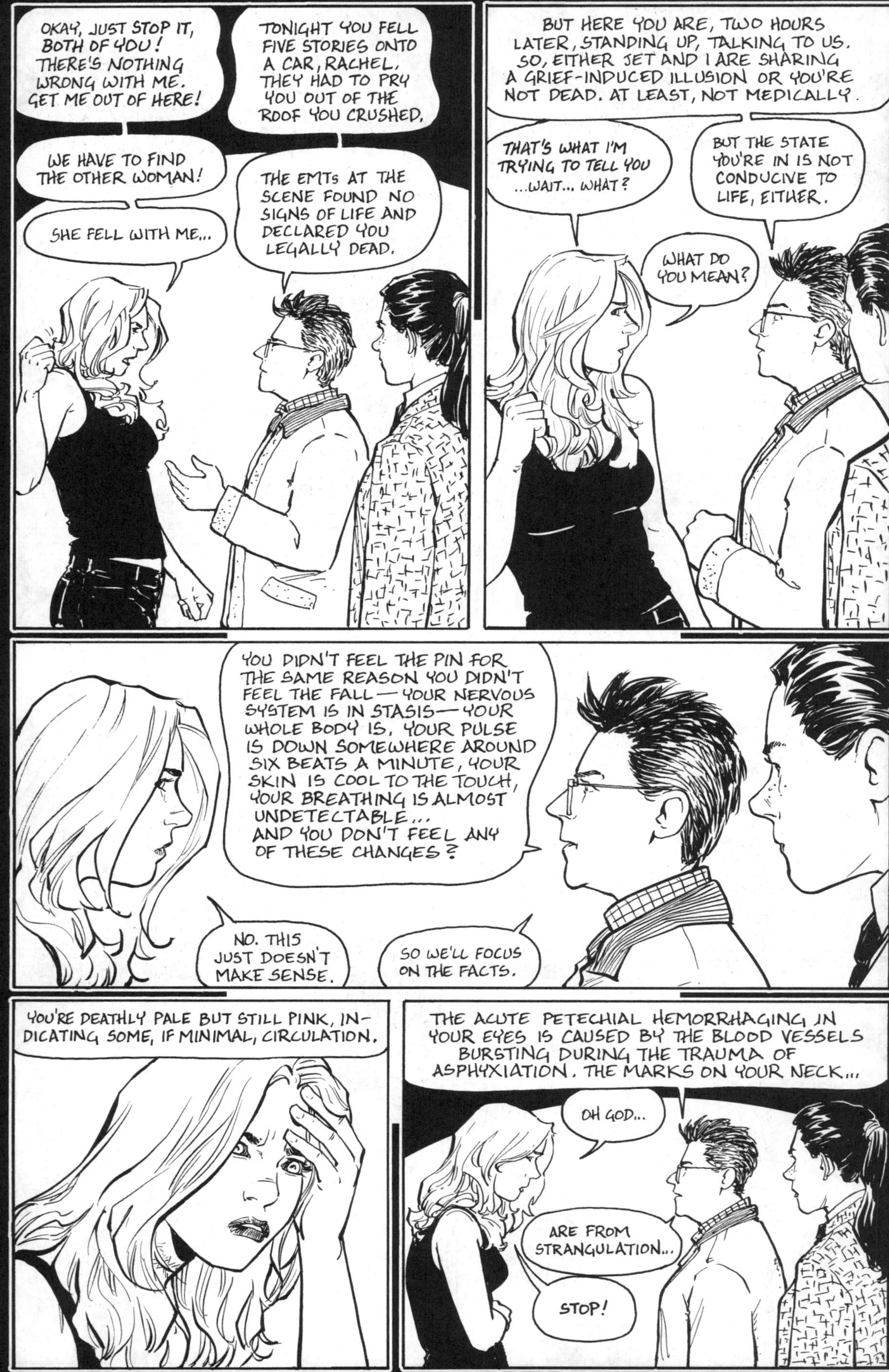
OKAY, JUST STOP IT, BOTH OF YOU! THERE'S NOTHING WRONG WITH ME. GET ME OUT OF HERE!
WE HAVE TO FIND THE OTHER WOMAN!
SHE FELL WITH ME...
TONIGHT YOU FELL FIVE STORIES ONTO A CAR, RACHEL. THEY HAD TO PRY YOU OUT OF THE ROOF YOU CRUSHED.
THE EMTs AT THE SCENE FOUND NO SIGNS OF LIFE AND DECLARED YOU LEGALLY DEAD.
BUT HERE YOU ARE, TWO HOURS LATER, STANDING UP, TALKING TO US. SO, EITHER JET AND I ARE SHARING A GRIEF-INDUCED ILLUSION OR YOU'RE NOT DEAD. AT LEAST, NOT MEDICALLY.
THAT'S WHAT I'M TRYING TO TELL YOU ...WAIT... WHAT?
BUT THE STATE YOU'RE IN IS NOT CONDUCIVE TO LIFE, EITHER.
WHAT DO YOU MEAN?
YOU DIDN'T FEEL THE PIN FOR THE SAME REASON YOU DIDN'T FEEL THE FALL—YOUR NERVOUS SYSTEM IS IN STASIS—YOUR WHOLE BODY IS. YOUR PULSE IS DOWN SOMEWHERE AROUND SIX BEATS A MINUTE, YOUR SKIN IS COOL TO THE TOUCH, YOUR BREATHING IS ALMOST UNDETECTABLE... AND YOU DON'T FEEL ANY OF THESE CHANGES?
NO. THIS JUST DOESN'T MAKE SENSE.
SO WE'LL FOCUS ON THE FACTS.
YOU'RE DEATHLY PALE BUT STILL PINK, INDICATING SOME, IF MINIMAL, CIRCULATION.
THE ACUTE PETECHIAL HEMORRHAGING IN YOUR EYES IS CAUSED BY THE BLOOD VESSELS BURSTING DURING THE TRAUMA OF ASPHYXIATION. THE MARKS ON YOUR NECK...
OH GOD...
ARE FROM STRANGULATION...
STOP!

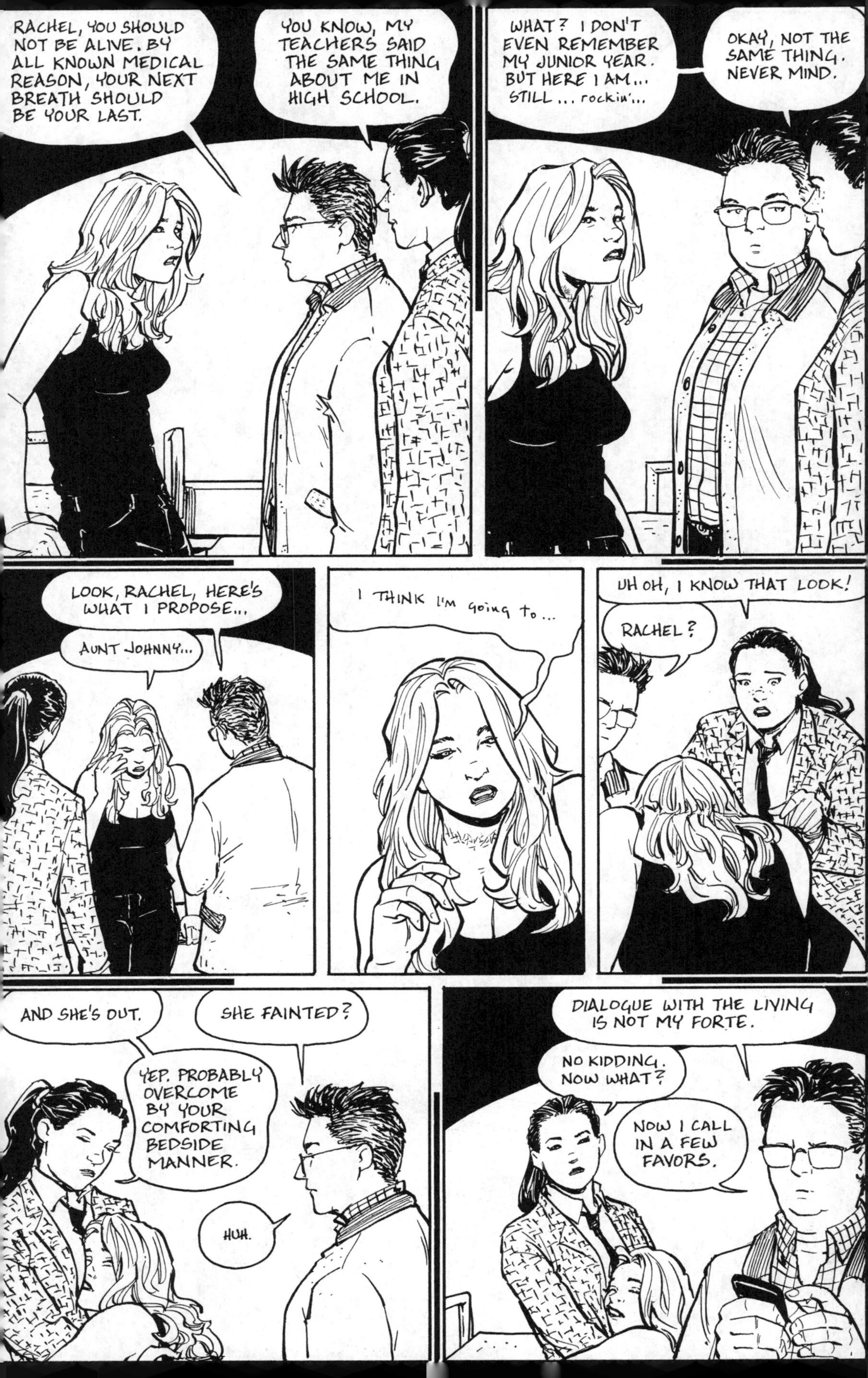
RACHEL, YOU SHOULD NOT BE ALIVE. BY ALL KNOWN MEDICAL REASON, YOUR NEXT BREATH SHOULD BE YOUR LAST.
YOU KNOW, MY TEACHERS SAID THE SAME THING ABOUT ME IN HIGH SCHOOL.
WHAT? I DON'T EVEN REMEMBER MY JUNIOR YEAR. BUT HERE I AM... STILL... rockin'...
OKAY, NOT THE SAME THING. NEVER MIND.
LOOK, RACHEL, HERE'S WHAT I PROPOSE...
AUNT JOHNNY...
I THINK I'M going to...
UH OH, I KNOW THAT LOOK!
RACHEL?
AND SHE'S OUT.
SHE FAINTED?
YEP. PROBABLY OVERCOME BY YOUR COMFORTING BEDSIDE MANNER.
HUH.
DIALOGUE WITH THE LIVING IS NOT MY FORTE.
NO KIDDING. NOW WHAT?
NOW I CALL IN A FEW FAVORS.

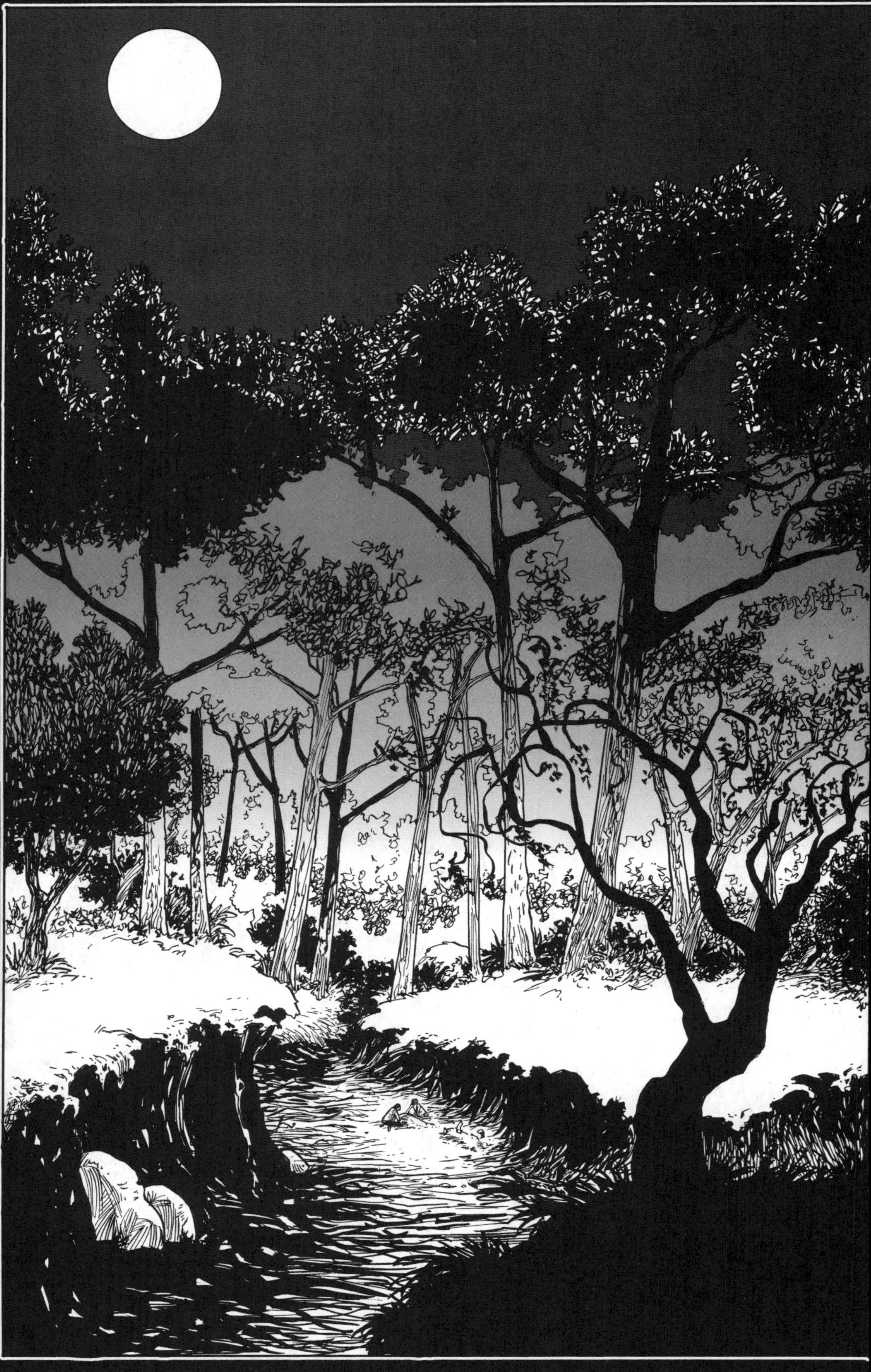

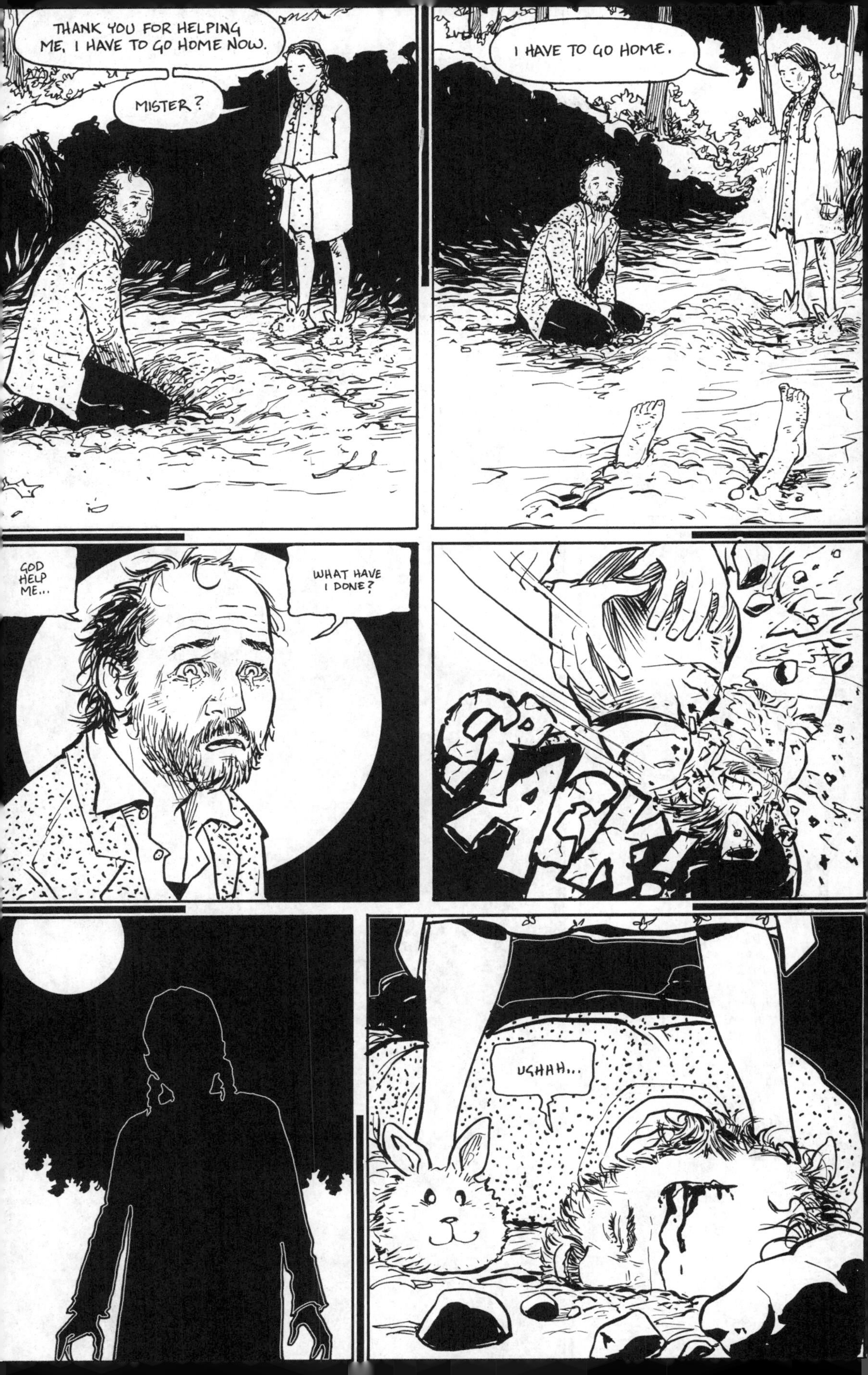
THANK YOU FOR HELPING ME, I HAVE TO GO HOME NOW.
MISTER?
I HAVE TO GO HOME.
GOD HELP ME...
WHAT HAVE I DONE?
UGHHH...

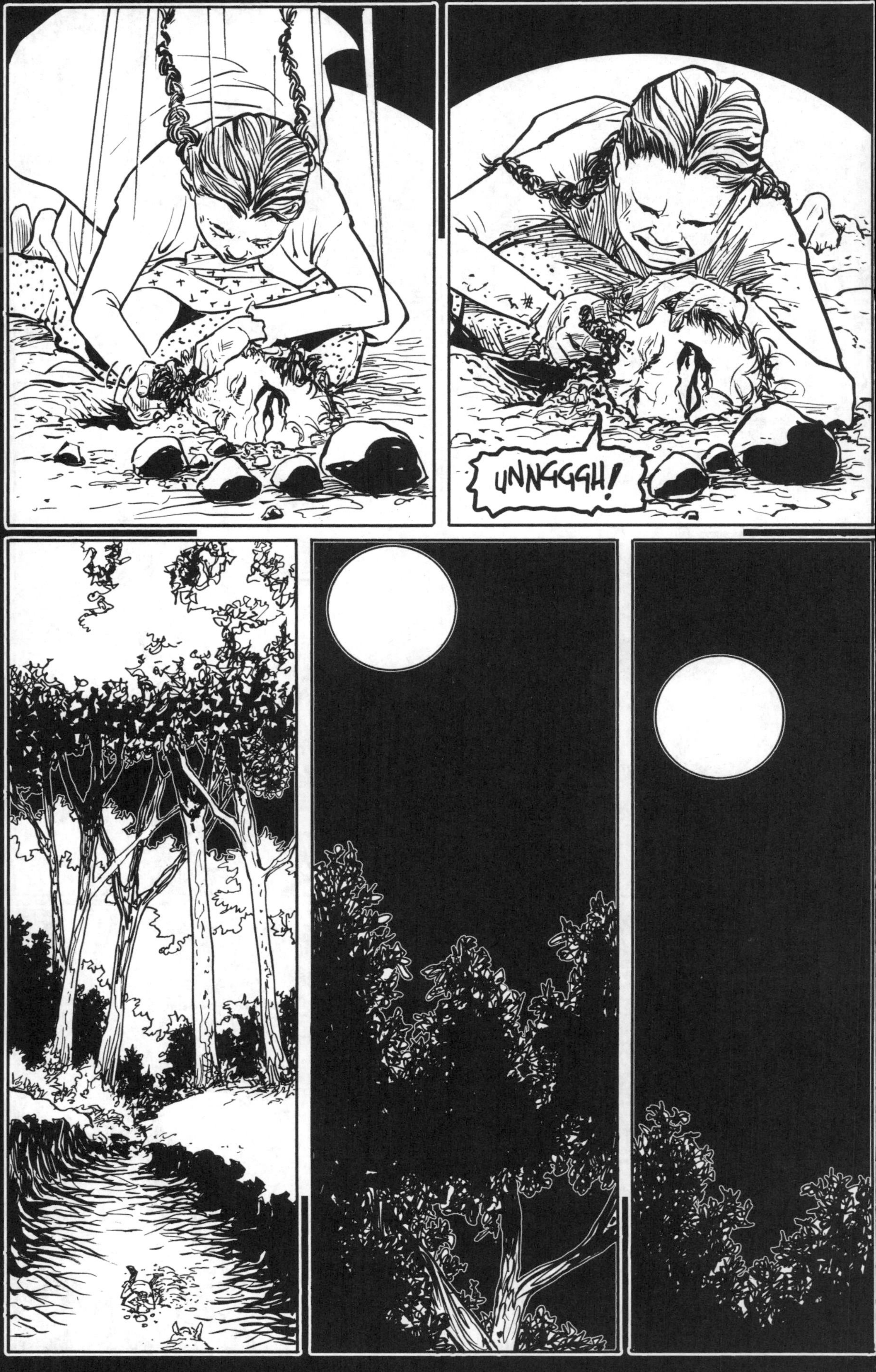
UNNGGGH!

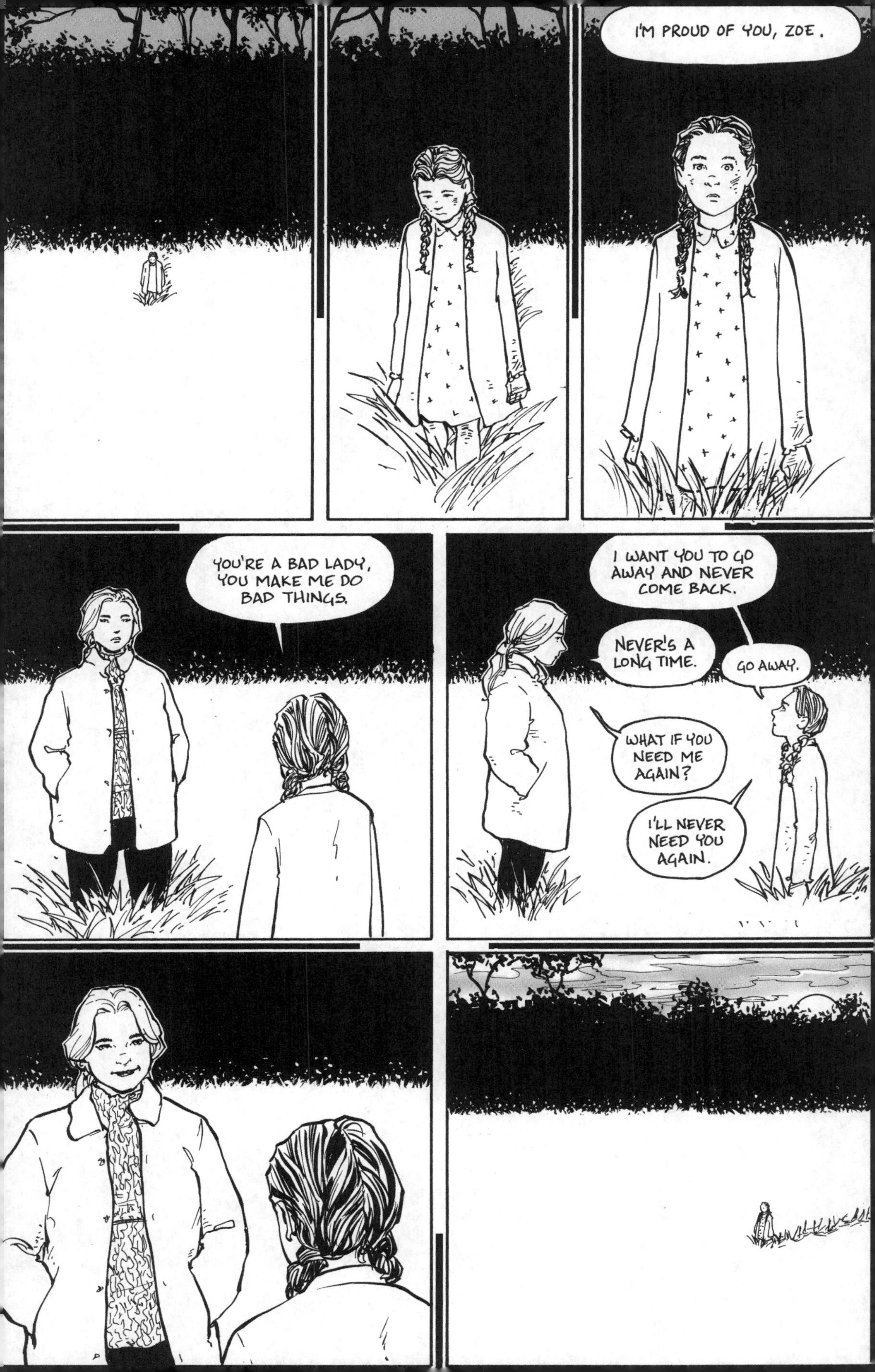
I'M PROUD OF YOU, ZOE.
YOU'RE A BAD LADY, YOU MAKE ME DO BAD THINGS.
I WANT YOU TO GO AWAY AND NEVER COME BACK.
NEVER'S A LONG TIME.
GO AWAY.
WHAT IF YOU NEED ME AGAIN?
I'LL NEVER NEED YOU AGAIN.

TERRY MOORE

# RACHEL RISING

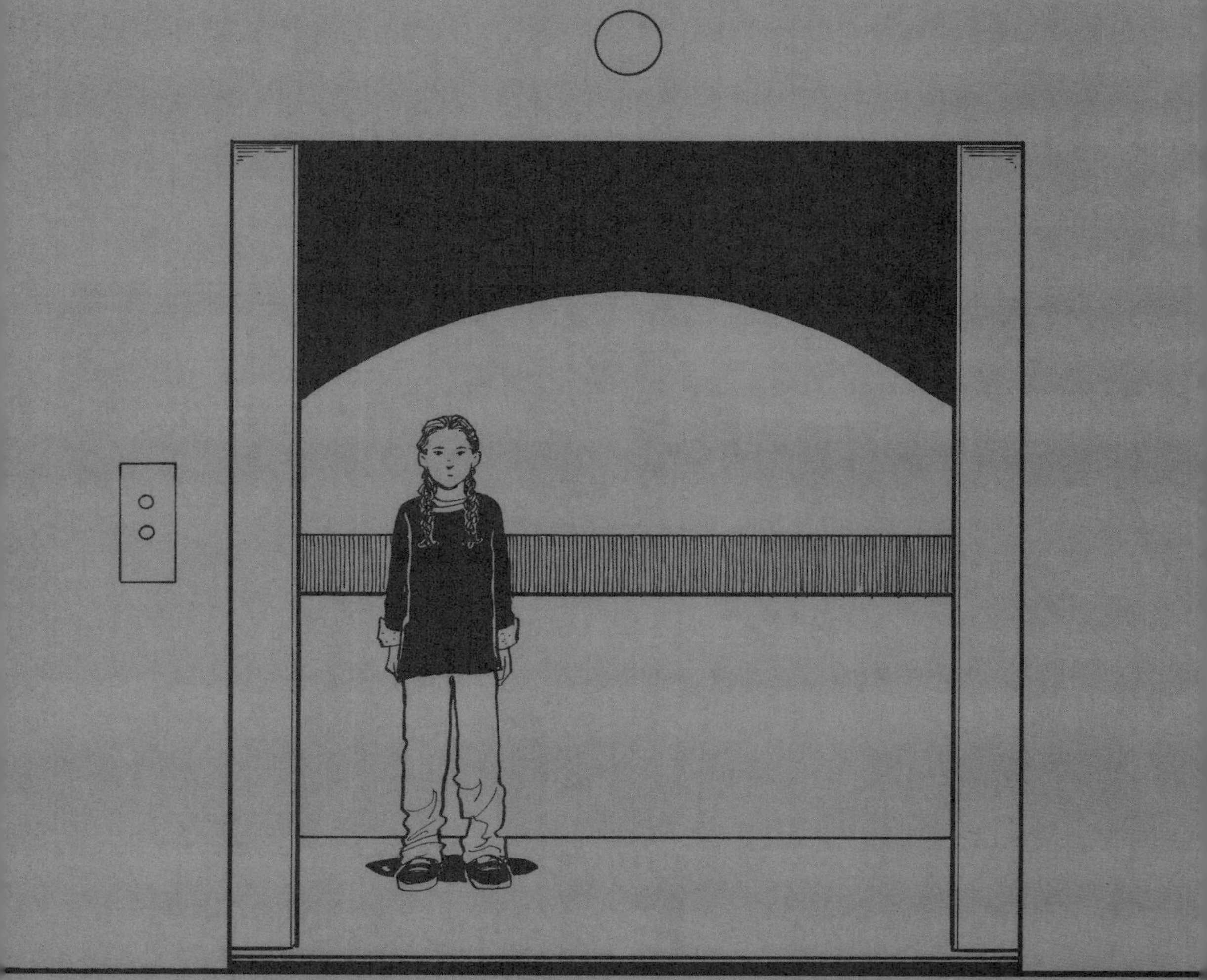

5

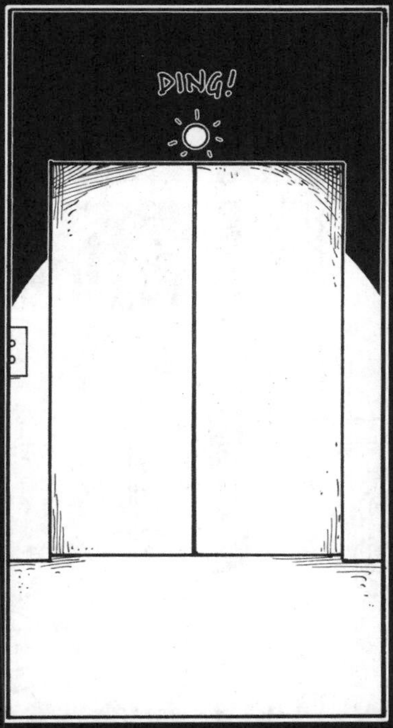
DING!

IN VIOLENCE WE FORGET WHO WE ARE.
—MARY MCCARTHY

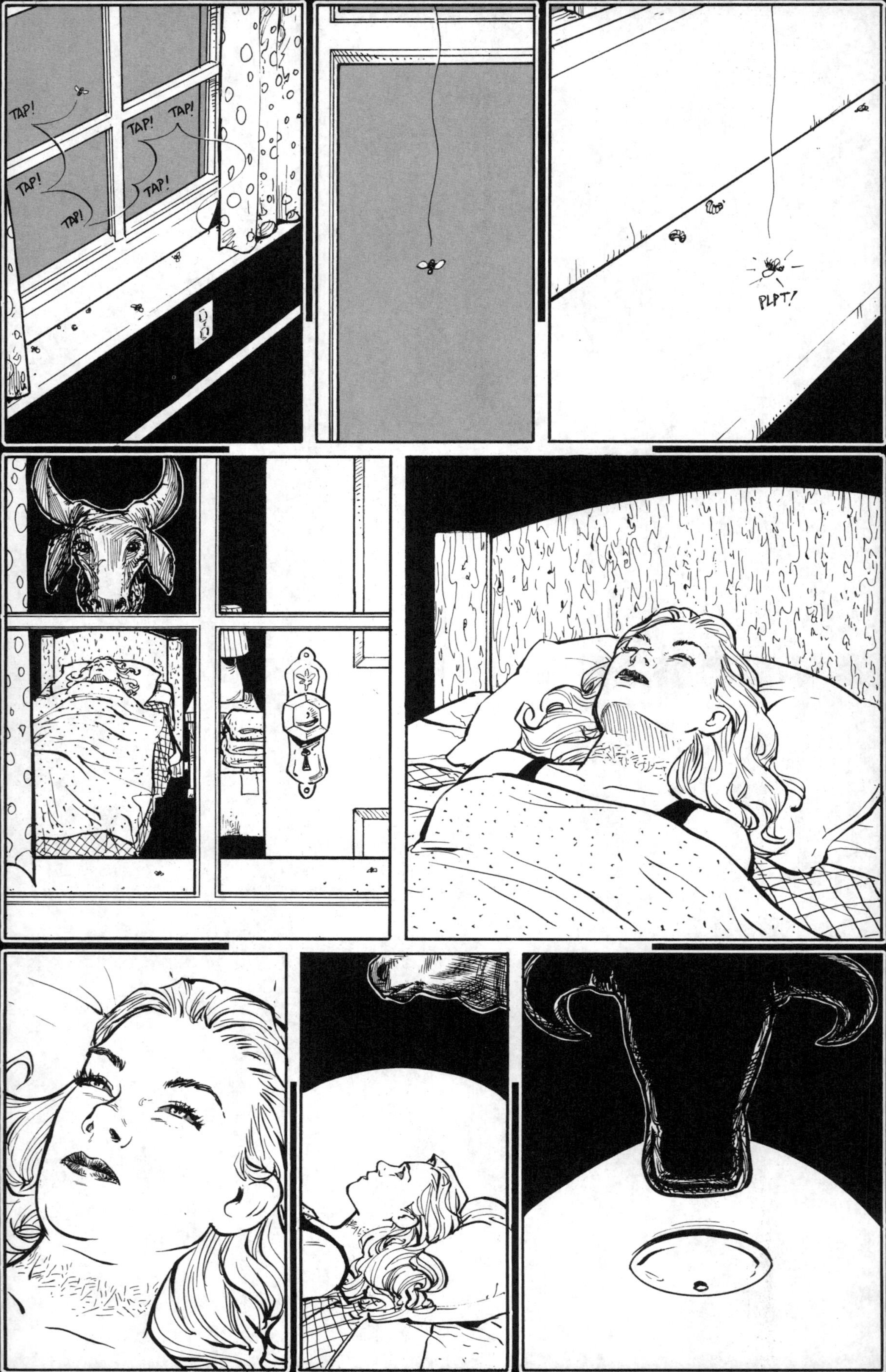
TAP!
TAP!
TAP!
TAP!
TAP!
TAP!
PLPT!

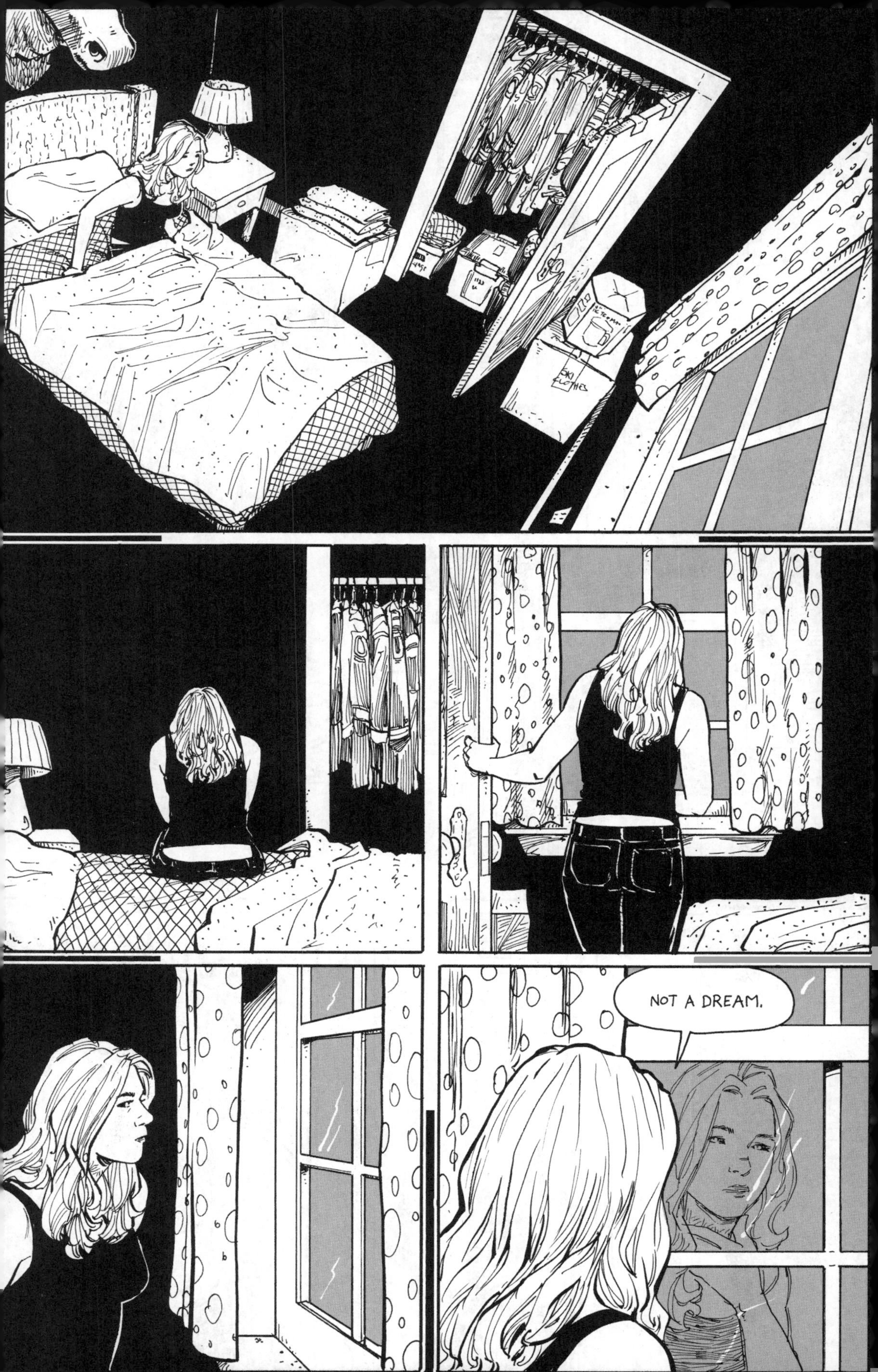
NOT A DREAM.

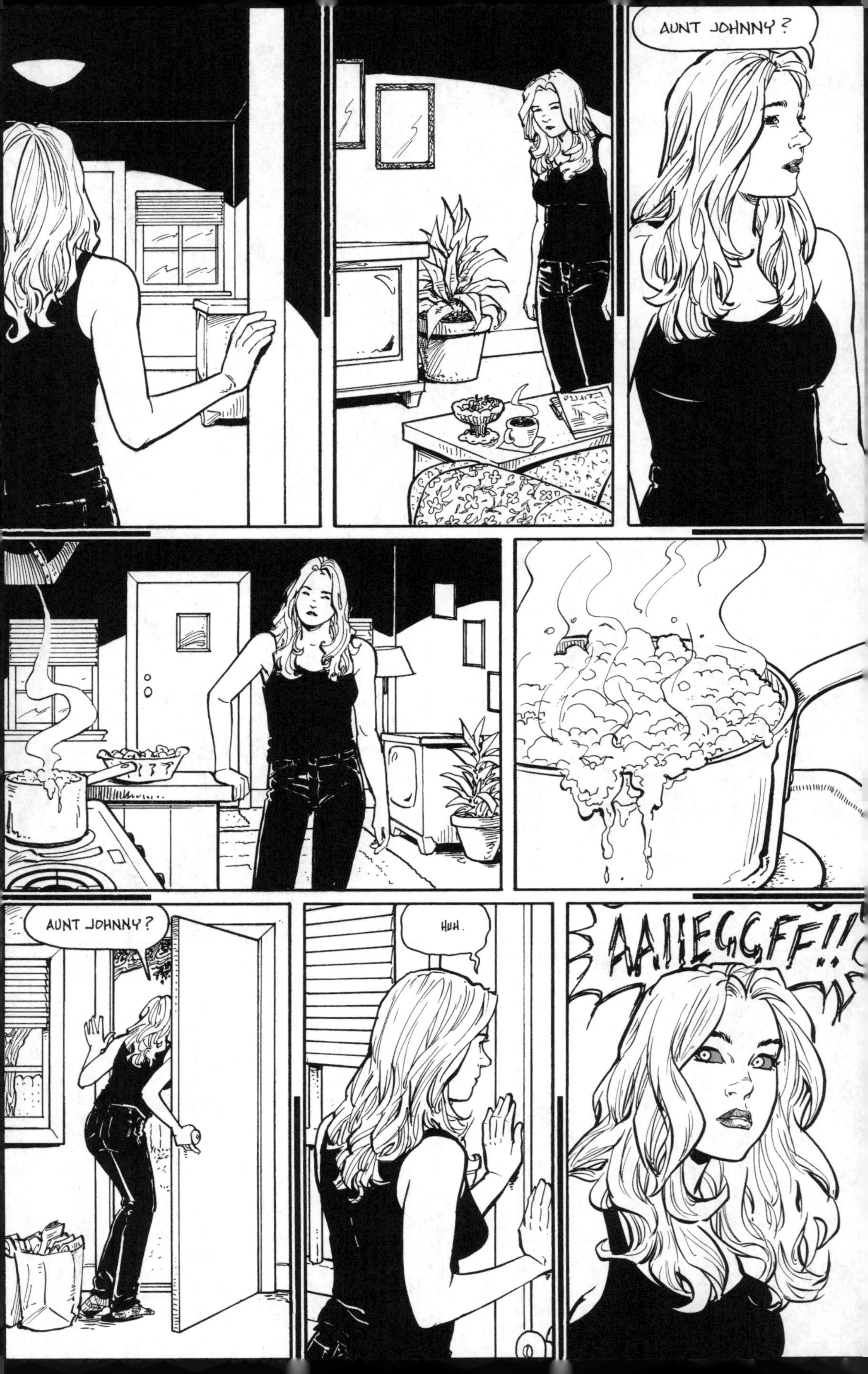
AUNT JOHNNY?
AUNT JOHNNY?
HUH.
AAIIEGGFF!!

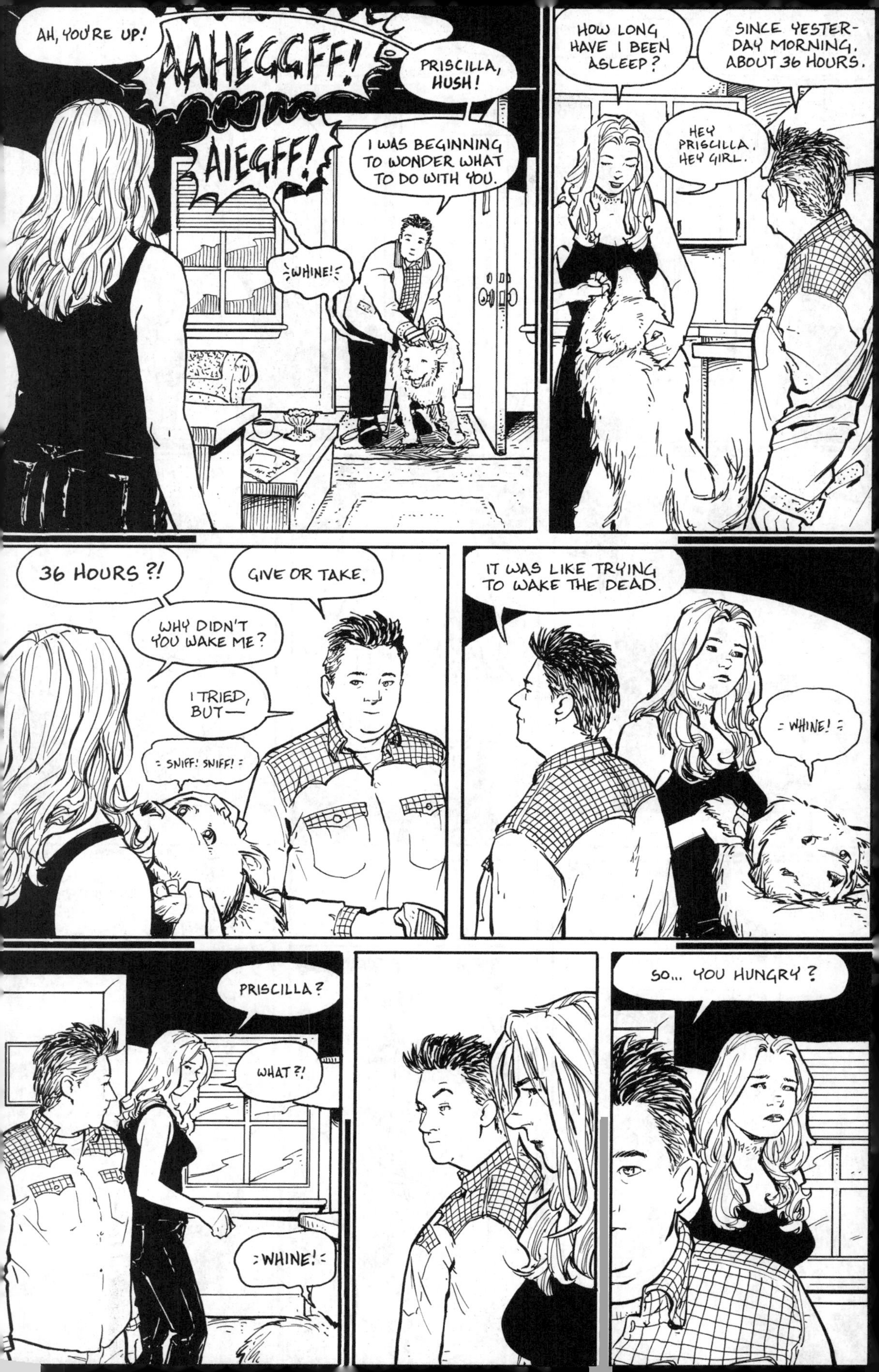

AH, YOU'RE UP!
AAHEGGFF!
AIEGFF!
PRISCILLA, HUSH!
I WAS BEGINNING TO WONDER WHAT TO DO WITH YOU.
WHINE!
HOW LONG HAVE I BEEN ASLEEP?
SINCE YESTERDAY MORNING. ABOUT 36 HOURS.
HEY PRISCILLA. HEY GIRL.
36 HOURS?!
GIVE OR TAKE.
WHY DIDN'T YOU WAKE ME?
I TRIED, BUT—
SNIFF! SNIFF!
IT WAS LIKE TRYING TO WAKE THE DEAD.
WHINE!
PRISCILLA?
WHAT?!
WHINE!
SO... YOU HUNGRY?

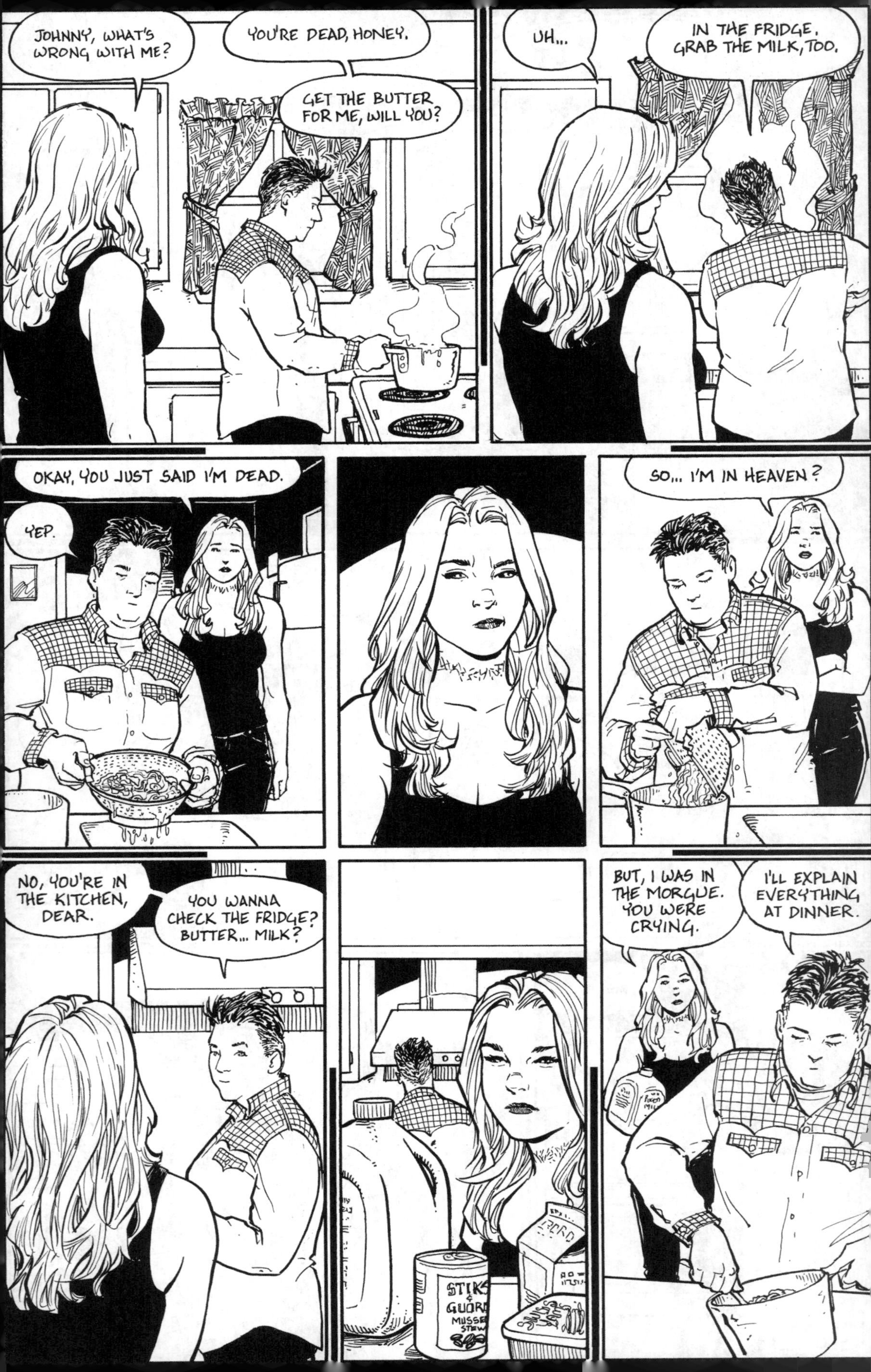
JOHNNY, WHAT'S WRONG WITH ME?
YOU'RE DEAD, HONEY.
GET THE BUTTER FOR ME, WILL YOU?
UH...
IN THE FRIDGE. GRAB THE MILK, TOO.
OKAY, YOU JUST SAID I'M DEAD.
YEP.
SO... I'M IN HEAVEN?
NO, YOU'RE IN THE KITCHEN, DEAR.
YOU WANNA CHECK THE FRIDGE? BUTTER... MILK?
BUT, I WAS IN THE MORGUE. YOU WERE CRYING.
I'LL EXPLAIN EVERYTHING AT DINNER.

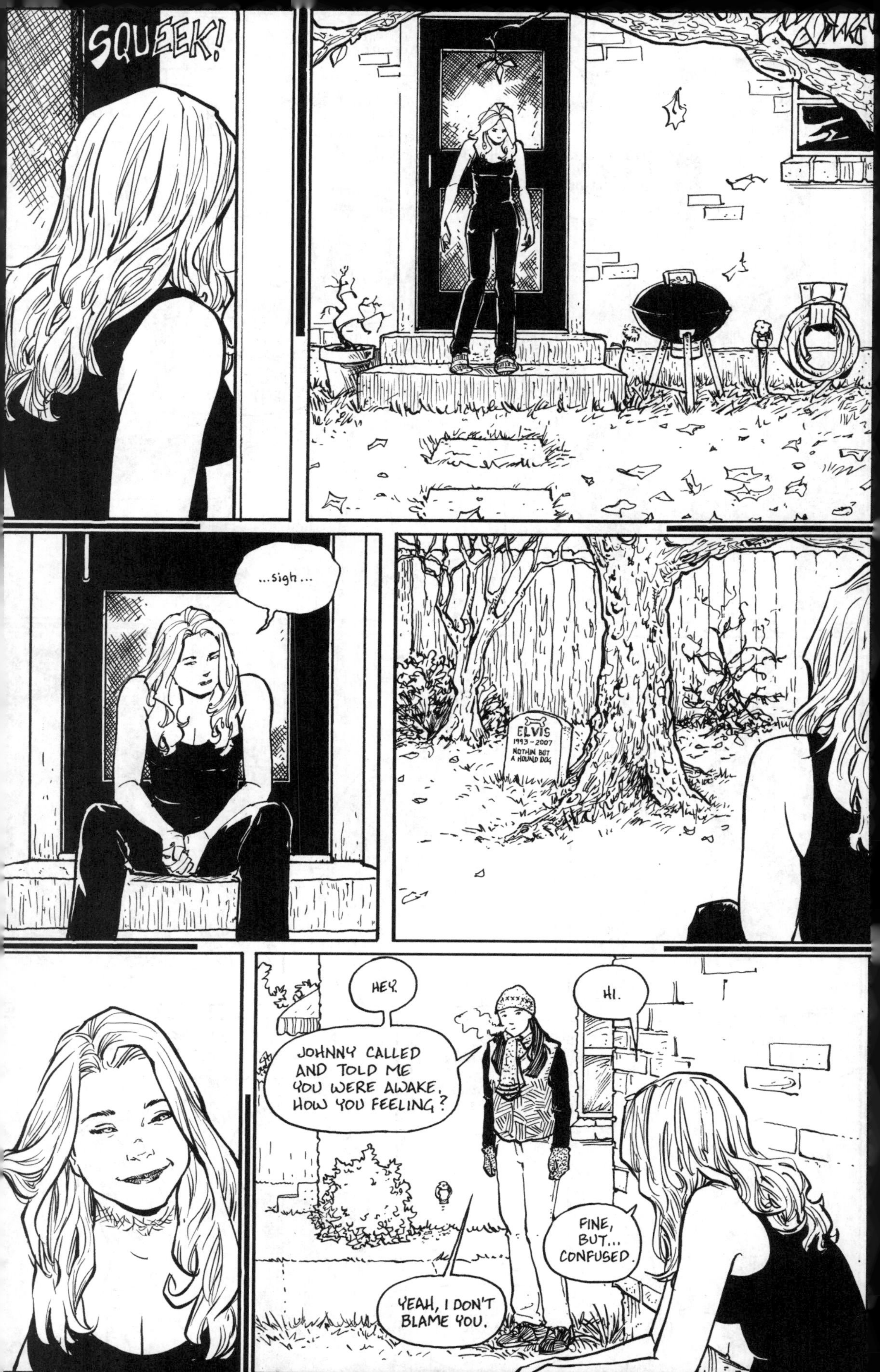
SQUEEK!
...sigh...
ELVIS
1993 - 2007
NOTHIN BUT A HOUND DOG
HEY.
HI.
JOHNNY CALLED AND TOLD ME YOU WERE AWAKE. HOW YOU FEELING?
FINE, BUT... CONFUSED.
YEAH, I DON'T BLAME YOU.

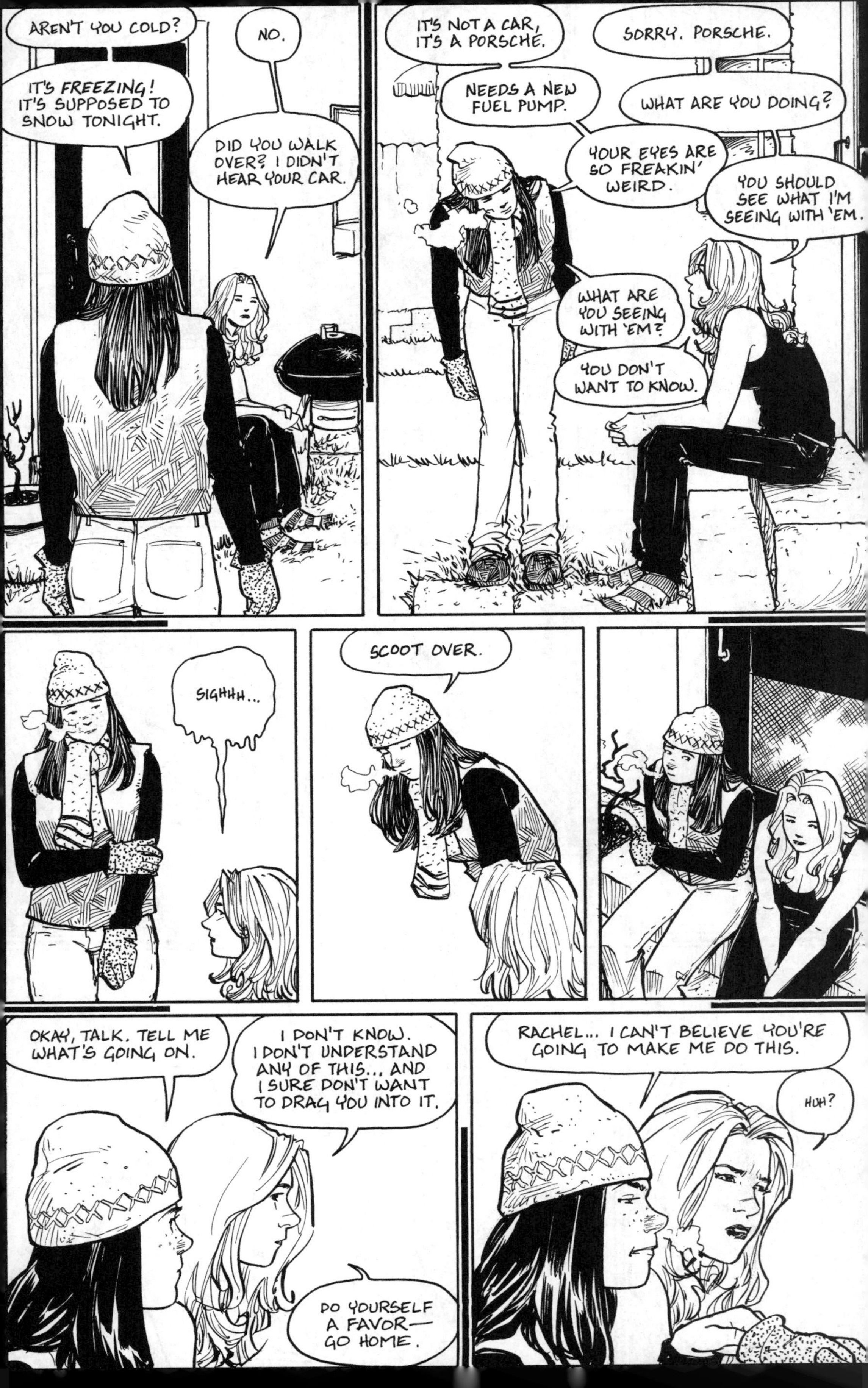
AREN'T YOU COLD?
IT'S FREEZING! IT'S SUPPOSED TO SNOW TONIGHT.
NO.
DID YOU WALK OVER? I DIDN'T HEAR YOUR CAR.
IT'S NOT A CAR, IT'S A PORSCHE.
NEEDS A NEW FUEL PUMP.
SORRY. PORSCHE.
WHAT ARE YOU DOING?
YOUR EYES ARE SO FREAKIN' WEIRD.
YOU SHOULD SEE WHAT I'M SEEING WITH 'EM.
WHAT ARE YOU SEEING WITH 'EM?
YOU DON'T WANT TO KNOW.
SIGHHH...
SCOOT OVER.
OKAY, TALK. TELL ME WHAT'S GOING ON.
I DON'T KNOW. I DON'T UNDERSTAND ANY OF THIS... AND I SURE DON'T WANT TO DRAG YOU INTO IT.
DO YOURSELF A FAVOR— GO HOME.
RACHEL... I CAN'T BELIEVE YOU'RE GOING TO MAKE ME DO THIS.
HUH?

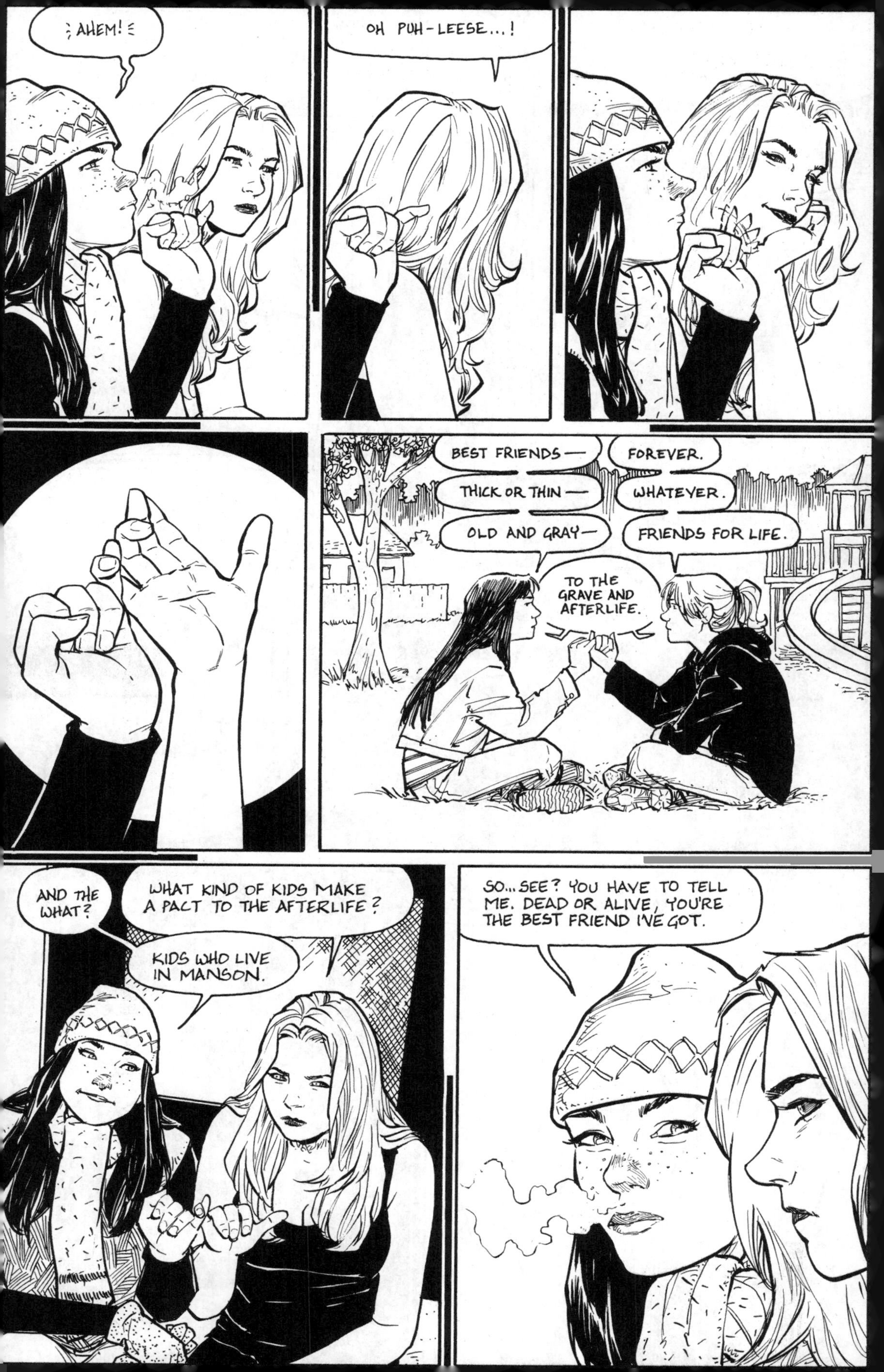
AHEM!
OH PUH-LEESE...!
BEST FRIENDS—
FOREVER.
THICK OR THIN—
WHATEVER.
OLD AND GRAY—
FRIENDS FOR LIFE.
TO THE GRAVE AND AFTERLIFE.
WHAT KIND OF KIDS MAKE A PACT TO THE AFTERLIFE?
AND THE WHAT?
KIDS WHO LIVE IN MANSON.
SO... SEE? YOU HAVE TO TELL ME. DEAD OR ALIVE, YOU'RE THE BEST FRIEND I'VE GOT.

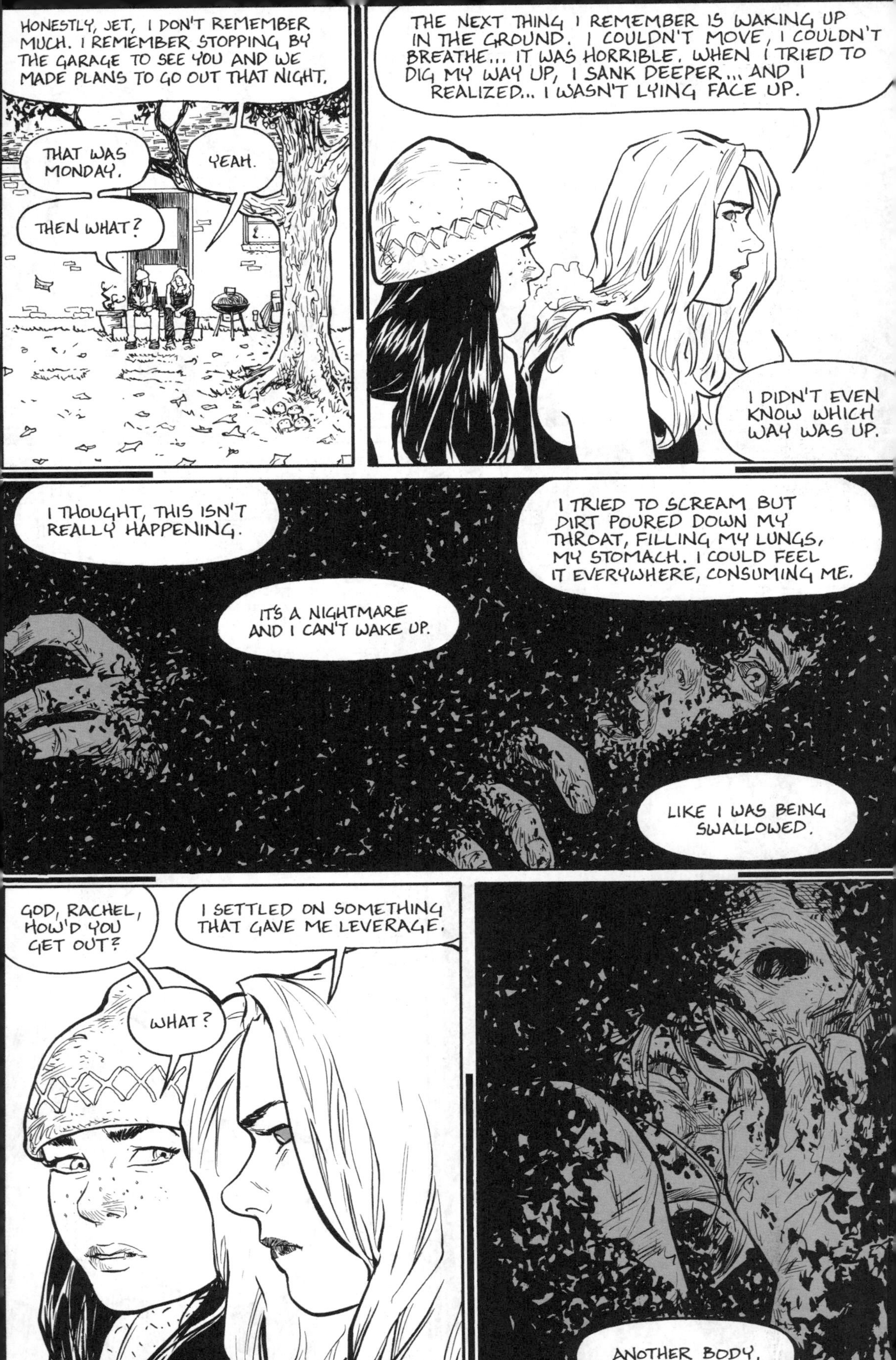
HONESTLY, JET, I DON'T REMEMBER MUCH. I REMEMBER STOPPING BY THE GARAGE TO SEE YOU AND WE MADE PLANS TO GO OUT THAT NIGHT.
THAT WAS MONDAY.
YEAH.
THEN WHAT?
THE NEXT THING I REMEMBER IS WAKING UP IN THE GROUND. I COULDN'T MOVE, I COULDN'T BREATHE... IT WAS HORRIBLE. WHEN I TRIED TO DIG MY WAY UP, I SANK DEEPER... AND I REALIZED... I WASN'T LYING FACE UP.
I DIDN'T EVEN KNOW WHICH WAY WAS UP.
I THOUGHT, THIS ISN'T REALLY HAPPENING.
IT'S A NIGHTMARE AND I CAN'T WAKE UP.
I TRIED TO SCREAM BUT DIRT POURED DOWN MY THROAT, FILLING MY LUNGS, MY STOMACH. I COULD FEEL IT EVERYWHERE, CONSUMING ME.
LIKE I WAS BEING SWALLOWED.
GOD, RACHEL, HOW'D YOU GET OUT?
I SETTLED ON SOMETHING THAT GAVE ME LEVERAGE.
WHAT?
ANOTHER BODY.

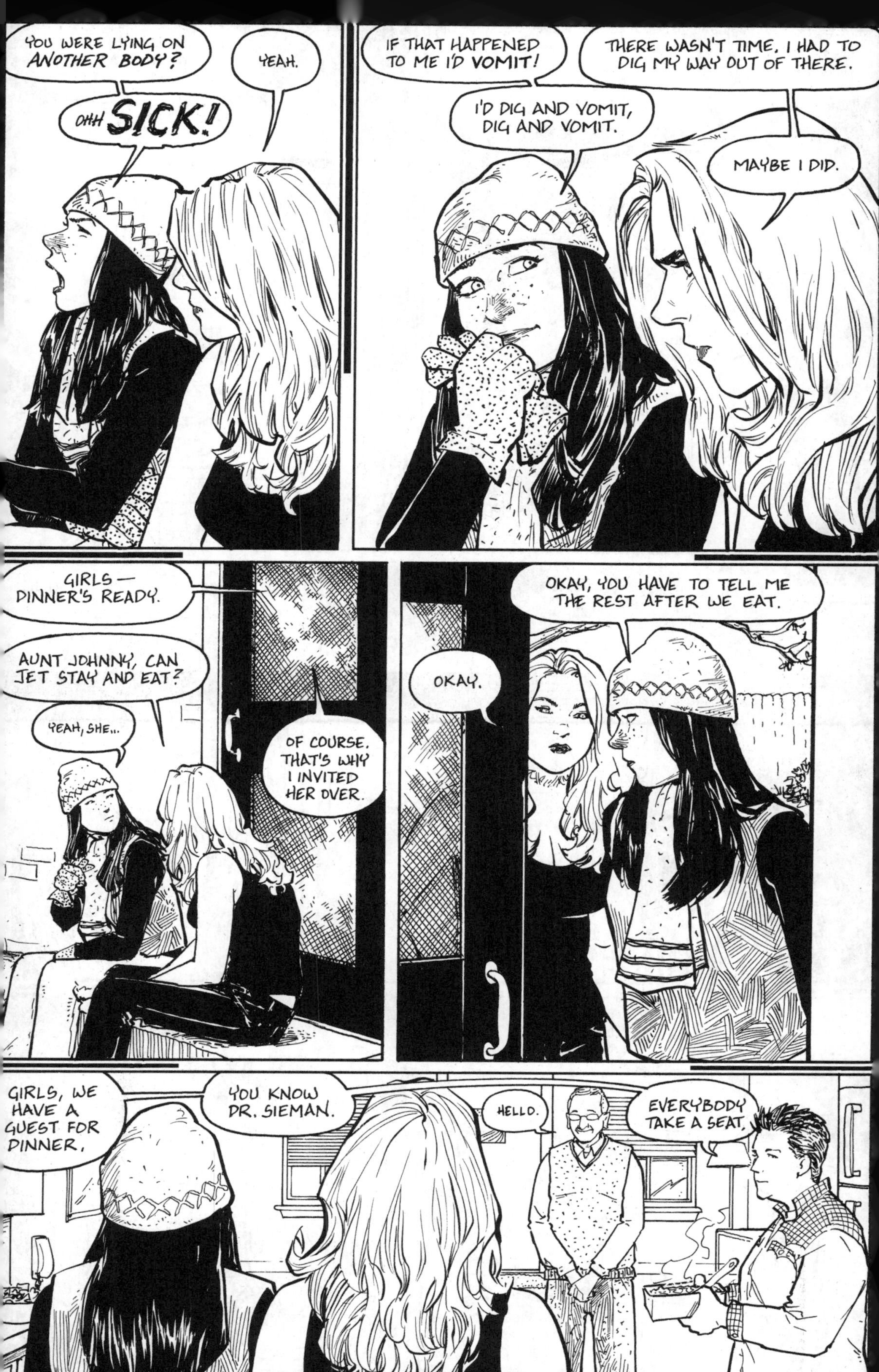
YOU WERE LYING ON ANOTHER BODY?
OHH SICK!
YEAH.
IF THAT HAPPENED TO ME I'D VOMIT!
I'D DIG AND VOMIT, DIG AND VOMIT.
THERE WASN'T TIME. I HAD TO DIG MY WAY OUT OF THERE.
MAYBE I DID.
GIRLS— DINNER'S READY.
AUNT JOHNNY, CAN JET STAY AND EAT?
YEAH, SHE...
OF COURSE. THAT'S WHY I INVITED HER OVER.
OKAY, YOU HAVE TO TELL ME THE REST AFTER WE EAT.
OKAY.
GIRLS, WE HAVE A GUEST FOR DINNER.
YOU KNOW DR. SIEMAN.
HELLO.
EVERYBODY TAKE A SEAT.

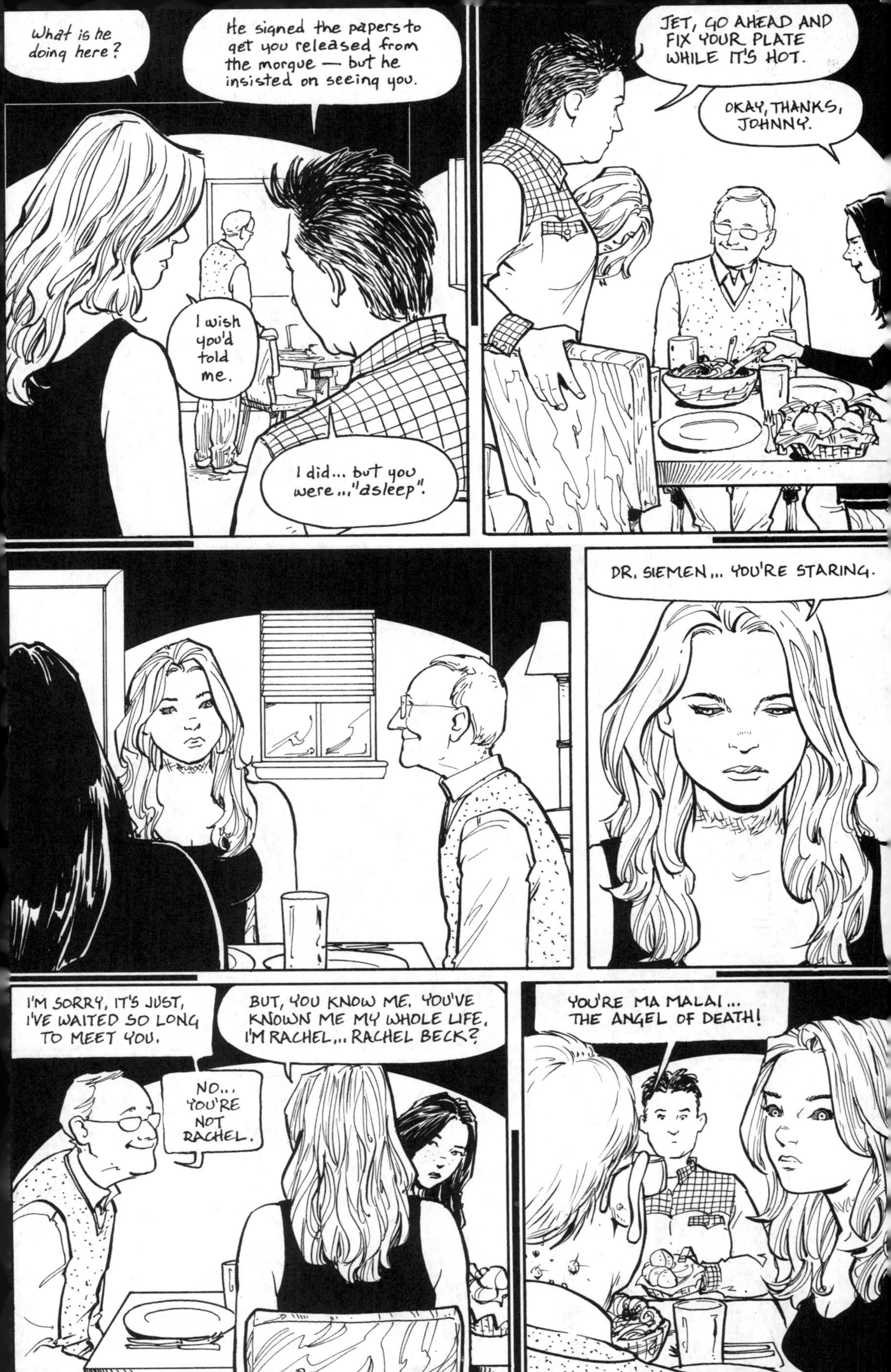
What is he doing here?
He signed the papers to get you released from the morgue — but he insisted on seeing you.
I wish you'd told me.
I did... but you were..."asleep".
JET, GO AHEAD AND FIX YOUR PLATE WHILE IT'S HOT.
OKAY, THANKS, JOHNNY.
DR. SIEMEN... YOU'RE STARING.
I'M SORRY, IT'S JUST, I'VE WAITED SO LONG TO MEET YOU.
BUT, YOU KNOW ME. YOU'VE KNOWN ME MY WHOLE LIFE. I'M RACHEL... RACHEL BECK?
NO... YOU'RE NOT RACHEL.
YOU'RE MA MALAI... THE ANGEL OF DEATH!

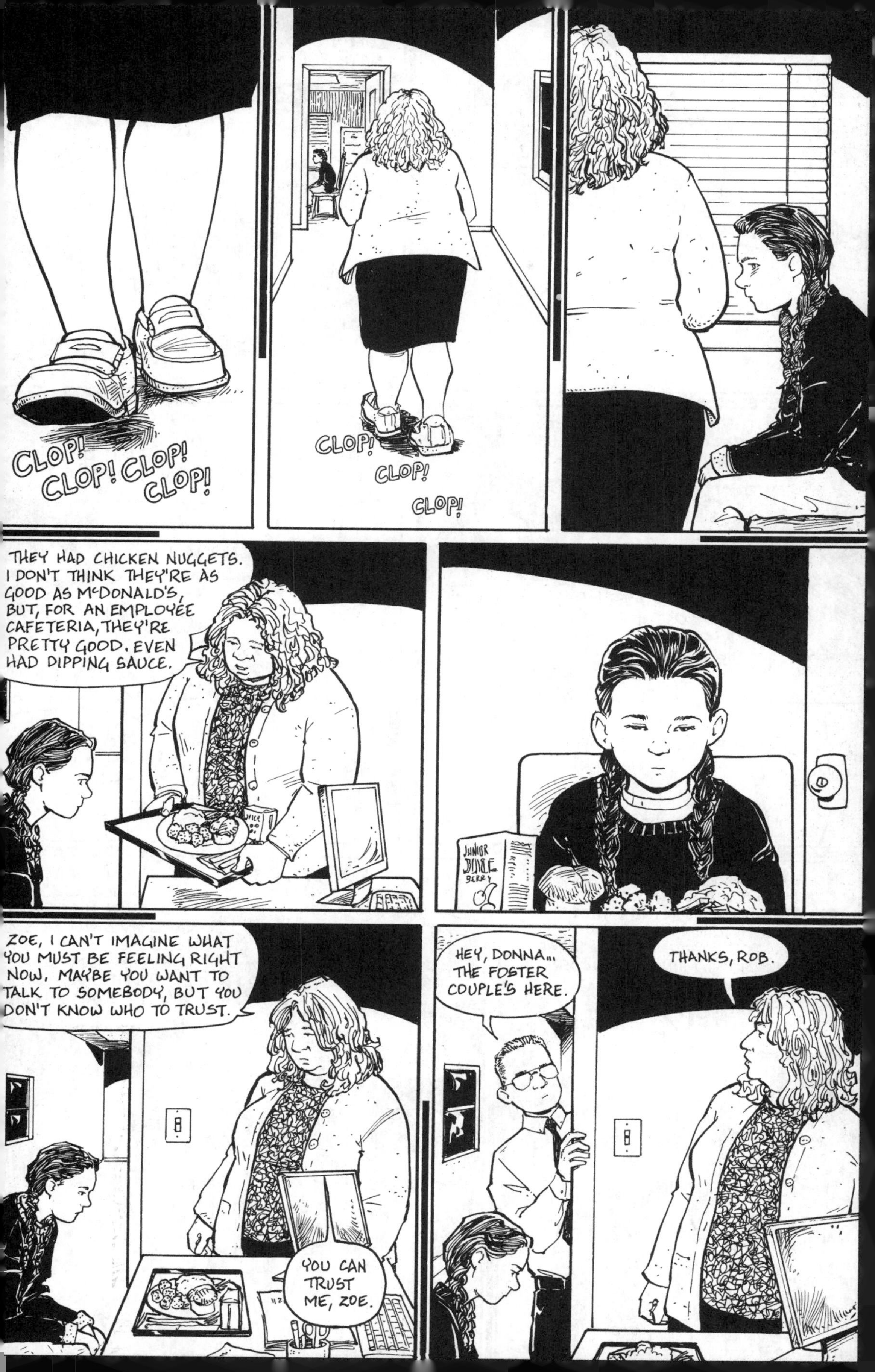
CLOP! CLOP! CLOP! CLOP!
CLOP! CLOP! CLOP!
THEY HAD CHICKEN NUGGETS. I DON'T THINK THEY'RE AS GOOD AS McDONALD'S, BUT, FOR AN EMPLOYEE CAFETERIA, THEY'RE PRETTY GOOD. EVEN HAD DIPPING SAUCE.
JUNIOR JUICE BERRY
ZOE, I CAN'T IMAGINE WHAT YOU MUST BE FEELING RIGHT NOW. MAYBE YOU WANT TO TALK TO SOMEBODY, BUT YOU DON'T KNOW WHO TO TRUST.
YOU CAN TRUST ME, ZOE.
HEY, DONNA... THE FOSTER COUPLE'S HERE.
THANKS, ROB.

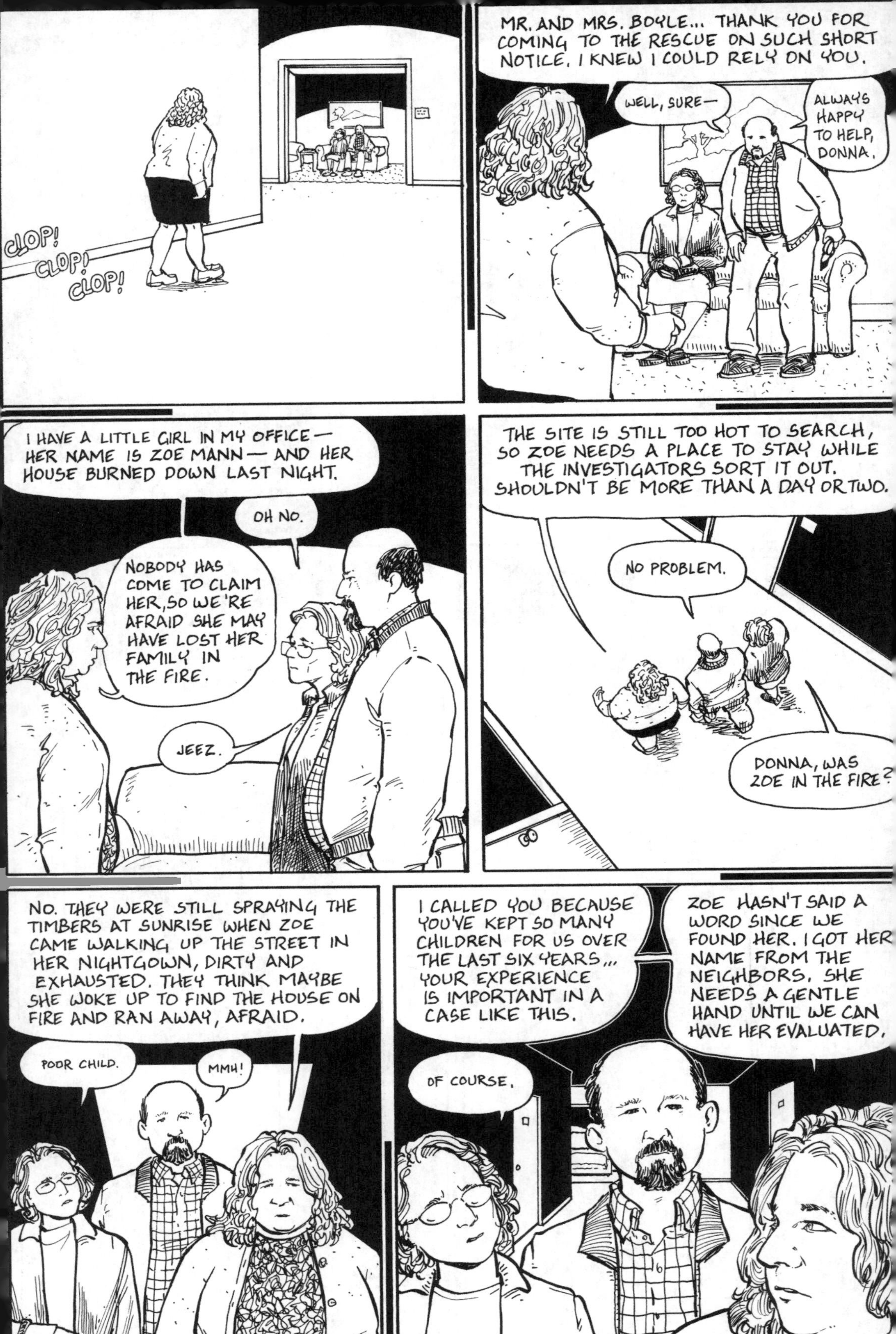
CLOP!
CLOP!
CLOP!
MR. AND MRS. BOYLE... THANK YOU FOR COMING TO THE RESCUE ON SUCH SHORT NOTICE. I KNEW I COULD RELY ON YOU.
WELL, SURE—
ALWAYS HAPPY TO HELP, DONNA.
I HAVE A LITTLE GIRL IN MY OFFICE— HER NAME IS ZOE MANN— AND HER HOUSE BURNED DOWN LAST NIGHT.
OH NO.
NOBODY HAS COME TO CLAIM HER, SO WE'RE AFRAID SHE MAY HAVE LOST HER FAMILY IN THE FIRE.
JEEZ.
THE SITE IS STILL TOO HOT TO SEARCH, SO ZOE NEEDS A PLACE TO STAY WHILE THE INVESTIGATORS SORT IT OUT. SHOULDN'T BE MORE THAN A DAY OR TWO.
NO PROBLEM.
DONNA, WAS ZOE IN THE FIRE?
NO. THEY WERE STILL SPRAYING THE TIMBERS AT SUNRISE WHEN ZOE CAME WALKING UP THE STREET IN HER NIGHTGOWN, DIRTY AND EXHAUSTED. THEY THINK MAYBE SHE WOKE UP TO FIND THE HOUSE ON FIRE AND RAN AWAY, AFRAID.
POOR CHILD.
MMH!
I CALLED YOU BECAUSE YOU'VE KEPT SO MANY CHILDREN FOR US OVER THE LAST SIX YEARS... YOUR EXPERIENCE IS IMPORTANT IN A CASE LIKE THIS.
ZOE HASN'T SAID A WORD SINCE WE FOUND HER. I GOT HER NAME FROM THE NEIGHBORS. SHE NEEDS A GENTLE HAND UNTIL WE CAN HAVE HER EVALUATED.
OF COURSE.

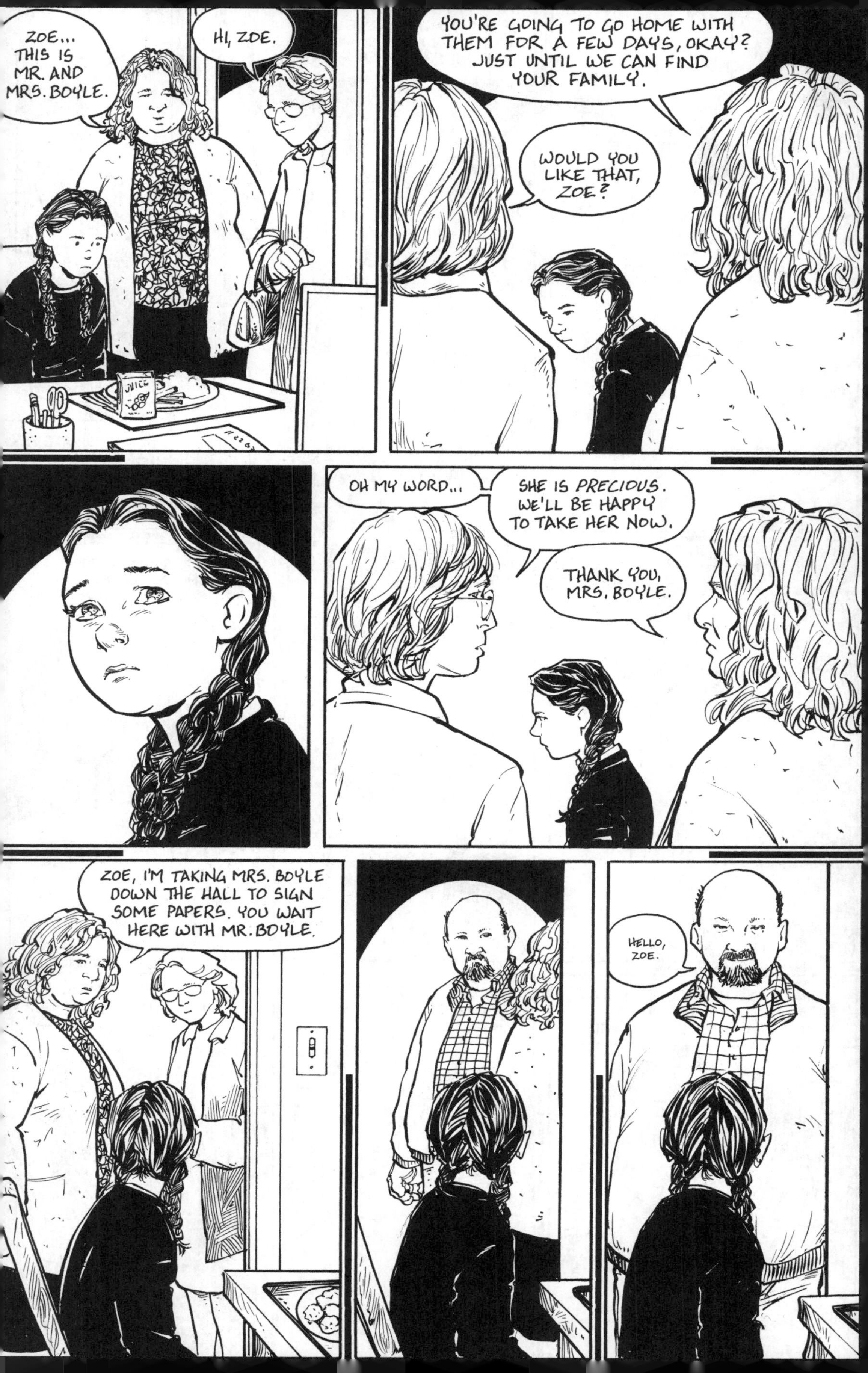
ZOE... THIS IS MR. AND MRS. BOYLE.
HI, ZOE.
YOU'RE GOING TO GO HOME WITH THEM FOR A FEW DAYS, OKAY? JUST UNTIL WE CAN FIND YOUR FAMILY.
WOULD YOU LIKE THAT, ZOE?
OH MY WORD...
SHE IS PRECIOUS. WE'LL BE HAPPY TO TAKE HER NOW.
THANK YOU, MRS. BOYLE.
ZOE, I'M TAKING MRS. BOYLE DOWN THE HALL TO SIGN SOME PAPERS. YOU WAIT HERE WITH MR. BOYLE.
HELLO, ZOE.

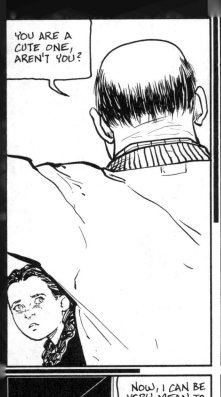

YOU ARE A CUTE ONE, AREN'T YOU?

IF YOU WANNA COME HOME WITH ME, WE'RE GONNA HAVE AN UNDERSTANDING.

YOU DO WHATEVER I SAY AND WE'RE GONNA GET ALONG JUST FINE. GOT IT?

NOW, I CAN BE VERY MEAN TO YOU OR I CAN BE VERY NICE. IT ALL DEPENDS ON YOU. DO YOU WANT ME TO BE MEAN?

OR... DO YOU WANT ME TO BE NICE? WHAT'S IT GOING TO BE, HUH?

ZOE? LOOK AT ME WHEN I'M TALKING TO YOU, GIRL. ZOE!

WHAT'S THE MATTER WITH YOU, ARE YOU DEAF AND DUMB? DON'T PLAY GAMES WITH ME.

YOU'RE A BAD MAN. YOU HURT CHILDREN.

IF YOU TOUCH ME AGAIN, I'LL TELL MISS DONNA.

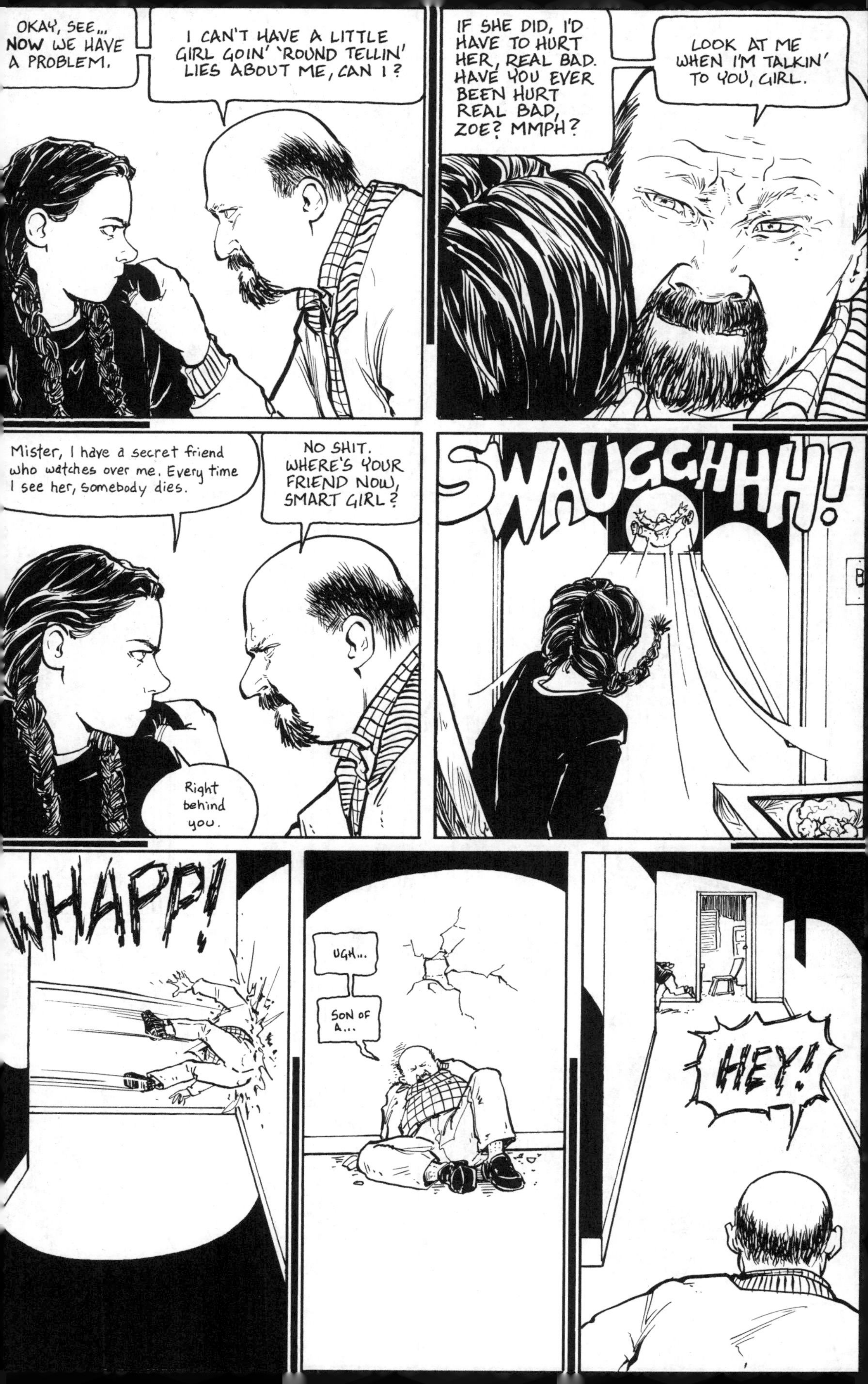
OKAY, SEE... NOW WE HAVE A PROBLEM.
I CAN'T HAVE A LITTLE GIRL GOIN' 'ROUND TELLIN' LIES ABOUT ME, CAN I?
IF SHE DID, I'D HAVE TO HURT HER, REAL BAD. HAVE YOU EVER BEEN HURT REAL BAD, ZOE? MMPH?
LOOK AT ME WHEN I'M TALKIN' TO YOU, GIRL.
Mister, I have a secret friend who watches over me. Every time I see her, somebody dies.
NO SHIT. WHERE'S YOUR FRIEND NOW, SMART GIRL?
Right behind you.
SWAUGGHHH!
WHAPP!
UGH...
SON OF A...
HEY!

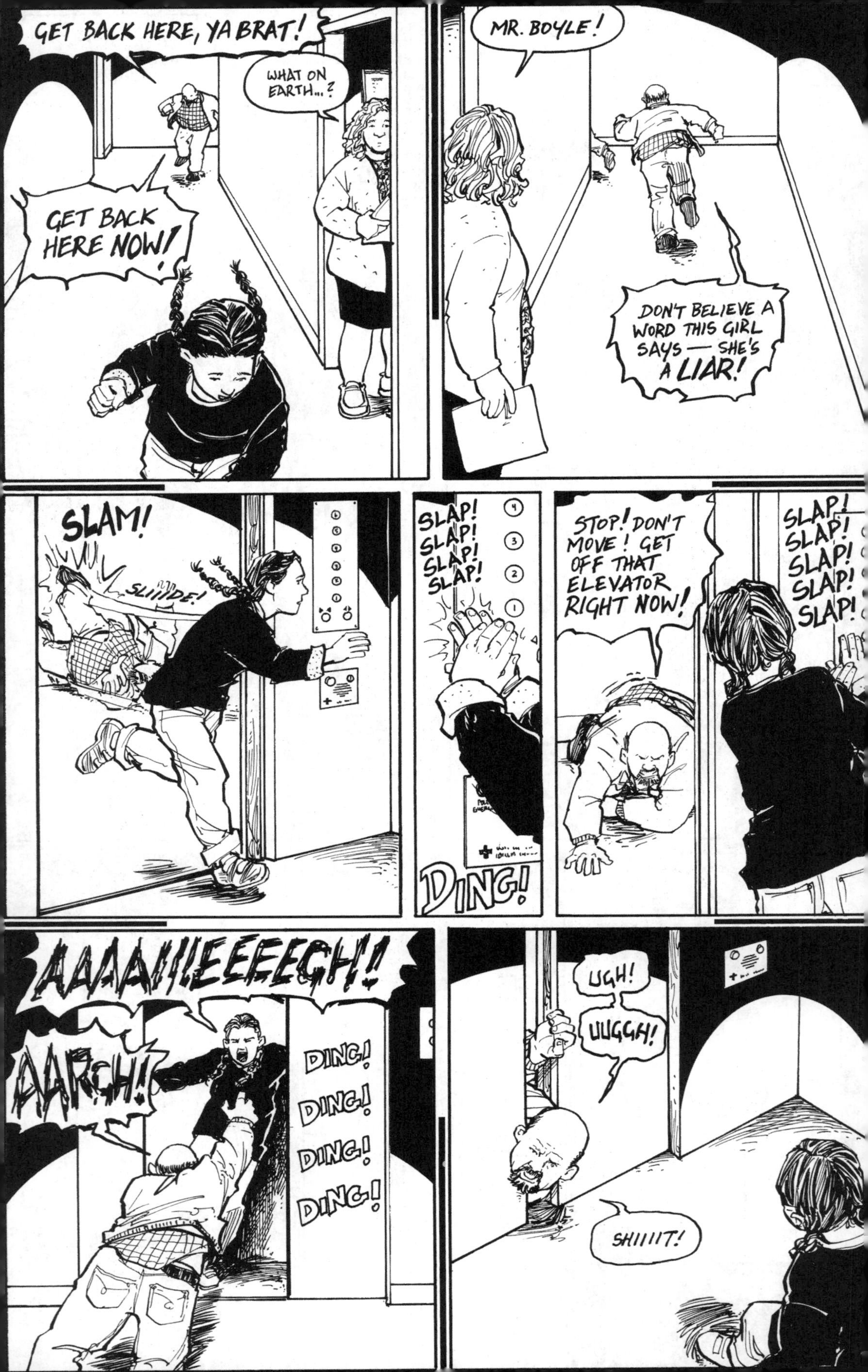
GET BACK HERE, YA BRAT!
WHAT ON EARTH...?
GET BACK HERE NOW!
MR. BOYLE!
DON'T BELIEVE A WORD THIS GIRL SAYS — SHE'S A LIAR!
SLAM!
SLIIIDE!
SLAP! SLAP! SLAP! SLAP!
DING!
STOP! DON'T MOVE! GET OFF THAT ELEVATOR RIGHT NOW!
SLAP! SLAP! SLAP! SLAP! SLAP!
AAAAIIIEEEECH!
AARGH!
DING! DING! DING! DING!
UGH!
UUGGH!
SHIIIIT!

OH MY WORD! HANK?!
ZOE, OPEN THE DOOR!
BAM! BAM! BAM!
OPEN THE DOOR, RIGHT NOW, ZOE!
AGH! HELP!
SO HELP ME, GOD, WHEN I GET MY HANDS ON YOU...!
WHA...? WHAT?!
DING!
WHOA! NO! WAIT! STOP! STOP!
CRUNCH!
DING!
KIRBY LN EXIT

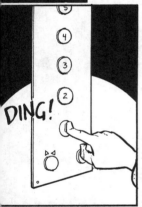

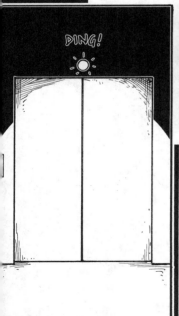

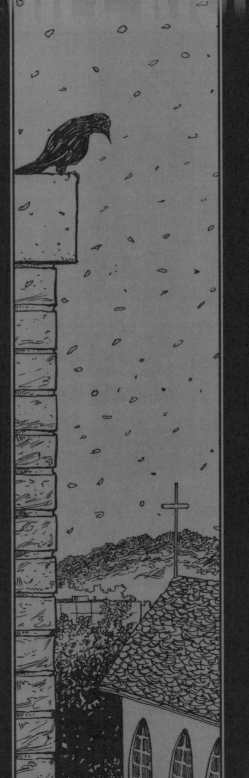

TERRY MOORE

# RACHEL RISING

6

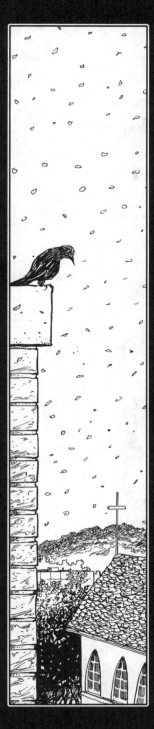

WE SHALL RISE LIKE OAKS
AND THEY SHALL FALL LIKE SNOW
AND WE SHALL WEAR THEM
LIKE A HUMAN COAT.

—VA DAMDIELD LIETCHEN

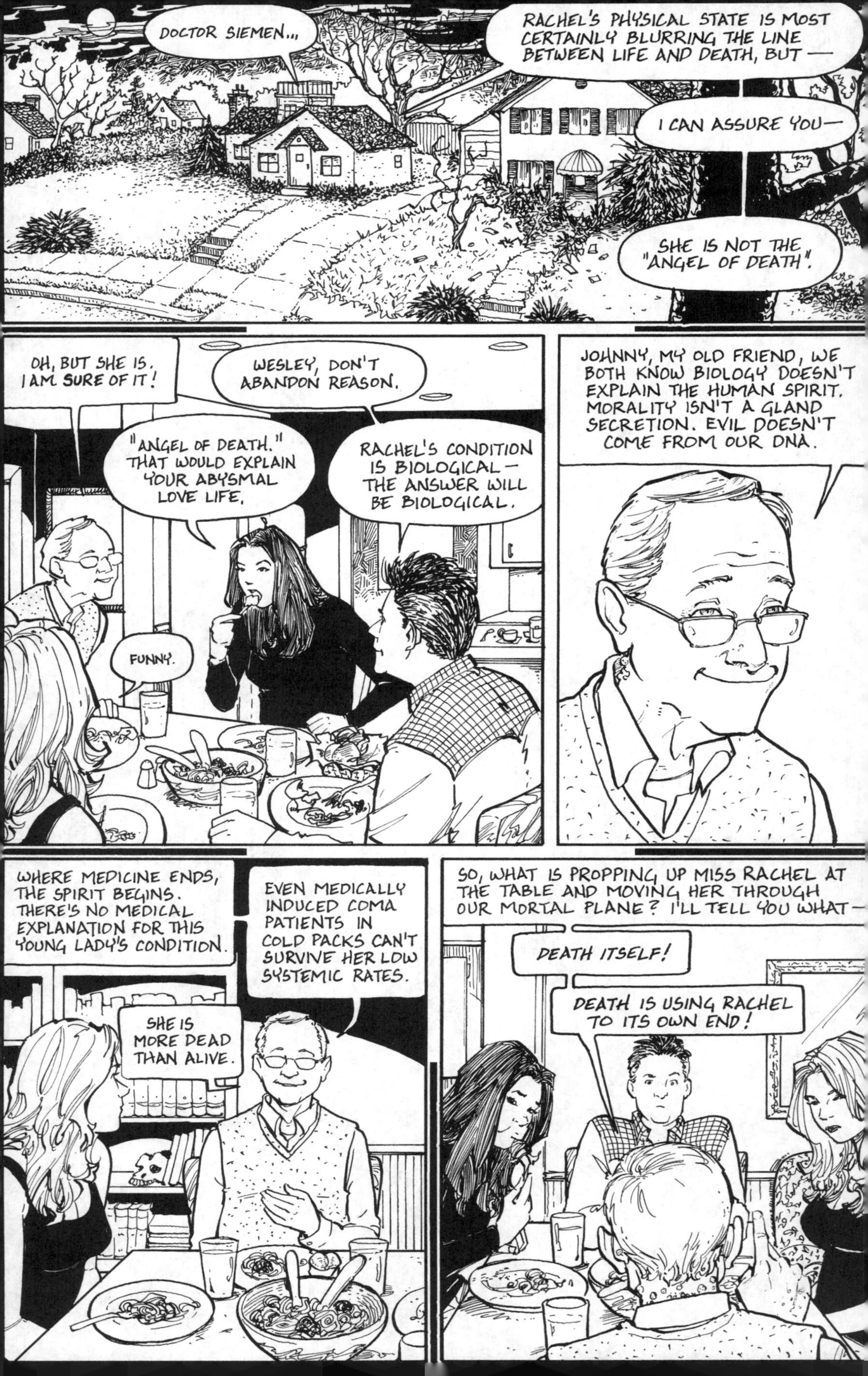
DOCTOR SIEMEN...
RACHEL'S PHYSICAL STATE IS MOST CERTAINLY BLURRING THE LINE BETWEEN LIFE AND DEATH, BUT —
I CAN ASSURE YOU—
SHE IS NOT THE "ANGEL OF DEATH".
OH, BUT SHE IS. I AM SURE OF IT!
WESLEY, DON'T ABANDON REASON.
"ANGEL OF DEATH." THAT WOULD EXPLAIN YOUR ABYSMAL LOVE LIFE.
RACHEL'S CONDITION IS BIOLOGICAL — THE ANSWER WILL BE BIOLOGICAL.
FUNNY.
JOHNNY, MY OLD FRIEND, WE BOTH KNOW BIOLOGY DOESN'T EXPLAIN THE HUMAN SPIRIT. MORALITY ISN'T A GLAND SECRETION. EVIL DOESN'T COME FROM OUR DNA.
WHERE MEDICINE ENDS, THE SPIRIT BEGINS. THERE'S NO MEDICAL EXPLANATION FOR THIS YOUNG LADY'S CONDITION.
EVEN MEDICALLY INDUCED COMA PATIENTS IN COLD PACKS CAN'T SURVIVE HER LOW SYSTEMIC RATES.
SHE IS MORE DEAD THAN ALIVE.
SO, WHAT IS PROPPING UP MISS RACHEL AT THE TABLE AND MOVING HER THROUGH OUR MORTAL PLANE? I'LL TELL YOU WHAT—
DEATH ITSELF!
DEATH IS USING RACHEL TO ITS OWN END!

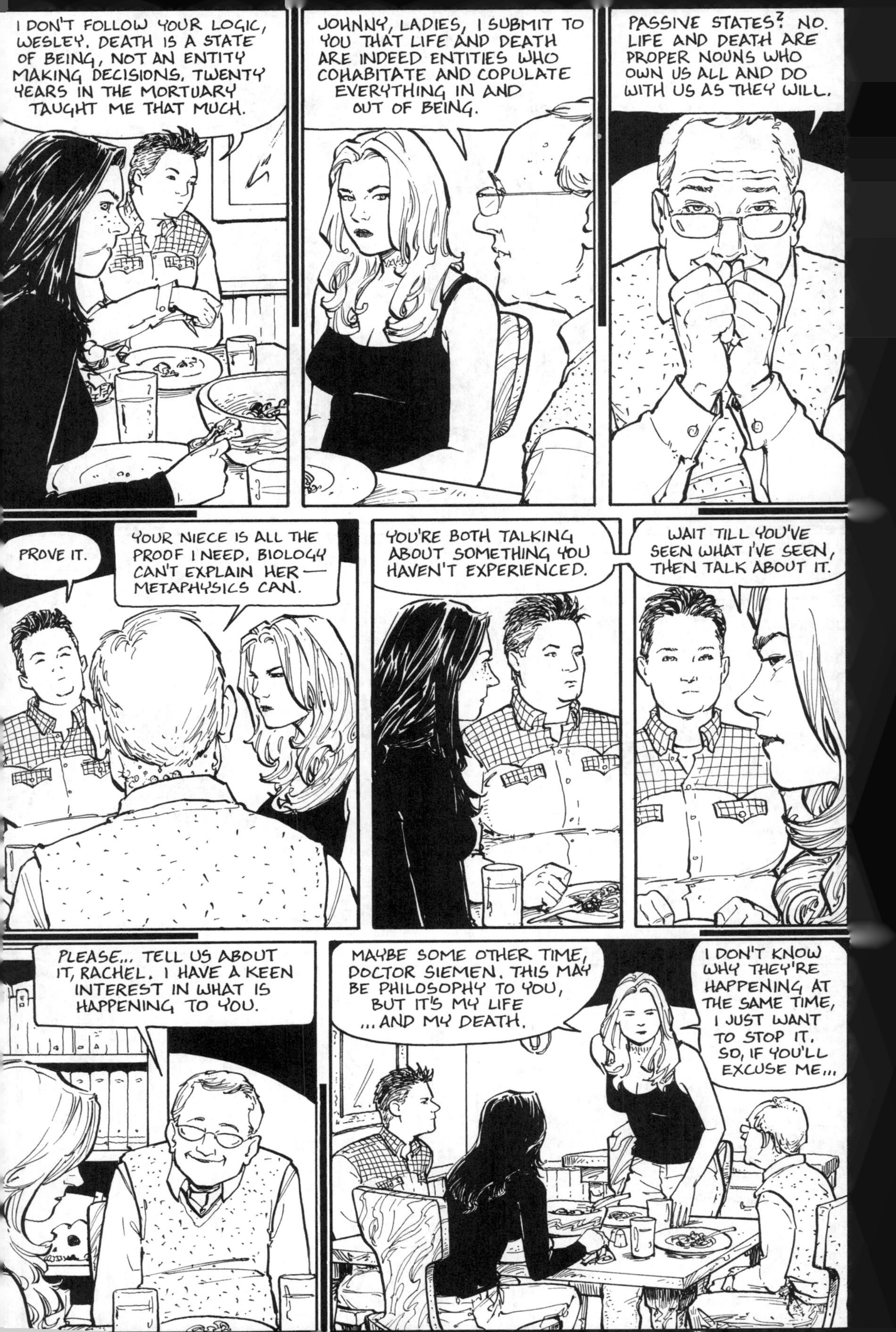

I DON'T FOLLOW YOUR LOGIC, WESLEY. DEATH IS A STATE OF BEING, NOT AN ENTITY MAKING DECISIONS. TWENTY YEARS IN THE MORTUARY TAUGHT ME THAT MUCH.
JOHNNY, LADIES, I SUBMIT TO YOU THAT LIFE AND DEATH ARE INDEED ENTITIES WHO COHABITATE AND COPULATE EVERYTHING IN AND OUT OF BEING.
PASSIVE STATES? NO. LIFE AND DEATH ARE PROPER NOUNS WHO OWN US ALL AND DO WITH US AS THEY WILL.
PROVE IT.
YOUR NIECE IS ALL THE PROOF I NEED. BIOLOGY CAN'T EXPLAIN HER— METAPHYSICS CAN.
YOU'RE BOTH TALKING ABOUT SOMETHING YOU HAVEN'T EXPERIENCED.
WAIT TILL YOU'VE SEEN WHAT I'VE SEEN, THEN TALK ABOUT IT.
PLEASE... TELL US ABOUT IT, RACHEL. I HAVE A KEEN INTEREST IN WHAT IS HAPPENING TO YOU.
MAYBE SOME OTHER TIME, DOCTOR SIEMEN. THIS MAY BE PHILOSOPHY TO YOU, BUT IT'S MY LIFE ...AND MY DEATH.
I DON'T KNOW WHY THEY'RE HAPPENING AT THE SAME TIME, I JUST WANT TO STOP IT. SO, IF YOU'LL EXCUSE ME...

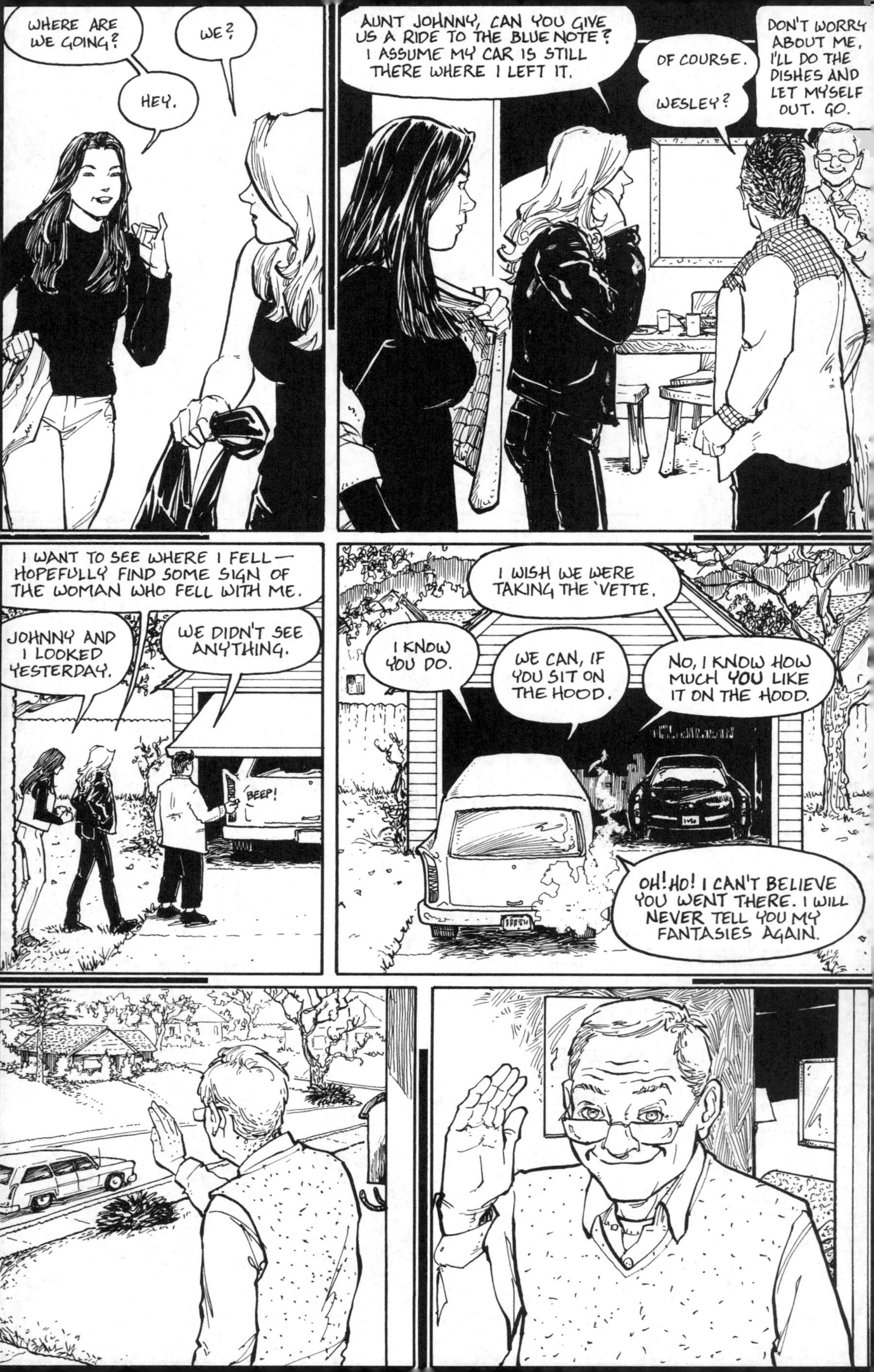
WHERE ARE WE GOING?
HEY.
WE?
AUNT JOHNNY, CAN YOU GIVE US A RIDE TO THE BLUE NOTE? I ASSUME MY CAR IS STILL THERE WHERE I LEFT IT.
OF COURSE.
WESLEY?
DON'T WORRY ABOUT ME, I'LL DO THE DISHES AND LET MYSELF OUT. GO.
I WANT TO SEE WHERE I FELL— HOPEFULLY FIND SOME SIGN OF THE WOMAN WHO FELL WITH ME.
JOHNNY AND I LOOKED YESTERDAY.
WE DIDN'T SEE ANYTHING.
BEEP!
I WISH WE WERE TAKING THE 'VETTE.
I KNOW YOU DO.
WE CAN, IF YOU SIT ON THE HOOD.
NO, I KNOW HOW MUCH YOU LIKE IT ON THE HOOD.
OH! HO! I CAN'T BELIEVE YOU WENT THERE. I WILL NEVER TELL YOU MY FANTASIES AGAIN.

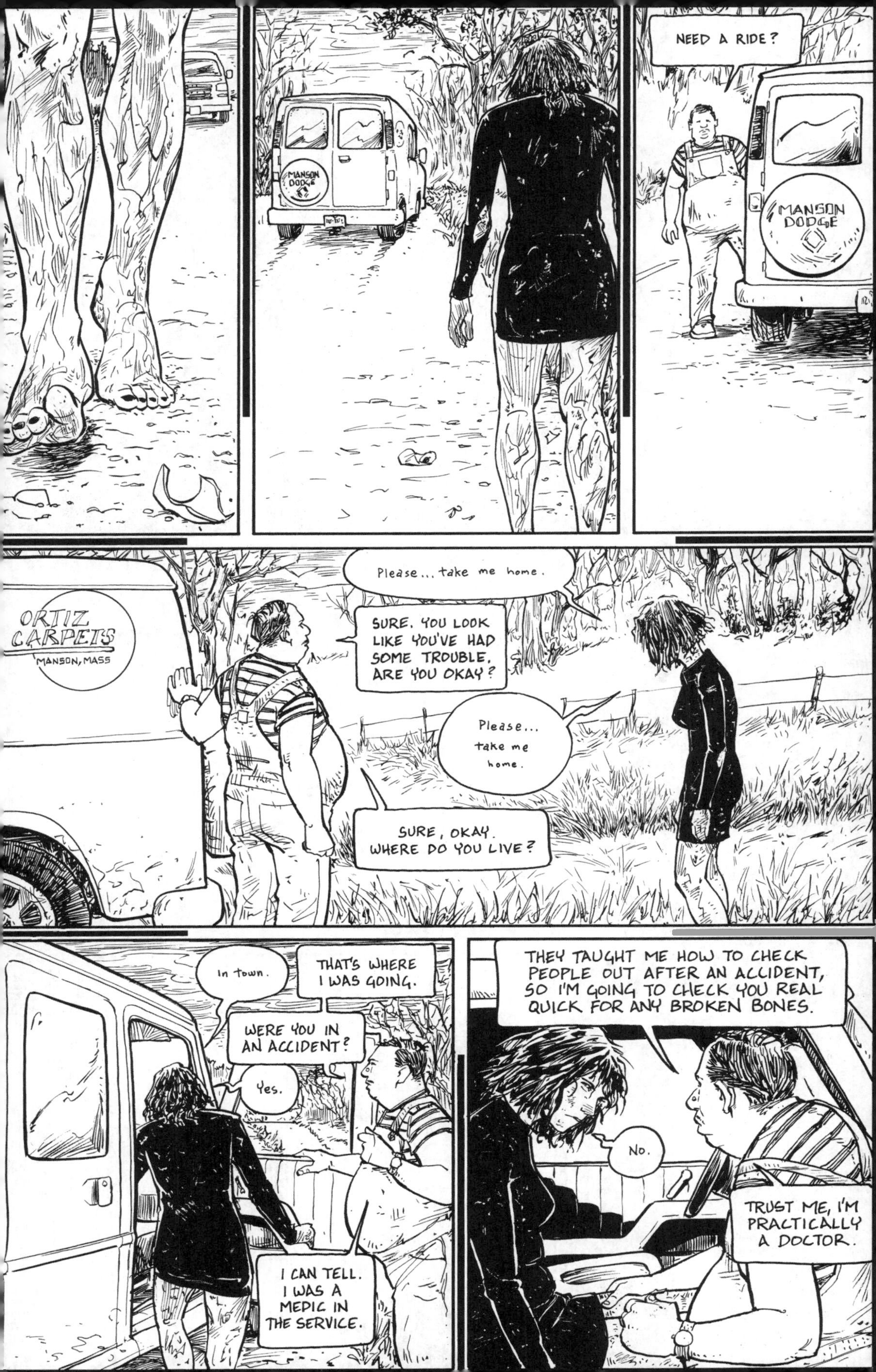
NEED A RIDE?
MANSON DODGE
Please... take me home.
ORTIZ CARPETS
MANSON, MASS
SURE. YOU LOOK LIKE YOU'VE HAD SOME TROUBLE. ARE YOU OKAY?
Please... take me home.
SURE, OKAY. WHERE DO YOU LIVE?
In town.
THAT'S WHERE I WAS GOING.
WERE YOU IN AN ACCIDENT?
Yes.
I CAN TELL. I WAS A MEDIC IN THE SERVICE.
THEY TAUGHT ME HOW TO CHECK PEOPLE OUT AFTER AN ACCIDENT, SO I'M GOING TO CHECK YOU REAL QUICK FOR ANY BROKEN BONES.
No.
TRUST ME, I'M PRACTICALLY A DOCTOR.

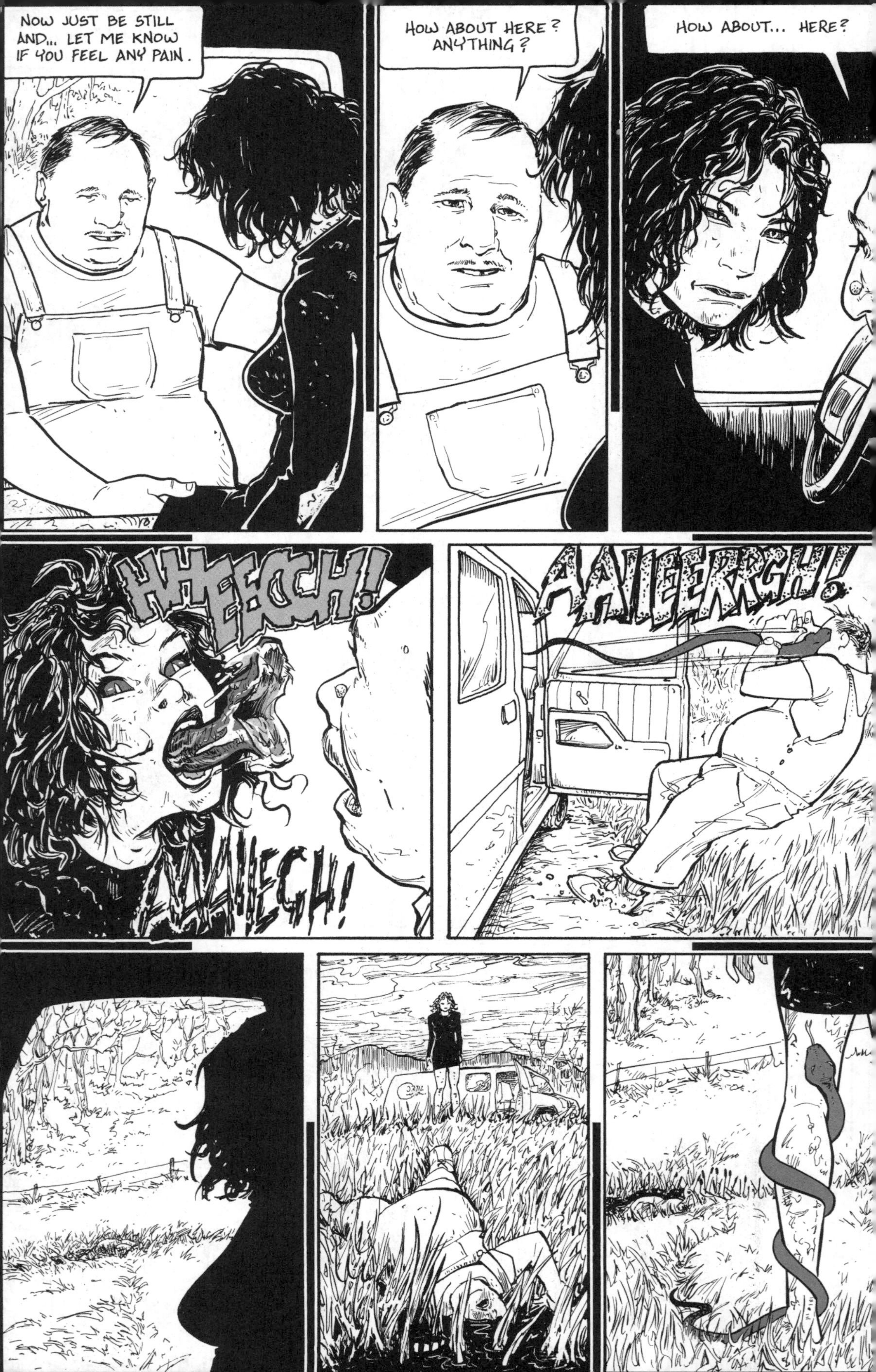
NOW JUST BE STILL AND... LET ME KNOW IF YOU FEEL ANY PAIN.
HOW ABOUT HERE? ANYTHING?
HOW ABOUT... HERE?
HHEECCH!
HHHECH!
AAIEERRGH!

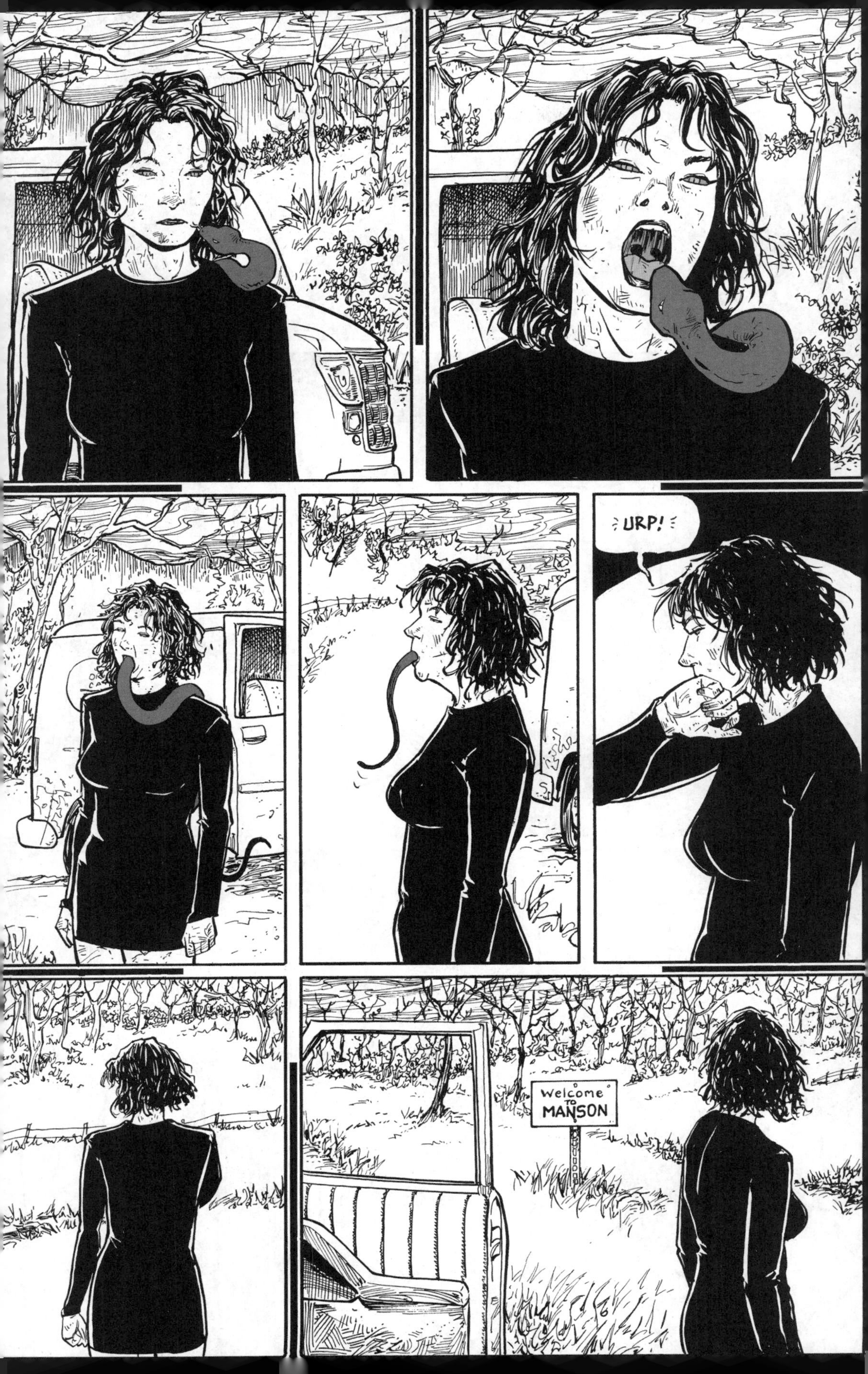
URP!
Welcome
TO
MANSON

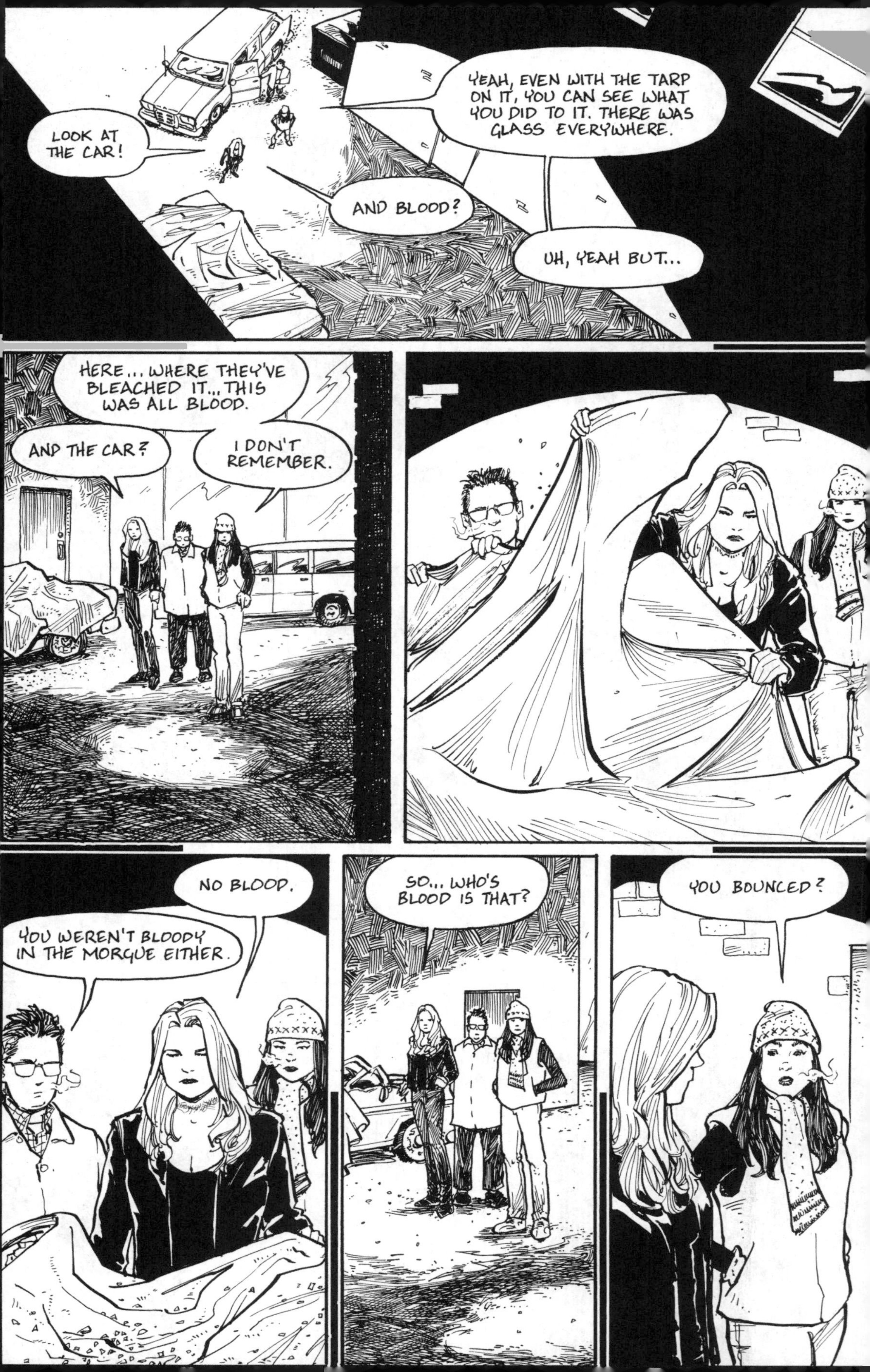

LOOK AT THE CAR!
YEAH, EVEN WITH THE TARP ON IT, YOU CAN SEE WHAT YOU DID TO IT. THERE WAS GLASS EVERYWHERE.
AND BLOOD?
UH, YEAH BUT...
HERE... WHERE THEY'VE BLEACHED IT... THIS WAS ALL BLOOD.
AND THE CAR?
I DON'T REMEMBER.
NO BLOOD.
YOU WEREN'T BLOODY IN THE MORGUE EITHER.
SO... WHO'S BLOOD IS THAT?
YOU BOUNCED?

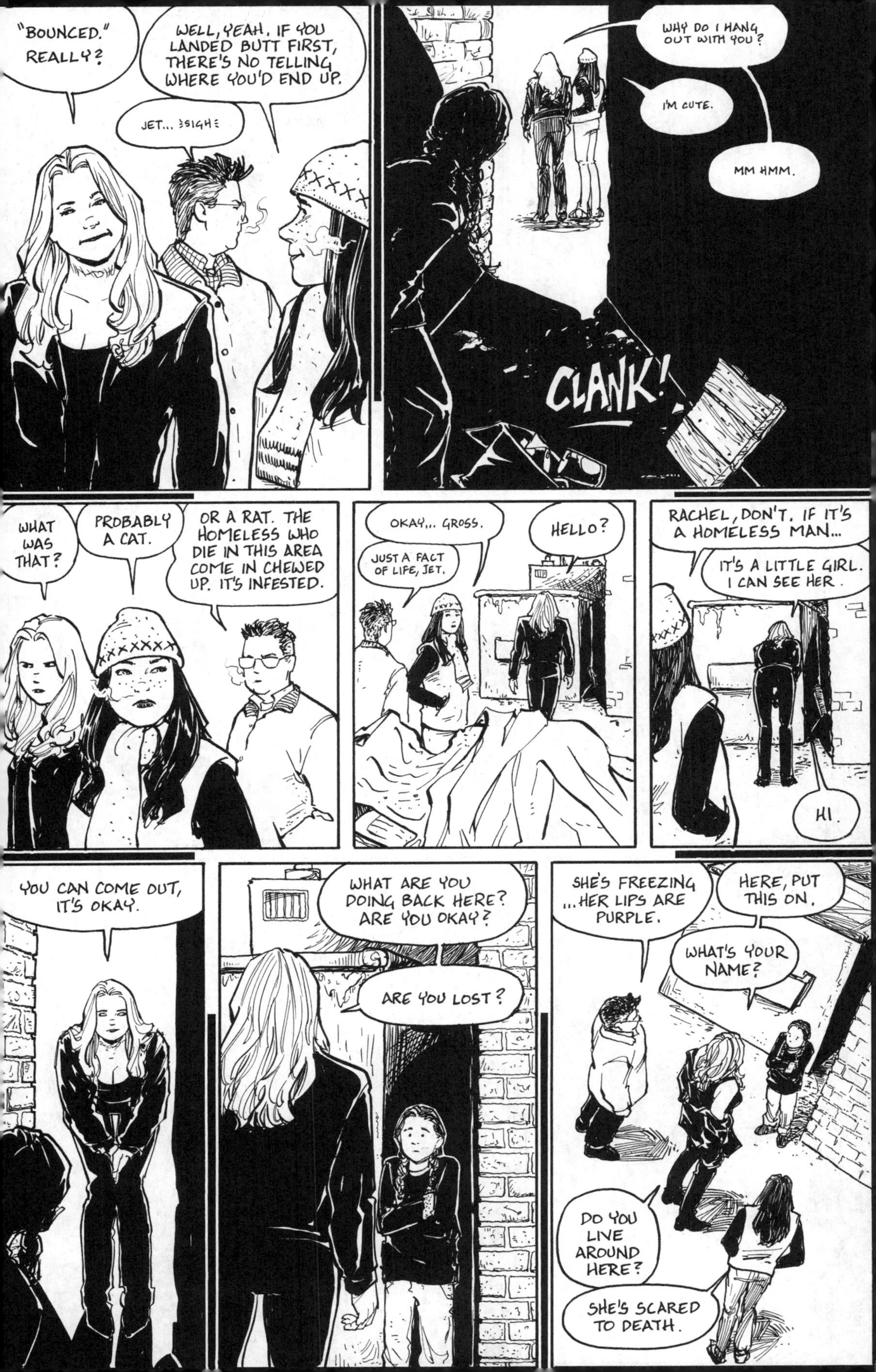
"BOUNCED." REALLY?
WELL, YEAH. IF YOU LANDED BUTT FIRST, THERE'S NO TELLING WHERE YOU'D END UP.
JET... ≋SIGH≋
WHY DO I HANG OUT WITH YOU?
I'M CUTE.
MM HMM.
CLANK!
WHAT WAS THAT?
PROBABLY A CAT.
OR A RAT. THE HOMELESS WHO DIE IN THIS AREA COME IN CHEWED UP. IT'S INFESTED.
OKAY... GROSS.
JUST A FACT OF LIFE, JET.
HELLO?
RACHEL, DON'T. IF IT'S A HOMELESS MAN...
IT'S A LITTLE GIRL. I CAN SEE HER.
HI.
YOU CAN COME OUT, IT'S OKAY.
WHAT ARE YOU DOING BACK HERE? ARE YOU OKAY?
ARE YOU LOST?
SHE'S FREEZING ...HER LIPS ARE PURPLE.
HERE, PUT THIS ON.
WHAT'S YOUR NAME?
DO YOU LIVE AROUND HERE?
SHE'S SCARED TO DEATH.

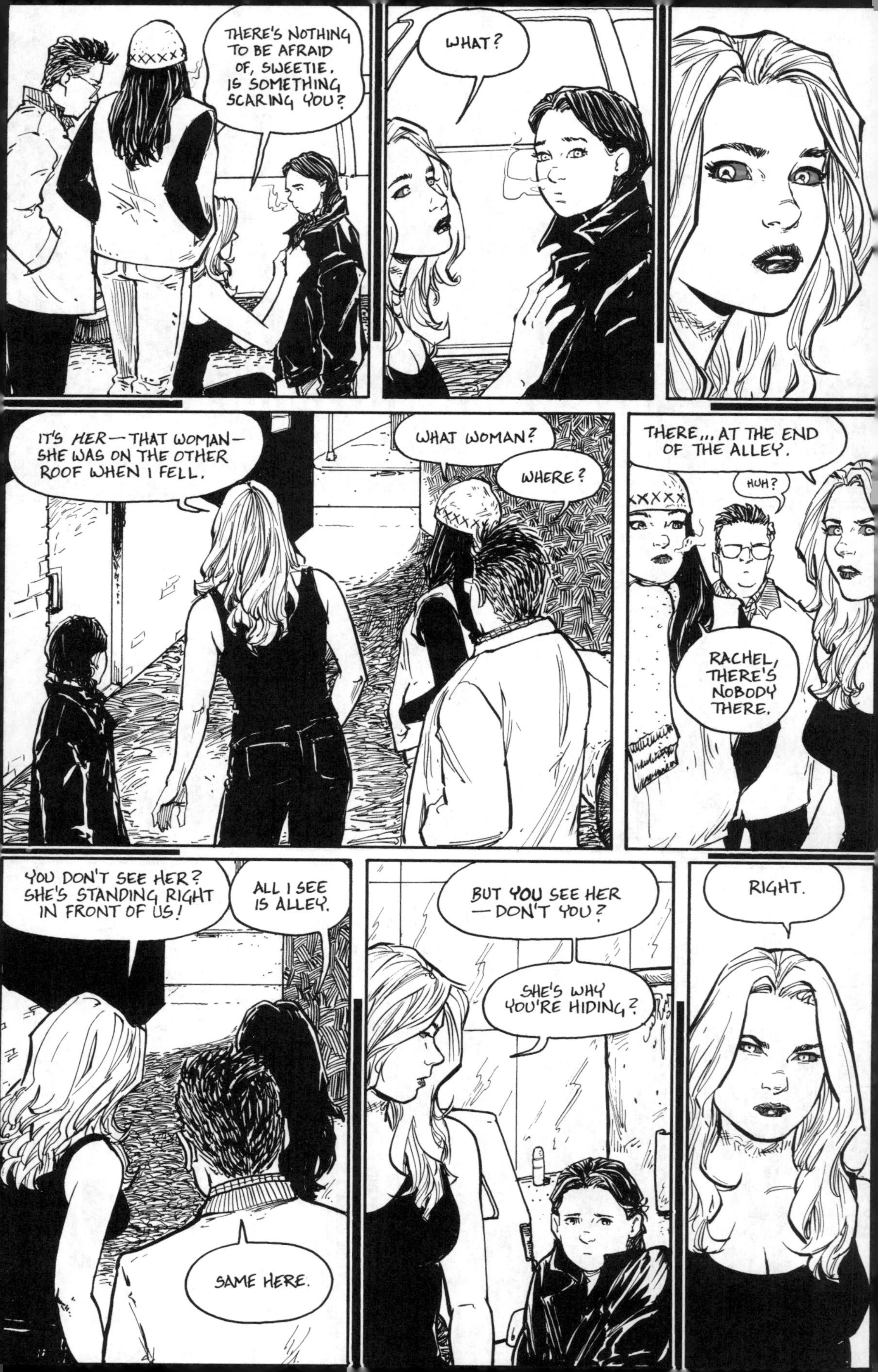
THERE'S NOTHING TO BE AFRAID OF, SWEETIE. IS SOMETHING SCARING YOU?
WHAT?
IT'S HER—THAT WOMAN—SHE WAS ON THE OTHER ROOF WHEN I FELL.
WHAT WOMAN?
WHERE?
THERE... AT THE END OF THE ALLEY.
HUH?
RACHEL, THERE'S NOBODY THERE.
YOU DON'T SEE HER? SHE'S STANDING RIGHT IN FRONT OF US!
ALL I SEE IS ALLEY.
SAME HERE.
BUT YOU SEE HER—DON'T YOU?
SHE'S WHY YOU'RE HIDING?
RIGHT.

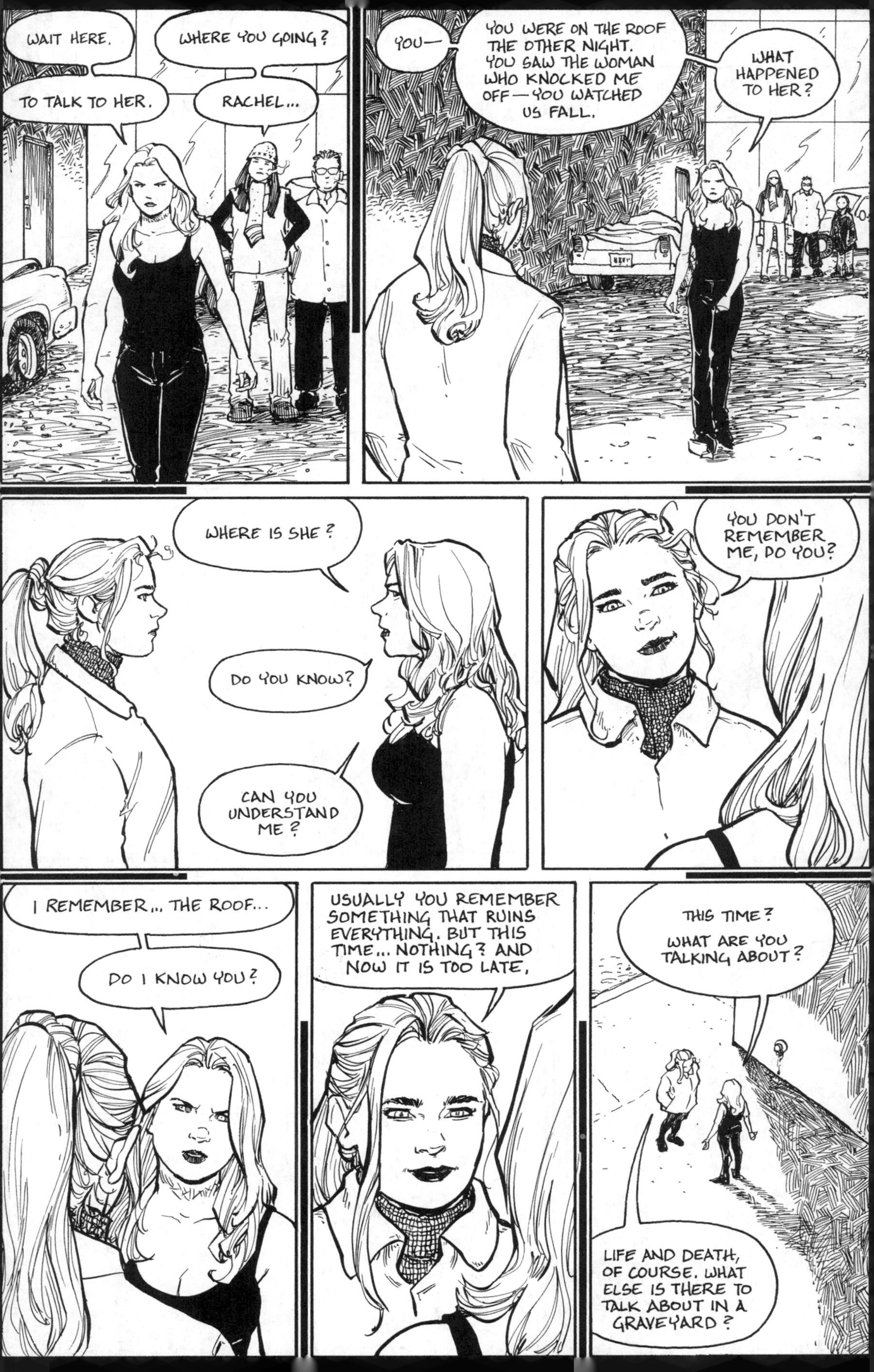
WAIT HERE.
WHERE YOU GOING?
TO TALK TO HER.
RACHEL...
YOU—
YOU WERE ON THE ROOF THE OTHER NIGHT. YOU SAW THE WOMAN WHO KNOCKED ME OFF—YOU WATCHED US FALL.
WHAT HAPPENED TO HER?
WHERE IS SHE?
DO YOU KNOW?
CAN YOU UNDERSTAND ME?
YOU DON'T REMEMBER ME, DO YOU?
I REMEMBER... THE ROOF...
DO I KNOW YOU?
USUALLY YOU REMEMBER SOMETHING THAT RUINS EVERYTHING. BUT THIS TIME... NOTHING? AND NOW IT IS TOO LATE.
THIS TIME?
WHAT ARE YOU TALKING ABOUT?
LIFE AND DEATH, OF COURSE. WHAT ELSE IS THERE TO TALK ABOUT IN A GRAVEYARD?

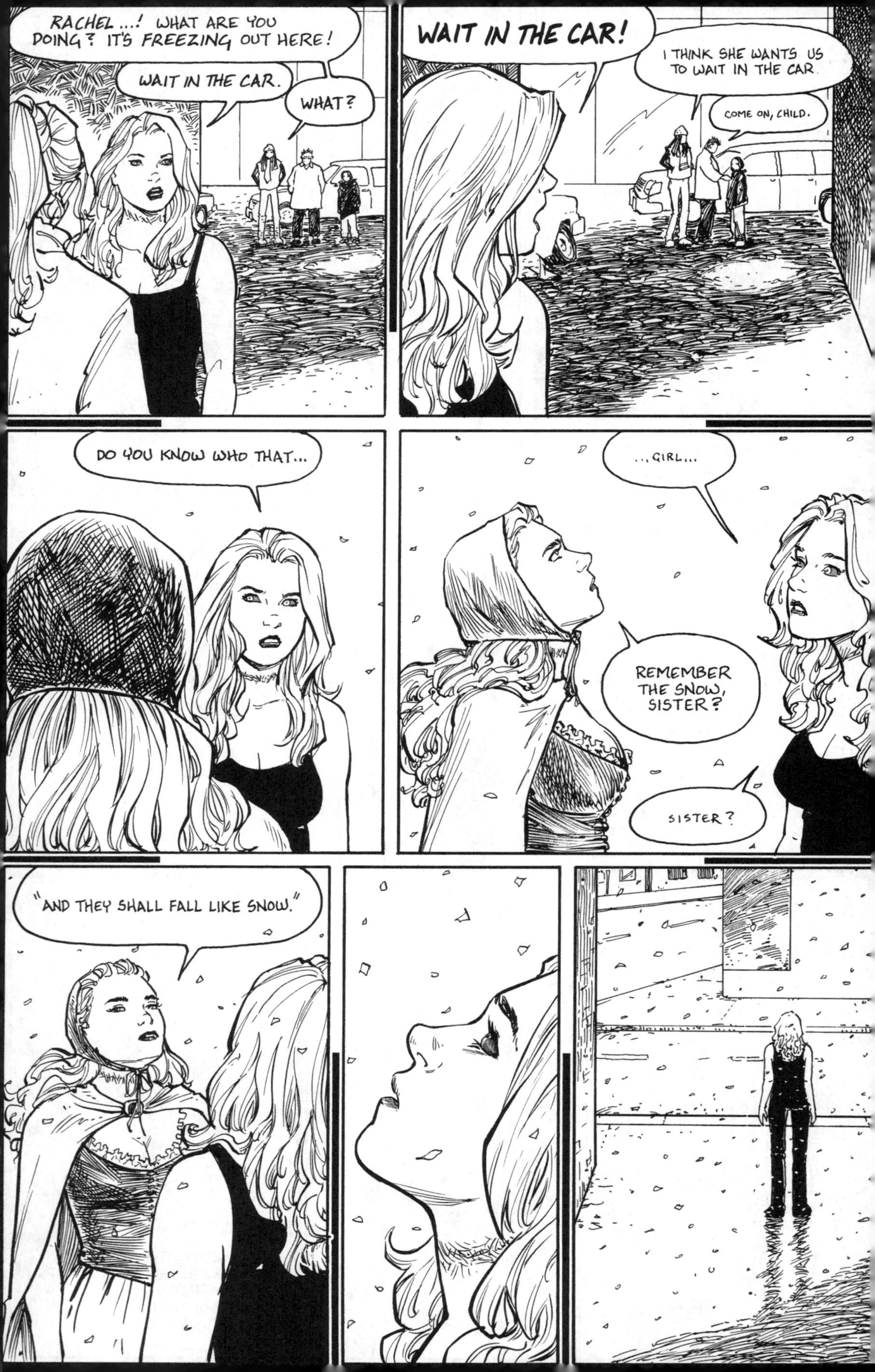
RACHEL ...! WHAT ARE YOU DOING? IT'S FREEZING OUT HERE!
WAIT IN THE CAR.
WHAT?
WAIT IN THE CAR!
I THINK SHE WANTS US TO WAIT IN THE CAR
COME ON, CHILD.
DO YOU KNOW WHO THAT...
...GIRL...
REMEMBER THE SNOW, SISTER?
SISTER?
"AND THEY SHALL FALL LIKE SNOW."

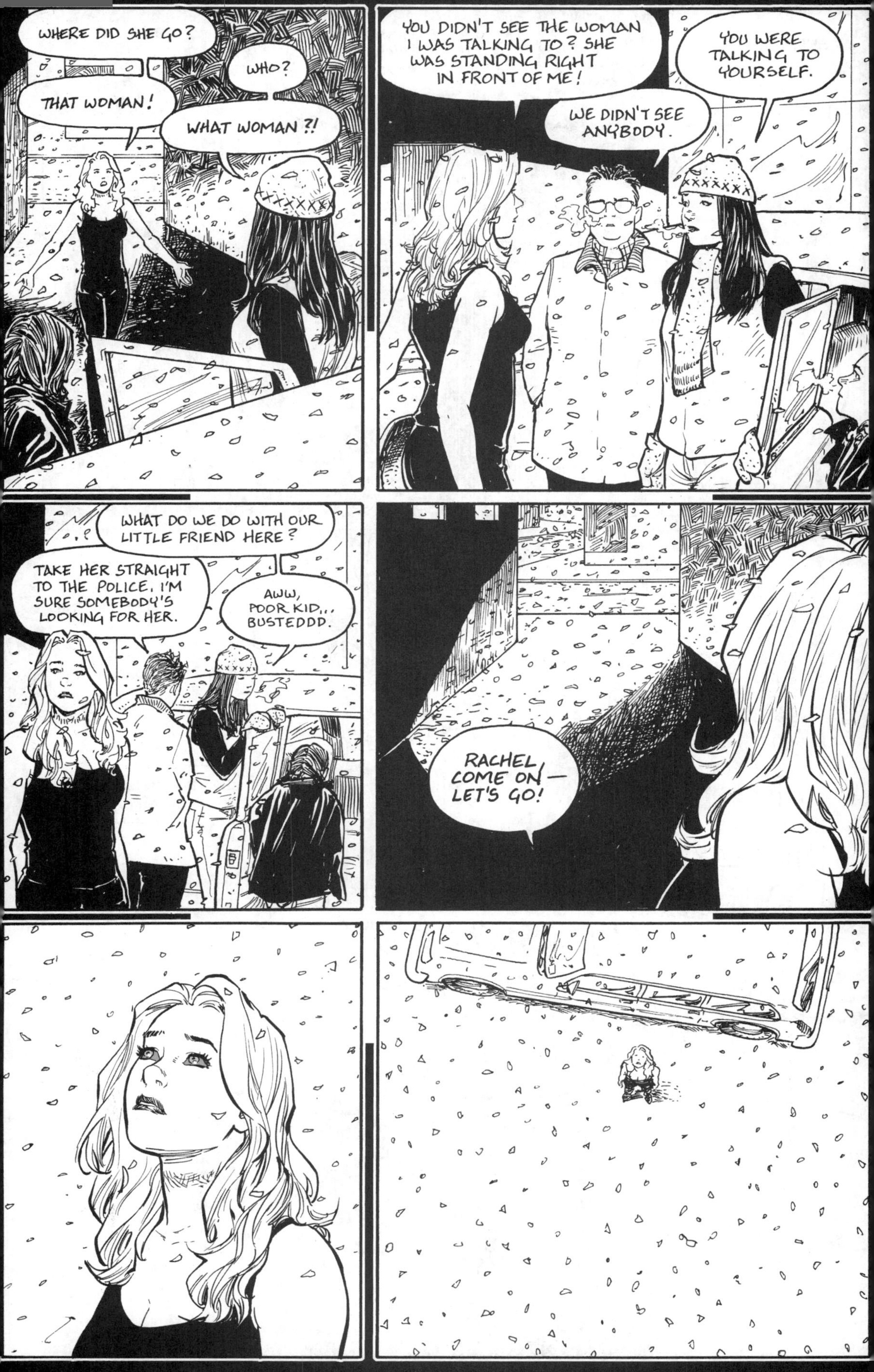
WHERE DID SHE GO?
WHO?
THAT WOMAN!
WHAT WOMAN?!
YOU DIDN'T SEE THE WOMAN I WAS TALKING TO? SHE WAS STANDING RIGHT IN FRONT OF ME!
YOU WERE TALKING TO YOURSELF.
WE DIDN'T SEE ANYBODY.
WHAT DO WE DO WITH OUR LITTLE FRIEND HERE?
TAKE HER STRAIGHT TO THE POLICE. I'M SURE SOMEBODY'S LOOKING FOR HER.
AWW, POOR KID... BUSTEDDD.
RACHEL, COME ON— LET'S GO!

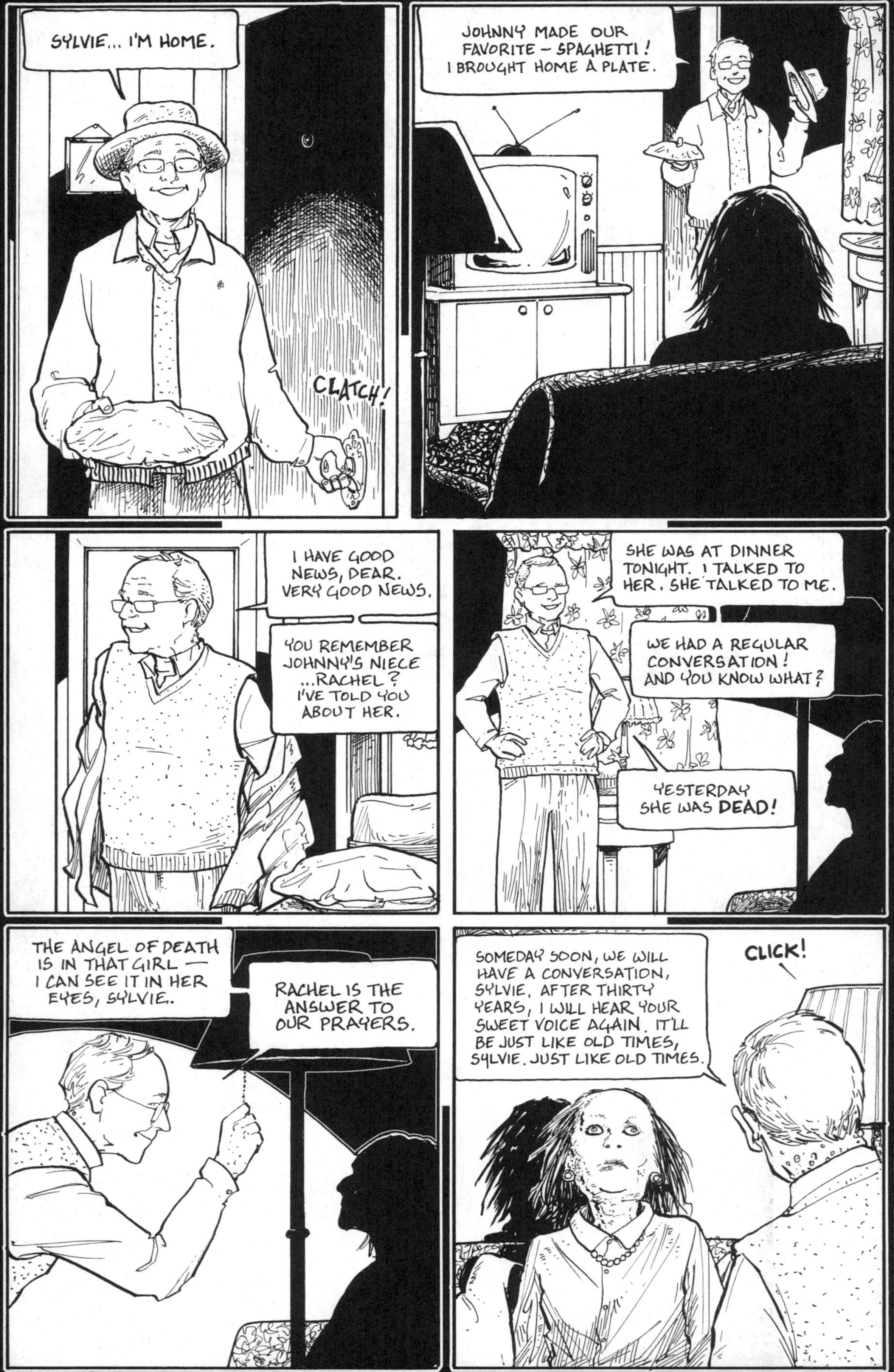
SYLVIE... I'M HOME.
CLATCH!
JOHNNY MADE OUR FAVORITE – SPAGHETTI! I BROUGHT HOME A PLATE.
I HAVE GOOD NEWS, DEAR. VERY GOOD NEWS.
YOU REMEMBER JOHNNY'S NIECE ...RACHEL? I'VE TOLD YOU ABOUT HER.
SHE WAS AT DINNER TONIGHT. I TALKED TO HER. SHE TALKED TO ME.
WE HAD A REGULAR CONVERSATION! AND YOU KNOW WHAT?
YESTERDAY SHE WAS DEAD!
THE ANGEL OF DEATH IS IN THAT GIRL — I CAN SEE IT IN HER EYES, SYLVIE.
RACHEL IS THE ANSWER TO OUR PRAYERS.
SOMEDAY SOON, WE WILL HAVE A CONVERSATION, SYLVIE. AFTER THIRTY YEARS, I WILL HEAR YOUR SWEET VOICE AGAIN. IT'LL BE JUST LIKE OLD TIMES, SYLVIE. JUST LIKE OLD TIMES.
CLICK!

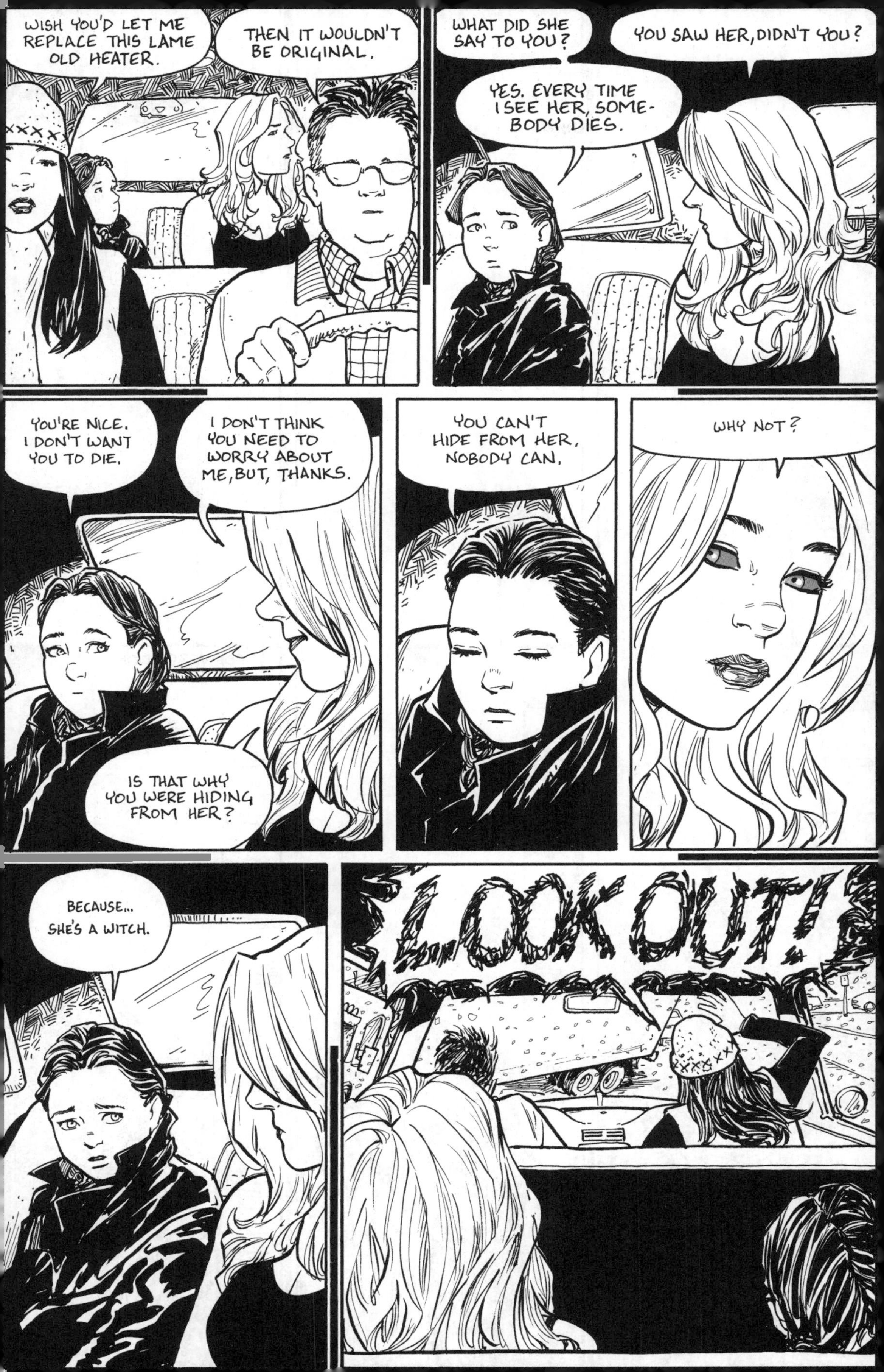
WISH YOU'D LET ME REPLACE THIS LAME OLD HEATER.
THEN IT WOULDN'T BE ORIGINAL.
WHAT DID SHE SAY TO YOU?
YOU SAW HER, DIDN'T YOU?
YES. EVERY TIME I SEE HER, SOMEBODY DIES.
YOU'RE NICE. I DON'T WANT YOU TO DIE.
I DON'T THINK YOU NEED TO WORRY ABOUT ME, BUT, THANKS.
IS THAT WHY YOU WERE HIDING FROM HER?
YOU CAN'T HIDE FROM HER, NOBODY CAN.
WHY NOT?
BECAUSE... SHE'S A WITCH.
LOOK OUT!

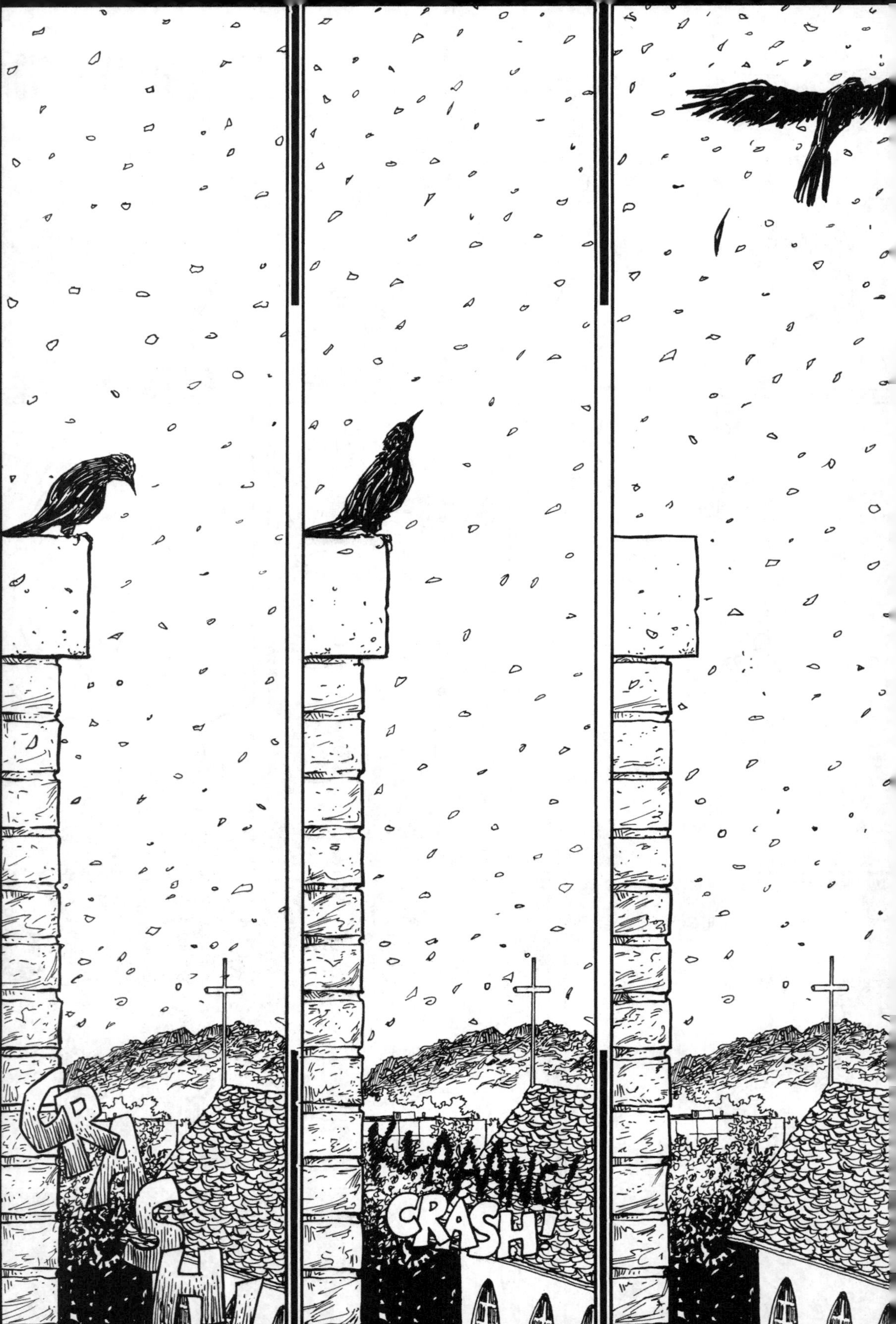
CRASH!
KLAAANG!
CRASH!

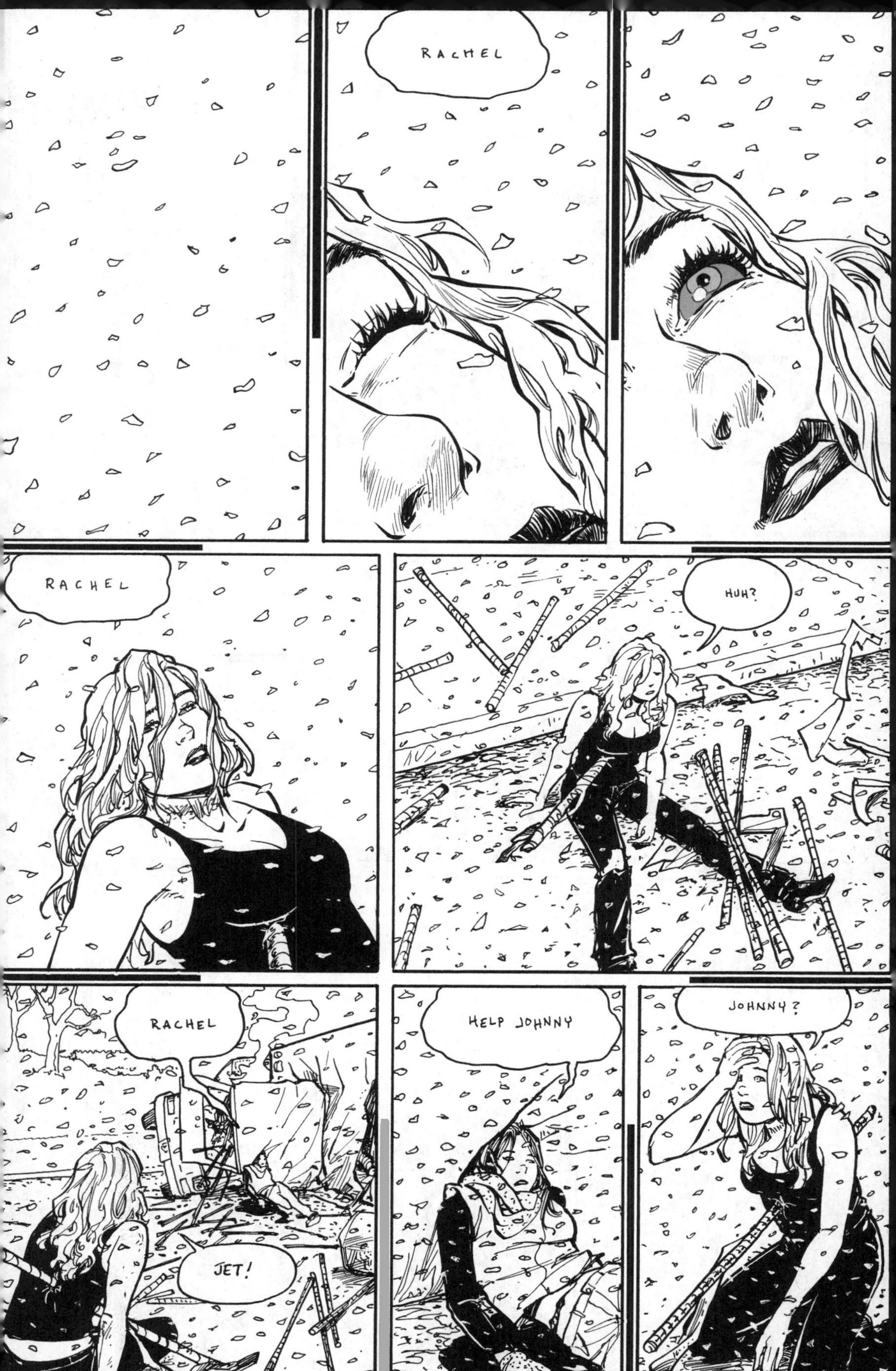
RACHEL
RACHEL
HUH?
RACHEL
JET!
HELP JOHNNY
JOHNNY?

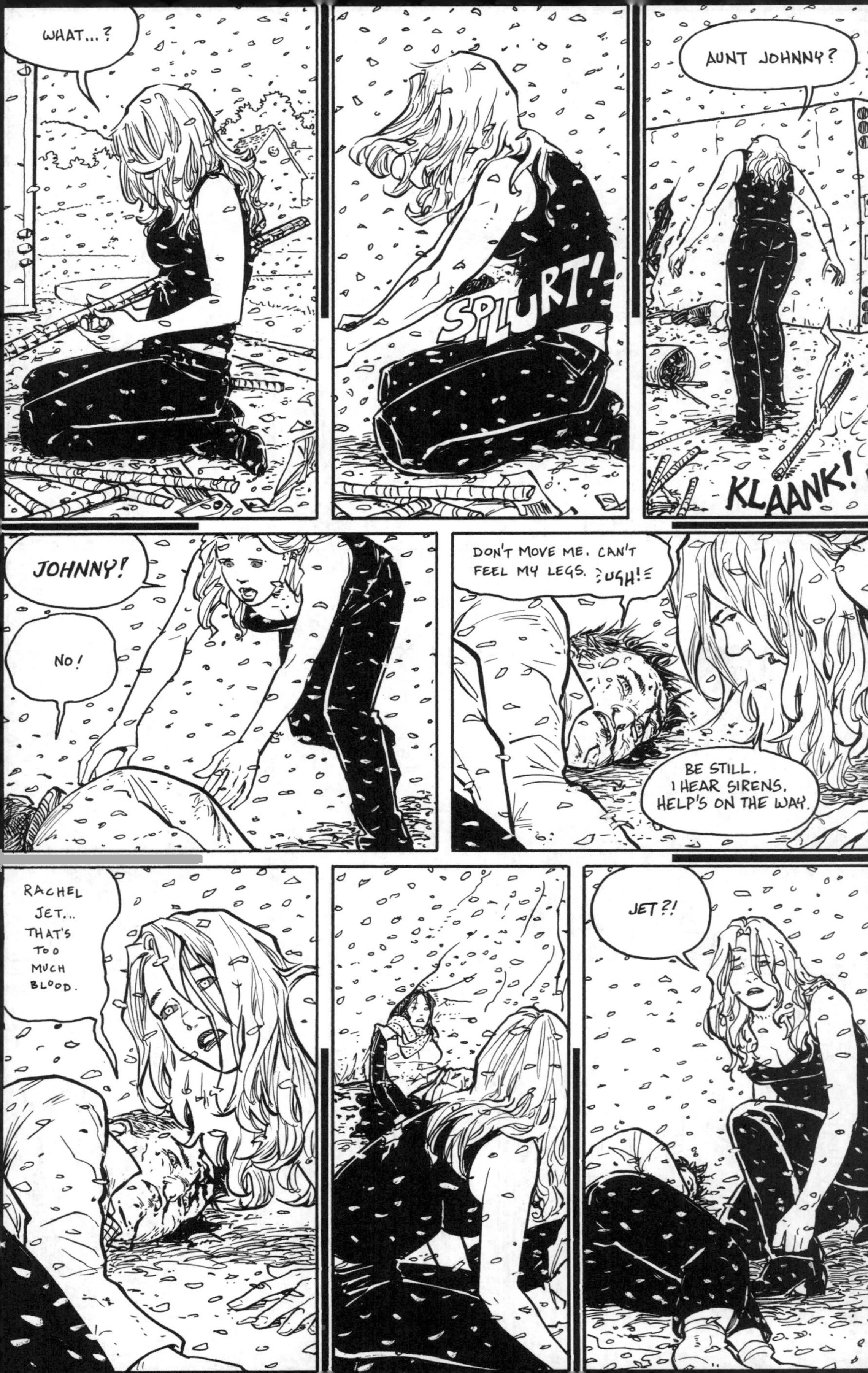
WHAT...?
SPLURT!
AUNT JOHNNY?
KLAANK!
JOHNNY!
NO!
DON'T MOVE ME. CAN'T FEEL MY LEGS. UGH!
BE STILL. I HEAR SIRENS. HELP'S ON THE WAY.
RACHEL JET... THAT'S TOO MUCH BLOOD.
JET?!

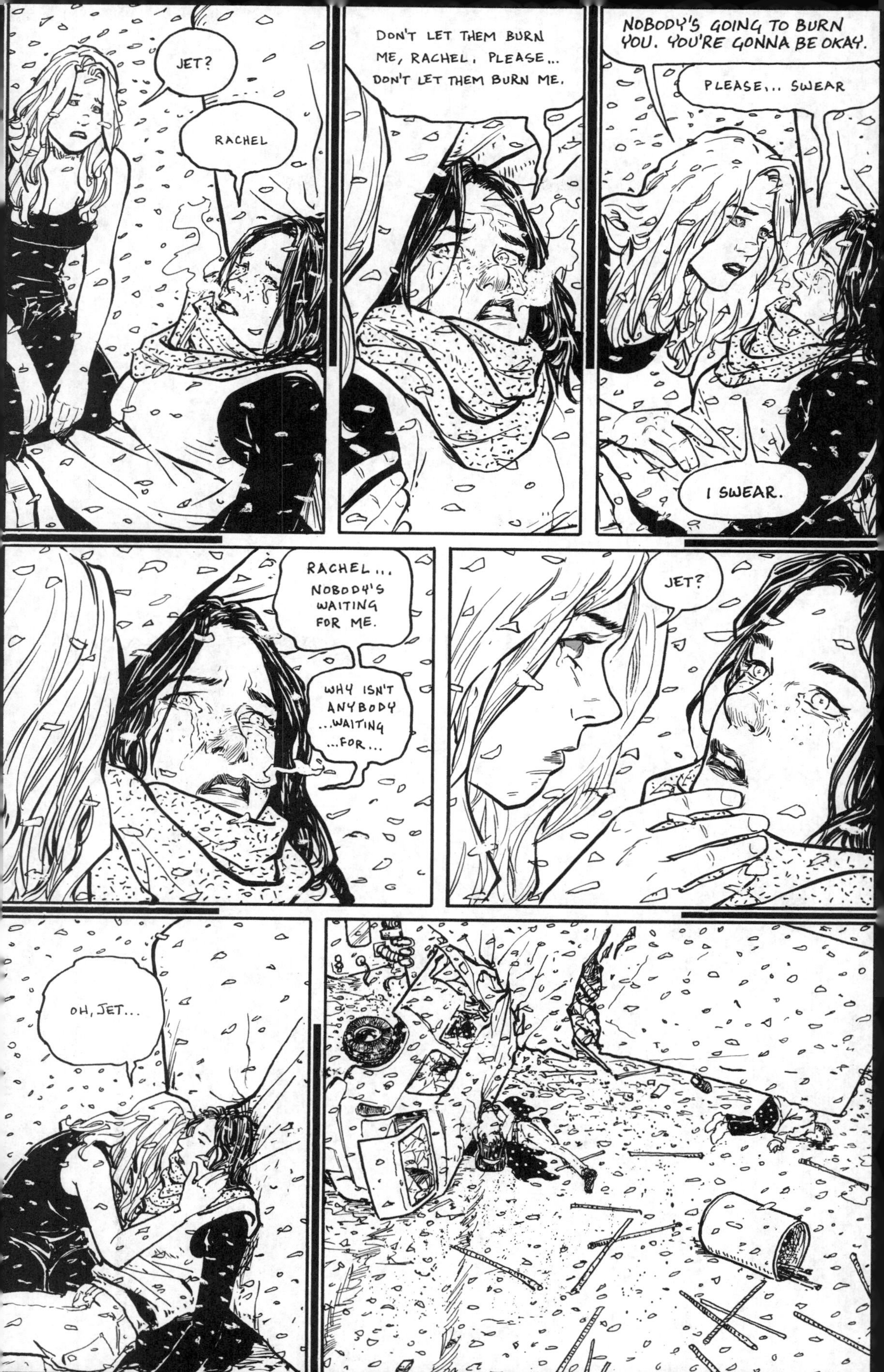
JET?
RACHEL
DON'T LET THEM BURN ME, RACHEL. PLEASE... DON'T LET THEM BURN ME.
NOBODY'S GOING TO BURN YOU. YOU'RE GONNA BE OKAY.
PLEASE... SWEAR
I SWEAR.
RACHEL... NOBODY'S WAITING FOR ME.
WHY ISN'T ANYBODY ...WAITING ...FOR...
JET?
OH, JET...

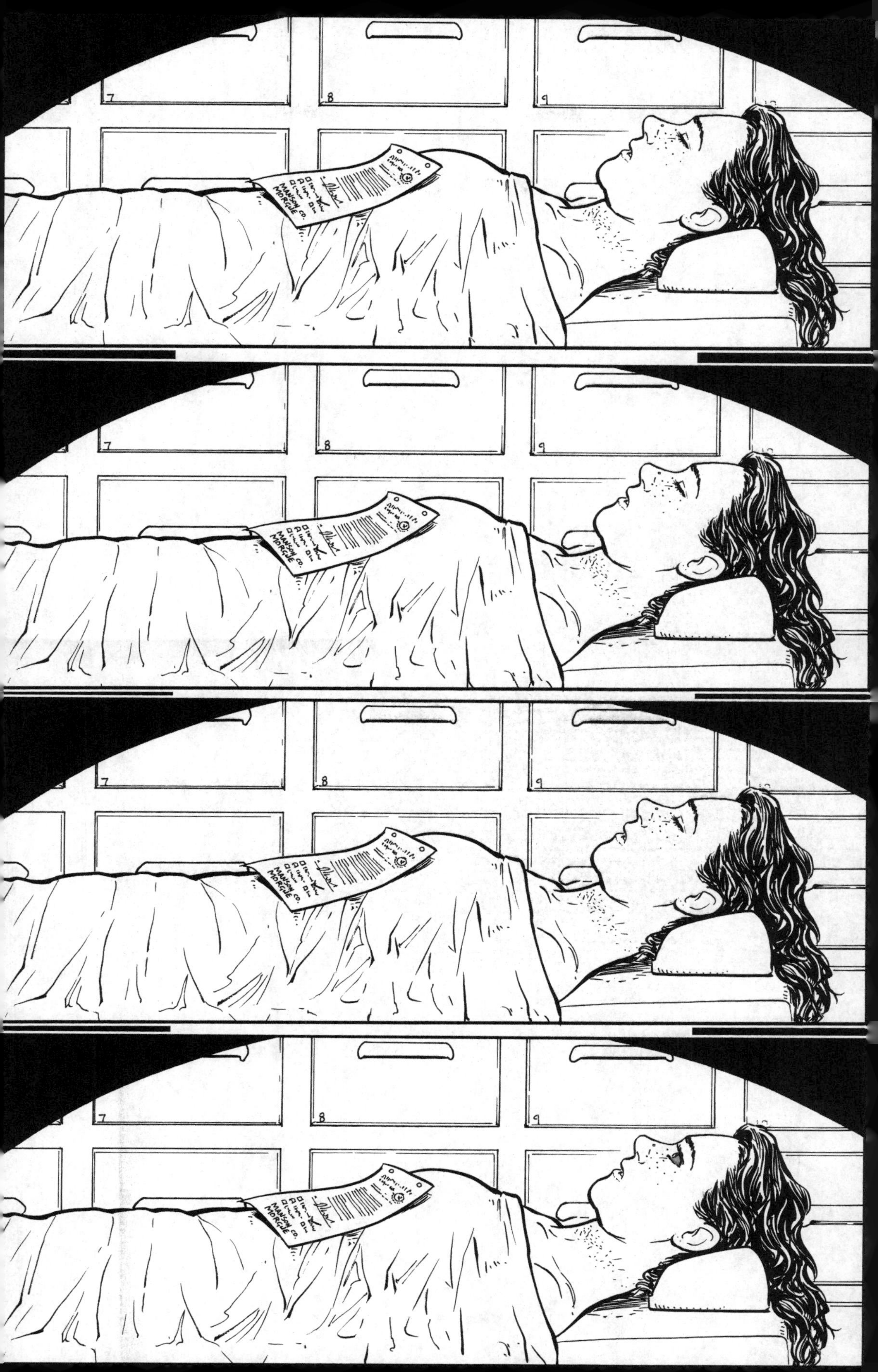
7
8
9
MANSON CO. MORGUE
7
8
9
MANSON CO. MORGUE
7
8
9
MANSON CO. MORGUE
7
8
9
MANSON CO. MORGUE

Story & Art
TERRY MOORE

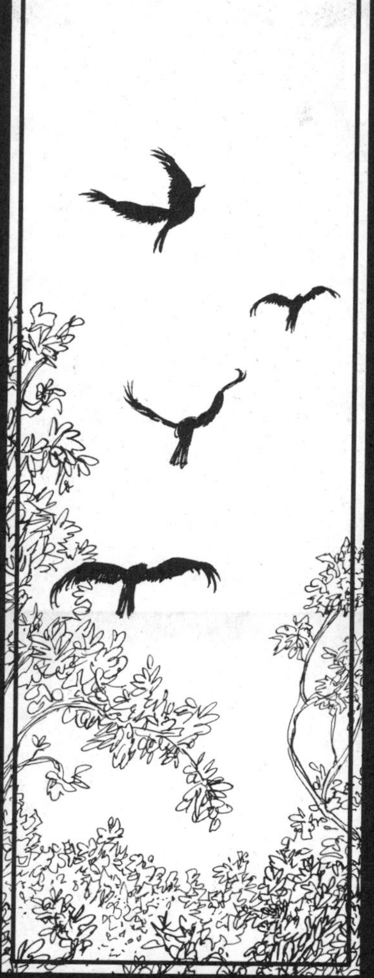

ROBYN MOORE
Publisher

Published by ABSTRACT STUDIO
P. O. Box 271487, Houston, Texas, 77277


Printed in Canada

# Rachel Rising

## Cover art for Upcoming Issues

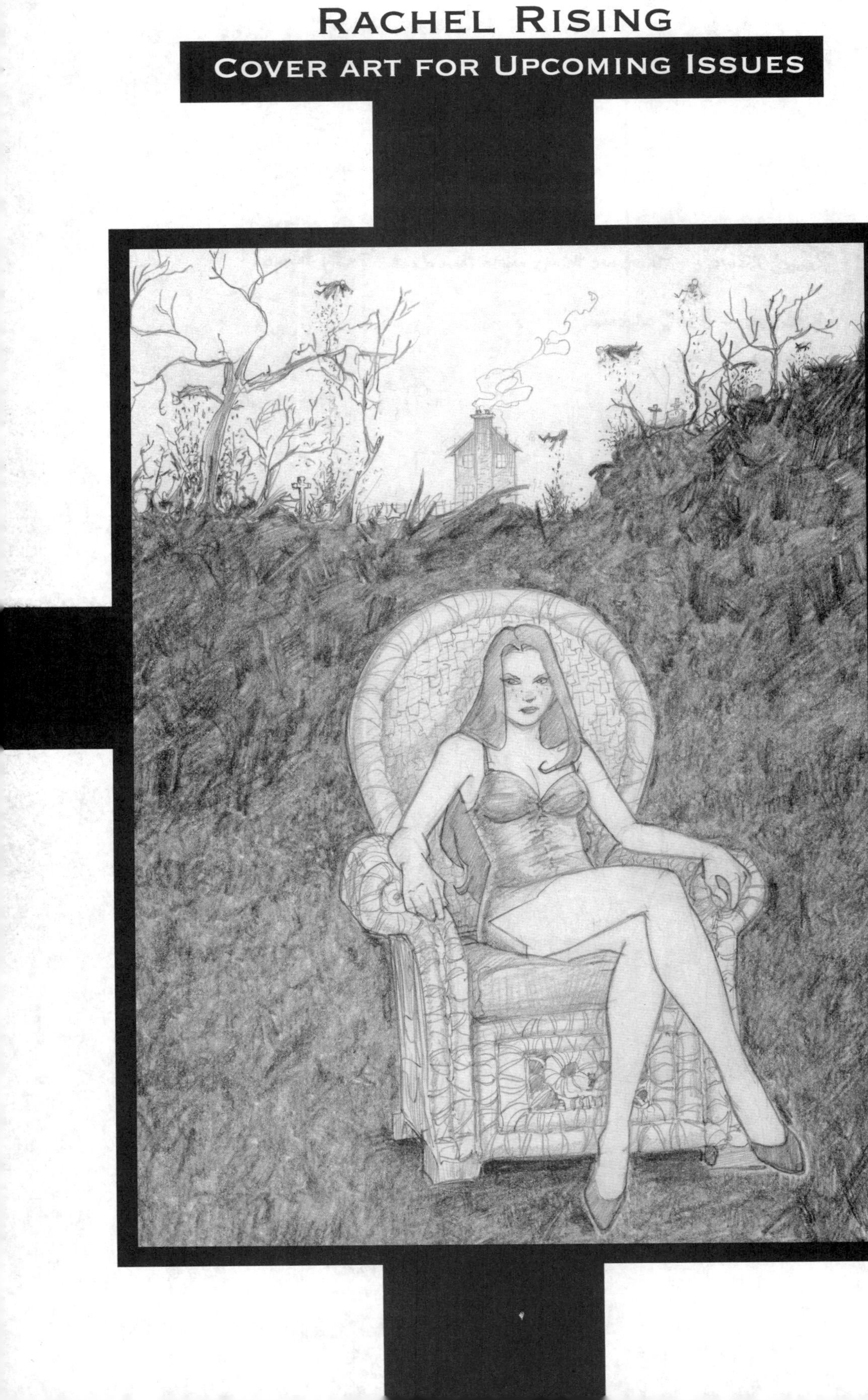

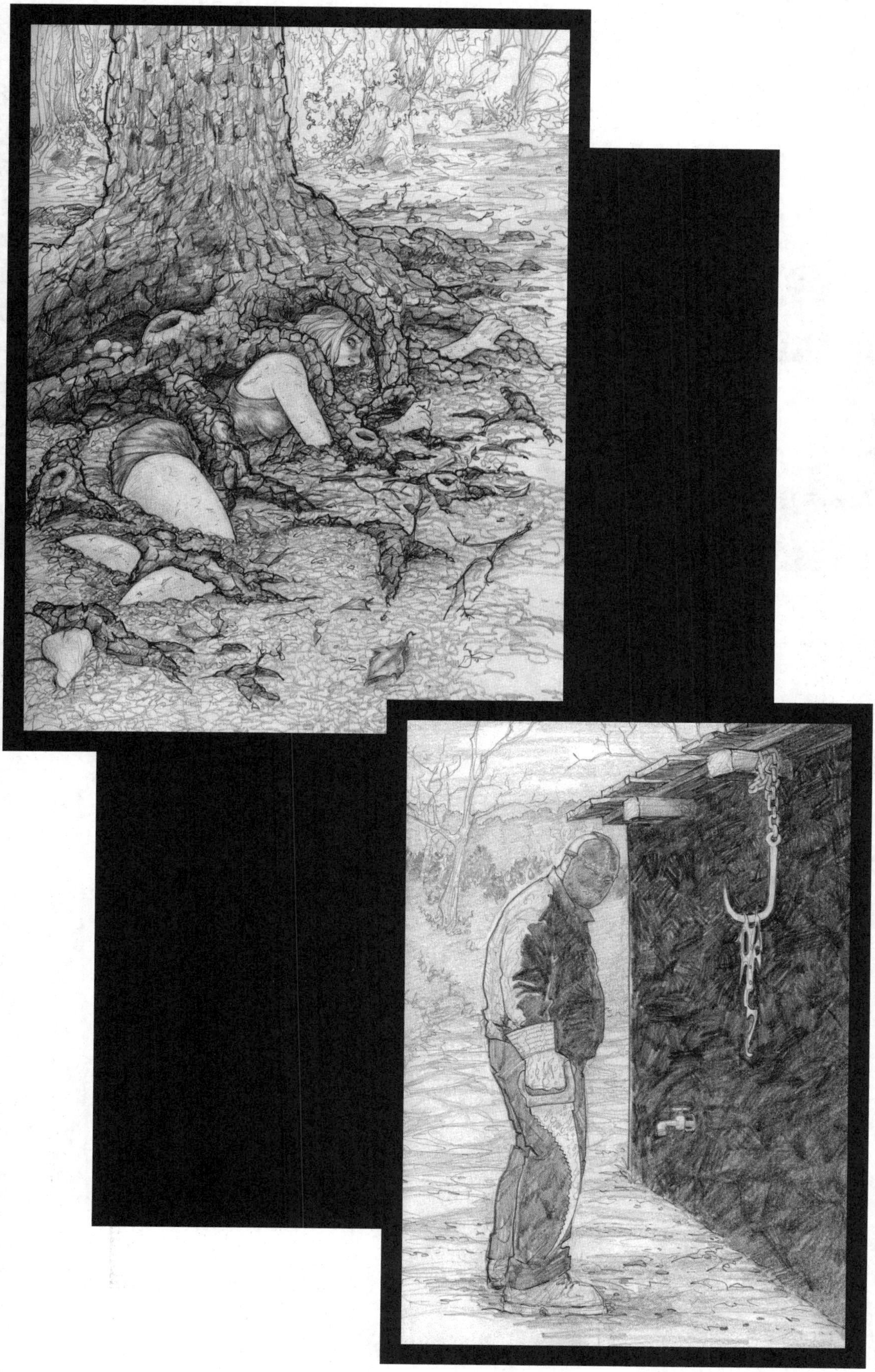

**TerryMooreArt.com**

**Also On Twitter & Facebook**

**Rachel Rising is Available Digitally At
ComiXology.com**

**email to
SIPNET@StrangersInParadise.com**

**Back Cover Art
Fabio Moon**